Relevance and Linguistic Meaning

The importance of discourse markers (words such as 'so', 'however' and 'well') lies in the theoretical questions they raise about the nature of discourse and the relationship between linguistic meaning and context. They are regarded as central to semantics because they raise problems for standard theories of meaning, and to pragmatics because they seem to play a role in the way discourse is understood. In this new and important study, Diane Blakemore argues that attempts to analyse these expressions within standard semantic frameworks raise even more problems, while their analysis as expressions that link segments of discourse has led to an unproductive and confusing exercise in classification. She concludes that the exercise in classification that has dominated discourse marker research should be replaced by the investigation of the way in which linguistic expressions contribute to the inferential processes involved in utterance understanding.

DIANE BLAKEMORE is Professor of Linguistics at the European Studies Research Institute and School of Languages, University of Salford. She is the author of *Semantic Constraints on Relevance* (1987) and *Understanding Utterances* (1992), as well as a range of articles in relevance-theoretic pragmatics in publications including *Journal of Linguistics, Lingua, Pragmatics and Cognition* and *Linguistics and Philosophy*.

CAMBRIDGE STUDIES IN LINGUISTICS

General Editors: P. AUSTIN, J. BRESNAN, B. COMRIE, W. DRESSLER,
C. J. EWEN, R. LASS, D. LIGHTFOOT, I. ROBERTS, S. ROMAINE, N. V. SMITH

In this series

Earlier issues not listed are also available

RELEVANCE AND LINGUISTIC MEANING

The semantics and pragmatics of discourse markers

DIANE BLAKEMORE

CAMBRIDGE
UNIVERSITY PRESS

PUBLISHED BY THE PRESS SYNDICATE OF THE UNIVERSITY OF CAMBRIDGE
The Pitt Building, Trumpington Street, Cambridge, United Kingdom

CAMBRIDGE UNIVERSITY PRESS
The Edinburgh Building, Cambridge CB2 2RU, UK
40 West 20th Street, New York, NY 10011-4211, USA
477 Williamstown Road, Port Melbourne, VIC 3207, Australia
Ruiz de Alarcón 13, 28014 Madrid, Spain
Dock House, The Waterfront, Cape Town 8001, South Africa

http://www.cambridge.org

First published 2002

Printed in the United Kingdom at the University Press, Cambridge

Typeface Times 10/13 pt   *System* LATEX 2_ε [TB]

A catalogue record for this book is available from the British Library

Library of Congress Cataloguing in Publication data

Blakemore, Diane.
Relevance and linguistic meaning : the semantics and pragmatics of discourse
markers / Diane Blakemore.
    p.   cm. – (Cambridge studies in linguistics; 99)
Includes bibliographical references and index.
ISBN 0 521 64007 5
1. Discourse markers.   2. Semantics.   3. Relevance.   4. Pragmatics.
I. Title.   II. Series.
P302.35 .B58   2002
401′.41 – dc21   2002019248

ISBN 0 521 64007 5 hardback

For Deirdre Wilson
with thanks

Contents

Acknowledgements

I have never known how to thank Deirdre Wilson for the part she has played in my life – a role which goes way beyond the intellectual inspiration and support she has given me, and which has continued long after I left University College London to make my own way in the world. In dedicating this book to her, I hope to convey how important she has been to me, and to express something of the gratitude I feel.

There are many people who have helped me on my way to and through this book. Robyn Carston, with whom I have shared my half-worked-out ideas, my New Zealandness, my frustrations and moments of understanding, has shown me the importance of not thinking or working alone. The importance that her work has had for mine shows on many pages of this book. Neil Smith and Bob Borsley have continued to support and encourage me in every aspect of my work, and I would like to take this opportunity of thanking them here. Over the last year my research has gained inspiration from Corinne Iten's work on concessives: she is perhaps the only other person I know who is willing to talk about *but* at a moment's notice.

Since I have been in Manchester I could not have done without the support and friendship of Wiebke Brockhaus: she has sorted my computer problems, entertained me, listened to me and, above all, has always been there. Thanks too to Celine Berthier for making my life smoother and happier.

I would like to thank the members of the School of Languages at the University of Salford and my colleagues in the North-West Centre for Linguistics for making me so welcome in Manchester.

Last, but certainly not least, I would like to thank my family in New Zealand for their love and support, and my daughter Anna for her music, her sense of humour and her patience. I wish I could promise her that I will never talk about *but* again.

Introduction

Titles of books are often deceptive. My discovery of a copy of Austin's (1962) *How to do things with words* in a bookshop amongst various manuals on composition and writing skills was amusing but understandable. While it is unlikely that this book will be incorrectly catalogued on the basis of its title, it is possible that it will give rise to expectations that it will not fulfil. Indeed, that is its point. For the aim of this book is to show that there is no justification for writing a book about discourse or discourse markers at all.

A book which has 'discourse markers' in its title suggests that there is a class of phenomena which can be called 'discourse markers'. In earlier work (Blakemore 1987, 1992) I refer to the expressions which appear in this book as 'discourse connectives', while other writers (e.g. Fraser 1990, Schiffrin 1987, Stubbs 1983) call them 'discourse markers'. The problem is that since there is no agreement on what counts as a discourse marker, it is difficult to know whether these are two labels for the same set of phenomena. Compare, for example, the discrepancies between the lists of discourse markers given by Fraser (1990) with the one given by Schiffrin (1987):

> consequently, also, above all, again, anyway, alright, alternatively, besides, conversely, in other words, in any event, meanwhile, more precisely, nevertheless, next, otherwise, similarly, or, and, equally, finally, in that case, in the meantime, incidentally, OK, listen, look, on the one hand, that said, to conclude, to return to my point, while I have you (Fraser 1990)

> oh, well, but, and, or, so, because, now, then, I mean, y'know, see, look, listen, here, there, why, gosh, boy, this is the point, what I mean is, anyway, whatever (Schiffrin 1987)

In spite of these discrepancies, it seems that the term 'discourse' is intended to underline the fact that their role must be described at the level of discourse rather than the sentence, while the term 'marker' is intended to underline the fact that their meanings must be analysed in terms of what they *indicate* or *mark* rather than what they describe. At the same time, however, it seems to be agreed

1

that discourse markers are not the only expressions which operate as indicators at the level of discourse. For example, discourse adverbials such as *frankly*, *unfortunately* and *reportedly*, interjections such as *yuk* and *oh* and expletives such as *damn* and *good grief* are also described in these terms. If the term 'discourse markers' does indeed refer to a particular class of expressions, then they must have a property which distinguishes them from other discourse indicators. This property is generally considered to be their function of marking relationships or connections among units of discourse. Thus Levinson (1983) draws attention to examples of words and phrases which not only have a 'component of meaning which resists truth-conditional treatment', but also 'indicate, often in very complex ways, just how the utterance that contains them is a response to, or a continuation of, some portion of the prior discourse' (1983:87–8).[1]

It is these two assumptions – the assumption that linguistic meaning can be non-truth conditional and the assumption that there are expressions that mark connections in discourse – which this book is really about. In this way, it is less a book about expressions classified as discourse connectives or markers as a book about the theoretical assumptions that are made by those writers who have analysed expressions as discourse connectives or markers. Accordingly, it is not a book crammed with analyses of particular discourse connectives. The analyses I give (largely in chapter 4) are given in support of an approach to the study of meaning and communication in which non-truth conditionality and discourse play no role at all.

In this book I do not make a distinction between discourse markers and discourse connectives. My arguments apply to authors who use either term inasmuch as their analyses are based on the two distinctions I have just mentioned, and my own use of the terms 'discourse marker' and 'discourse connective' is not intended to reflect a commitment to a class of discourse markers/connectives. The examples that I do discuss in detail are English expressions. In this sense, I may be considered guilty of perpetuating the over-dependence of discourse marker research on English (see Schourup 1999). However, my arguments are directed at the assumptions made in discourse marker/connective research, and hence apply to any classification or analysis made on the basis of these assumptions. Nevertheless, as we shall see, my approach does raise questions about how inferential procedures are encoded in particular languages, and, moreover, sheds light on the questions about the inter-translatability of discourse markers noted by Schourup (1999). The claim that expressions such as *but* and

---

[1] For an excellent overview of the literature on discourse connectives and discourse markers, see Schourup (1999).

so are non-truth conditional has been taken to mean that their meaning must be analysed within pragmatics rather than semantics. In chapter 1, I critically examine the assumption underlying this view, namely, that semantics = truth conditions, while pragmatics = meaning minus truth conditions (see Gazdar 1979). I shall argue that this approach to the semantics–pragmatics distinction is based on a view of linguistic semantics that cannot be maintained in a cognitive approach to meaning. Semantic representations delivered by the grammar do not encode truth conditions.

Within the framework of speech act theory, the distinction between truth conditional ('semantic') meaning and non-truth conditional ('pragmatic') meaning has been unpacked as a distinction between describing and indicating. Thus it is claimed that expressions such as *but* and *so* do not contribute to the descriptive content of the utterances that contain them but merely indicate how these utterances are to be interpreted. However, as Rieber (1997) has said, while many theorists have appealed to the speech act theoretic distinction between describing and indicating, there have been relatively few attempts to say what it means for an expression to indicate information rather than describe it. The exception to this trend is Grice (1989), whose notion of *conventional implicature* has played a prominent role in discussions of non-truth conditional meaning. In chapter 2, I examine the saying–indicating distinction in detail and show how Grice's (1989) notion of conventional implicature can be regarded as following in the speech act theoretic tradition. I shall argue that, in the end, saying that an expression carries a conventional implicature simply amounts to saying it is non-truth conditional, and hence does not provide an account of what it is that such an expression contributes to.

In chapter 3, I outline an alternative approach to linguistic meaning based on Sperber and Wilson's (1995) relevance theory.[2] For Sperber and Wilson, the distinction between semantics and pragmatics is a distinction between the two kinds of cognitive processes involved in utterance interpretation. Semantic meaning is the result of linguistic decoding processes which provide an input to inferential processes constrained by a single cognitive principle. As we shall see, this approach allows for two ways in which linguistic encoding may act as input to pragmatic inferencing and hence two kinds of linguistically encoded meaning: on the one hand, a linguistic expression or structure may encode a constituent of the conceptual representations that enter into pragmatic

---

[2] References in this book will be to the second (1995) edition of Sperber and Wilson's book rather than the first (1986) edition. However, note that, apart from the postscript, the pagination of the 1995 edition is identical with that of the 1986 edition.

inferences, while on the other, a linguistic expression may encode a constraint on pragmatic inferences. This is the distinction I arrived at in my earlier book (Blakemore 1987) and which has become known as the distinction between conceptual and procedural encoding.

However, the distinction I arrived at in 1987 is not really the distinction that is at the heart of this book. I originally envisaged this distinction as being a cognitive version of the truth conditional versus non-truth conditional distinction, and hence as being co-extensive with it. Subsequent research has shown that this cannot be the case: there are expressions which encode procedures but which contribute to what is thought of as truth conditional content, and there are expressions which encode concepts but which do not contribute to what is thought of as truth conditional content. The fact that the two distinctions cross-cut each other in this way leaves us with the question of which distinction is *the* distinction in a cognitive theory of semantics. Chapters 3 and 4 of this book are intended as an argument for abandoning the distinction between truth conditional and non-truth conditional meaning in favour of the distinction between procedural and conceptual encoding.

However, in spite of the amount of research that has been inspired by the notion of procedural meaning, the notion remains relatively poorly understood. Chapter 4 addresses some of the new questions that are raised by this new approach to linguistic meaning. In particular, it addresses the question of what exactly procedural meaning looks like. As it is defined in my 1987 book, it is information about the intended cognitive effect, or, in other words, constraints on the *results* of the pragmatic inferences involved in the recovery of implicit content. However, it is not clear that this very limited notion of procedural encoding can accommodate the full range of expressions that encode constraints on relevance. The analyses in chapter 4 are not just intended as a contribution to our understanding of the roles of the expressions discussed, but aim to show how my original notion of procedural encoding must be broadened to include constraints on all aspects of inferential processing.

The picture that emerges from chapters 3 and 4 is more complex than the picture that is drawn within the speech act theoretic framework described in chapter 2. Not all the expressions which have been classified as non-truth conditional indicators indicate in the same way. Some of these expressions encode concepts, while others encode procedures. And if my analyses in chapter 3 are right, there is not just one kind of procedural encoding. All this means that from a cognitive point of view, there is not a single class of discourse markers.

This conclusion will be unwelcome not only to those who are interested in discourse markers as examples of non-truth conditional meaning, but also to those who analyse them in terms of their function in discourse. The assumption that discourse markers operate at a discourse rather than a sentence level is based on the assumption that there is such a thing as discourse. As we shall see in chapter 5, there is more than one view of what discourse is, and accordingly more than one view of what it means for an expression to operate at discourse level. Some writers see discourse in terms of social behaviour or interaction, while others see it as an object with structural properties. On either view, discourse is an externalized object which can be investigated independently of the human mind. It is either behaviour or an abstract object. In this respect, both views must be contrasted with the one I shall argue for in this book. On this view, the object of study is not discourse, but the cognitive processes underlying successful linguistic communication, and the expressions which have been labelled as discourse markers must be analysed in terms of their input to those processes. The problem is that not all expressions classified as discourse markers make the same kind of contribution.

For those writers who do analyse these expressions in terms of their role in discourse, their most important property is their function of marking relations between discourse segments, or, in other words, their function as 'discourse glue' (Fraser 1990:385). What these expressions are assumed to connect varies according to the view of discourse that is adopted. Thus in a structural approach to discourse these expressions are analysed as marking relations between spans of discourse, while in a functional approach they are analysed as marking relations between acts or exchanges. Schiffrin (1987), who adopts a view of discourse which involves the integration of structural, semantic, pragmatic and social factors, argues that discourse markers operate on a number of different 'planes' of discourse, or that they must be analysed in terms of their role in integrating 'knowing, meaning, saying and doing' (1987:29). Building on the arguments in chapters 3 and 4, I shall argue that this view cannot be maintained, and that we can have a better understanding of the expressions which have been labelled as discourse markers if we abandon the idea that they mark connections in discourse, whether these be connections between discourse segments, connections between the propositions expressed by discourse segments or connections between social acts, and explore the idea that they contribute to relevance. This is not an argument for simply replacing the notion of discourse coherence by relevance so that we can speak of the encoding of relevance relations rather than discourse relations. Discourse, whether it is construed in structural or interactional terms, is an artifact with no psychological reality, and coherence is a property of that artifact. Relevance is not a property of discourse, but rather of an interpretation which is mentally represented and derived through cognitive processes.

It is clear that the arguments in all parts of this book depend on the acceptance of the view that utterance interpretation involves cognitive processes: thus the overall aim of the book is not so much that there is no justification at all for writing a book about discourse or discourse connectives, but rather that there is no justification from the point of view of a cognitively grounded theory of utterance interpretation. Accordingly, it is important to explain at the outset what it means to take this approach.

The cognitively grounded theory of utterance interpretation which underlies the arguments of this book is Sperber and Wilson's (1986, 1995) relevance theory, which I outline in chapter 3. As Carston (2000a) has observed, relevance theoretic pragmatics has certain fundamental aims and assumptions in common with generative grammar. In particular, like generative grammar, relevance theoretic pragmatics aims to give sub-personal explanations rather than explanations at a personal level. This means that both theories aim at full explicitness, 'leaving nothing to the intuitions of the reader or user, so that the description or mechanisms specified could be employed by a mindless automaton with the same results as in the human case' (Carston 2000a:91). Hence the talk of computations.

It has been argued that a theory which treats utterance interpretation in this way is 'disconnected from everyday communication and its problems' (Mey 1993:82), and that the mindless automaton is an inappropriate analogy when one is trying to explain what people do when they communicate. People are 'social beings' who interact in 'pre-existing [socially determined] conditions' (Mey 1993:82). Mindless automatons are not.

Mey is right that this approach to pragmatics does not attempt to explain how people communicate. As Chomsky points out, only a theory at the personal level could explain how people communicate – how they 'pronounce words, refer to cats, speak their thoughts, understand what others say' (Chomsky 1992:213). This is not to suggest, however, that people do not operate in socially determined conditions or that people's beliefs and assumptions do not include culturally determined assumptions or assumptions about social relationships and institutions. The point is that in communicating in a social context people are enabled by various sub-personal systems – grammatical competence, an inferencing system, the visual system – and these are more amenable to scientific enquiry than the person-level activity which Mey seems to have in mind. In order to show that this view of utterance interpretation is not justified, it would have to be shown either that communication in socially determined conditions is not enabled by a sub-personal inferencing system or that there is a theory of communication at a person-level. It seems that Mey's (1993), Leech's (1983) and Schiffrin's (1994) attempts to bridge what they call 'formalist' (or 'structuralist') approaches to language with functionalist approaches can be construed as an attempt to develop a person-level theory of communication. Thus Leech (1983) claims that 'we cannot understand the nature of language without studying both domains [grammar and pragmatics] and the interaction between them' (1983:4). In this book, I shall argue that this sort of enterprise cannot succeed since it does not explain how grammar, which according to Chomsky, is a mentally represented system, does interact with pragmatics, which according to Leech, Mey and Schiffrin, is a theory of something external to the human mind.[3]

The fact that relevance theoretic pragmatics is located in cognitive science and is aiming at sub-personal explanations means that it has the potential to provide a theory of utterance interpretation which is consistent with generative grammar. However, this should not be taken to mean that relevance theory aims to explain utterance interpretation within a grammatical model. As we shall see, according to relevance theory, communication involves two distinct cognitive mechanisms which are as different from each other as 'walking is from plane flight' (Sperber and Wilson 1995:3). If this is right, then it would be simply inappropriate to reduce communication to a single model. In particular, it would be inappropriate to explain communication within the model of generative grammar. For generative grammar can only provide an account of one of the cognitive mechanisms involved in utterance interpretation, namely, the coding–decoding mechanism. The contribution of relevance theory is to account for the other type of mechanism, which is, as I have already said, inferential.

In this respect, relevance theory differs not only from Leech's (1983) and Mey's (1993) social approaches to pragmatics, but also from the structural approaches to discourse mentioned above (for example, Mann and Thompson's (1987, 1988) rhetorical structure theory). For these approaches aim to develop a theory of interpretation within a grammatical model. Indeed, at the 1999 Conference on Economy in Language Design, Computation and Use (Lyon,

---

[3] In fact, it seems that many of these authors' examples of social interaction can be explained only if we assume that humans are able to make inferences to conclusions that are mental representations of another human's thoughts. In other words, the explanation of the fact that people can communicate in a socially determined context and affect social relationships lies in a sub-personal theory.

October 1999), pragmatic explanations were frequently praised on the grounds that they were like or analogous to grammatical explanations.

If the relevance theoretic view is right, and pragmatic explanations are *not* like grammatical explanations, then the exact nature of the relationship between the two systems has to be spelt out. Clearly, this cannot be done until it is shown how relevance theory works in actual cases of utterance interpretation. However, there are two general points which must be made in order to locate the chapters that follow within familiar theoretical paradigms in linguistics.

The first point concerns the distinction between competence and performance. According to some theorists, for example, Leech (1983) and Mey (1993), the distinction between Chomskyan linguistics and pragmatics is co-extensive with the distinction between competence and performance. Accordingly, they see the move towards an integrated theory of language (see above) as a move towards a theory in which a competence theory is complemented by a performance theory. By 'competence', both writers mean a language user's 'knowledge of the language and its rules (as e.g. described in transformational generative grammar' (Mey 1993:36)). By 'performance', they mean 'the way the individual user [goes] about using his or her language in everyday life' (Mey 1993:36). While this definition of competence in terms of knowledge is mentalistic, the definition of performance suggests socially determined behaviour.

It is clear that relevance theoretic pragmatics cannot be a performance theory in this sense. Does this mean that it belongs to the realm of competence? In chapter 1, I shall argue that there is no sense in which pragmatics can belong in the domain of semantic competence, since this is not enough to deliver the intended interpretation of an utterance. Chomsky (1980) has taken this to mean that alongside a theory of grammatical competence we need a theory of pragmatic competence or, in other words, a theory of speakers' knowledge of the conditions for appropriate use, of how to use grammatical and conceptual resources to achieve certain ends or purposes. While some writers, notably, Kasher (1991a, 1991b) have developed a view of pragmatic competence located outside the grammar, others, notably, Kuno (1990, 1987) and Prince (1985, 1988, 1997) have developed the idea that the grammar should include a pragmatic component, or in other words that there should be a theory of *linguistic* pragmatic (or discourse) competence.

Following Carston (2002), I shall argue that the idea of pragmatic competence, which has been developed by Kasher (1991a, 1991b), cannot be maintained, and that what is needed is not a competence theory, but a performance theory. This is not a theory of performance in the sense defined by Leech (1983) and Mey (1993) since it is concerned with cognitive performance mechanisms rather than social interaction. However, nor is it a theory of linguistic performance in the sense defined, for example, by Frazier (1987), since it is not concerned with linguistic performance mechanisms. As I have underlined throughout this introduction, pragmatic processing, according to relevance theory, is inferential.

While Prince (1988) recognizes that there are aspects of utterance comprehension which fall outside linguistics, she draws attention to a range of cases in which a particular linguistic form seems to encode information about the context in which the sentence that contains it should be used. For example, the cleft construction in (1a) has the same propositional content as the cleft in (1b) and yet only (1a) is appropriate as an answer to the question in (2):

(1) (a) It was Anna who found the money.
     (b) It was the money that Anna found.
(2) Who found the money?

As Carston (2000a) observes, there is a certain amount of controversy about this work (see Sperber and Wilson 1995:202–17). While these particular phenomena are not the ones I am concerned with in this book, it seems that the issue that Prince has raised is of central importance to the analysis of many of the phenomena that have been treated as discourse markers. For as we shall see, these expressions also seem to encode information about the contexts in which the utterances that contain them are appropriate rather than information about their propositional content. Thus all of the utterances in (3) have the same propositional content:

(3) (a) Anna is here. So Tom's got a meeting.
     (b) Anna is here. But Tom's got a meeting.
     (c) Anna is here. After all Tom's got a meeting.

This would seem to suggest that if Prince's phenomena are indeed to be explained in terms of a pragmatics sub-component of the grammar, so must the expressions in (3).

In this book, I argue that the explanation for these phenomena must indeed lie in the grammar, in the sense that the information that is conveyed is linguistically encoded. At the same time, I shall argue that these expressions encode information about pragmatic processes. However, these arguments assume an approach to semantics and pragmatics in which the analysis of these phenomena, although it makes reference to pragmatic information, is located in a theory of *semantic* competence.

As we shall see, this approach to the semantics–pragmatics distinction is grounded in a modular theory of mind. This brings us to the final point in the theoretical map I am attempting to draw. Generative grammar is based on a modular theory of mind in the sense that, first, the grammar is regarded as an autonomous system that does not have access to assumptions about the world, and, second, the grammar itself consists of autonomous but interacting sub-modules. Some writers have argued that pragmatics is modular in both senses. Thus Horn (1988) argues that pragmatics

> may be viewed as internally modular and interactionist, in the sense that the conceptually distinct sub-components . . . of pragmatic analysis may be simultaneously called upon within a single explanatory account of a single phenomenon, just as autonomous but interacting grammatical systems may interact to yield the simplest, most general, and most comprehensive treatment of some linguistic phenomenon (cf. the deconstruction of the passive in Chomsky 1982). (Horn 1988: 115)

Horn's analogy is derived from a view of pragmatics in which utterance interpretation is constrained by two distinct principles. In contrast, as we shall see, relevance theory argues that all aspects of inferential pragmatic processing are constrained by a single principle. Clearly, a theory which has only one principle cannot be modular in the second sense described above.[4]

While relevance theory is not modular in Horn's sense, it does assume a modular theory of mind in the sense that grammatical processes are different in kind from other cognitive processes, in particular, inferential pragmatic processes, and that they do not have access to the propositional world knowledge which is involved in inferential pragmatic processing. This raises the question of whether pragmatics is itself a module in the sense defined by Fodor (1983). Fodor himself argued that the human inference system is not modular but a central system which integrates and performs inferences on information derived from modular input systems (such as the visual system and the grammar) and memory. However, recently, Sperber (1994) has argued for a more radical view of modularity in which not only is pragmatics a distinct module dedicated to utterance comprehension, but also individual concepts are modules with their own inferential procedures and data bases of encyclopedic information. This argument lies outside the scope of this book (for further discussion, see Carston 2000a, 2002). My aim here has been simply to outline the theoretical assumptions underlying the discussion that will follow, and to compare them with the

---

[4] Carston (2000a, 2002) has argued that Horn's two pragmatic principles do not in fact interact in the way that grammatical principles do.

assumptions made by functional person-level approaches to language on the one hand, and cognitive sub-personal approaches, on the other.

Research on discourse connectives or markers grows daily. However, as far as I can tell, there are two distinct groups of researchers – those whose interest derives from an interest in the philosophy of language, and those whose interest derives from an interest in discourse. The two groups go to different conferences, read different literature and have different heros. Indeed, as we shall see, they have even adopted different expressions as their favourites. I am hoping that this book will be read by both groups. More particularly, I am hoping that those whose interest lies in the non-truth conditional properties of discourse connectives do not stop reading before chapter 5, and those whose interest lies in the role that these expressions play in discourse do not skip the first two chapters. The investigation of the semantics of these expressions cannot ignore their role in communication. Equally, the study of the function of these expressions in communication cannot ignore questions about the kind of information that linguistic expressions can encode.

I refer to the speaker as 'he' and the hearer as 'she'. This does not have any intended contextual implications. Examples are numbered consecutively within each chapter.

1 *Meaning and truth*

1.1 Introduction

The expressions which occupy centre stage throughout this book have played a number of different roles. In this part of the book, we shall examine the role they have played in the move towards a non-unitary theory of meaning. As we shall see, this move is itself not always a move towards the same sort of distinction, and the purpose of this and the following two chapters is to tease these distinctions apart, and to argue for a distinction between two kinds of meaning that is grounded in human cognition.

For many writers, this distinction is the distinction between semantics and pragmatics, and the significance of the expressions which I am calling discourse connectives lies in the role they have played in arguments for the existence of pragmatic meaning. Chapter 2 will examine the attempts that have been made to develop the notion of pragmatic meaning within the framework of speech act theory. This chapter focusses on the view of semantics which underlies the argument that expressions such as *but* and *well* have pragmatic meaning rather than semantic meaning.

This view is implicit in Gazdar's (1979) definition of pragmatics:

> PRAGMATICS = MEANING MINUS TRUTH CONDITIONS
> (Gazdar 1979:2)

According to this view, discourse connectives such as *but* must have pragmatic meaning rather than semantic meaning because they do not contribute to the truth conditional content of the utterances that contain them. And indeed, this is usually believed to be the case. For example, Rieber's (1997) analysis of *but* is based on the assumption that the suggestion that there is a contrast between the two segments of (1) is due to the presence of *but*, but that the truth of (1) depends only on the truth of the proposition in (2):

(1)   Sheila is rich but she is unhappy.
(2)   Sheila is rich and she is unhappy.

12

But may be a notorious example of non-truth conditional meaning, but it is not the only one. All the expressions discussed in this book will be recognized as examples of expressions which convey suggestions that are not part of the truth conditional content of the utterances that contain them. Moreover, as we shall see in the following chapter, there is a whole variety of expressions and constructions which fall outside the scope of this book which are also considered to be non-truth conditional. According to the view under investigation, the analysis of all of these phenomena cannot be provided by a semantic theory because semantics is restricted to the study of truth conditions.

Gazdar's decision to define semantics as the study of truth conditions has its origins in formal logic rather than linguistics. However, it is a decision which has been embraced by many linguists, including linguists working in the Chomskyan tradition (for example, Higginbotham 1988). In the next section we will explore the implications of bringing these two traditions together and ask whether the semantic component of a grammar, conceived in the Chomskyan sense, can indeed be truth conditional, or in other words, whether the semantic representations generated by the grammar have truth values.

Gazdar (1979) not only argues that the grammar of natural language has a truth conditional semantics component but also seems to assume that language 'has' a pragmatics (Gazdar 1979:2), or in other words, that linguistic competence includes pragmatic competence. As we have seen, this pragmatics component would include within its domain linguistically encoded non-truth conditional phenomena such as *but*. However, as Grice (1989) has shown us, the interpretation of an utterance includes information which is not part of its truth conditional content and which cannot be obtained through decoding linguistic form. For example, according to Grice (1989) the information in (3b) is an implicature derived from B's utterance in (3a) on the basis of contextual information and the assumption that the speaker is conforming to a general principle or maxim of conversation (in this case, the maxim of relation).

(3)   (a) A: Is Anna here?
             B: She's got a meeting.
         (b) Anna is not here.

Since the truth of B's utterance would not be affected by the falsity of (3b) (it would be possible to say, 'She's got a meeting but she's here'), this implicature would, by Gazdar's criterion, be included within the domain of pragmatics. This would in itself be regarded as uncontroversial. The problem is that the inclusion of this sort of phenomenon in pragmatics along with the suggestion conveyed by *but* would seem to suggest a pragmatics that is both a component and not a component of the grammar, or, in other words, a pragmatics which spreads across the linguistic/non-linguistic boundary.

In fact, as we shall see in section 3 of this chapter, a case has been made both for a theory of pragmatic competence whose domain includes the role of the context and general pragmatic principles in the interpretation of utterances and for a theory of linguistic pragmatic competence whose domain includes the role that certain (non-truth conditional) expressions play in the interpretation of the utterances that contain them. Thus while Kasher (1991a, 1991b) has argued for a notion of pragmatic competence which is analogous to the notion of grammatical competence but whose domain is the area of interpretation that involves inference mechanisms constrained by general principles of communication, Prince (1988) has focussed on a range of linguistically encoded structures whose use seems to depend on the speaker's knowledge of the contexts in which they are appropriate. I shall argue, first, that while Kasher's principles may be pragmatic, they are not part of a theory of pragmatic *competence*, and second, that while Prince is right to say that linguistic structures may encode information about the way an utterance is interpreted in context, these expressions should not necessarily be excluded from the domain of semantic competence.

Clearly, non-truth conditional expressions can be included within the domain of linguistic semantics only if linguistic semantics is not itself truth conditional. In section 4 I discuss the implications of this position, and, in particular, Levinson's (2000) charge that it constitutes a position of 'semantic retreat'. I shall argue that Levinson's own position is itself the result of a confusion between two different conceptions of semantics, and that in divorcing linguistic semantics from truth conditional semantics one is not necessarily abandoning the idea that there are relations between representations and the real world. There *are* relations between mental representations and the world, but these are not captured within a linguistic theory or grammar.

1.2   Meaning, truth and grammar

It is generally agreed by linguists working within the generative tradition that meaning is one of the concerns of a generative grammar. Thus according to a recent textbook on generative syntax, 'grammar is not just concerned with the principles which determine the formation of words, phrases and sentences, but also with the principles which tell us how to *interpret* (= assign meaning to) words, phrases and sentences' (Radford 1997:1). However, it seems that the notion of meaning that Radford has in mind is limited to 'structural' aspects of meaning such as the assignment of case features, and a student-reader might be forgiven for wondering whether the theory of meaning that is meant to be the domain of generative grammar has anything to do with the theory, that she has just been introduced to in her introductory semantics course, which pairs sentences such as (4) to truth conditions in so-called T sentences such as the one in (5).

(4)   Snow is white.
(5)   'Snow is white' if and only if snow is white.

Our student will have been told that a semantics which provided a T sentence for every sentence of the language would capture the intuition that language is used to talk about the world – that there is a relationship between language and the world. But what does this mean?

For philosophers such as Davidson (1984) or Lewis (1972), it means that language itself says something about the world. This means that the meaning of a sentence is captured by a T sentence of the sort in (4) while the meanings of words are analysed in terms of their contribution to the truth conditions of the sentences containing them. For these philosophers, a language is an abstract system defined independently of the minds of the people who use it, and the goal of semantics is to construct a model of the conditions in the world that would make each sentence in that system true. In other words, their theories are the product of what Chomsky (1986) calls an externalized conception of language (*E-language*).

In contrast, within the framework of generative syntax, a language is regarded as a cognitive system that is internalized in the human brain/mind – that is, as *I-language* (Chomsky 1986). The question is whether a theory which pairs sentences with truth conditions could be part of a theory of such an internalized cognitive system.

To say that the semantic component of a generative grammar is truth conditional would be to say that the semantic representations it generates are representations of states of affairs that make them true. That is, it would be to say that semantic representations are encodings of propositions. However, it is well known that the grammatically determined semantic representations are not fully propositional because they contain expressions whose reference cannot be determined independently of the context in which they are uttered – for example, expressions such as *here*, *tomorrow*, *you* and *this*.

Within the mind-external framework of formal semantics, context dependence is accommodated by extending the formal apparatus devised for assigning truth conditions to sentences so that it assigns truth conditions to sentence-context pairs. Thus Lewis (1972) proposed a set of contextual co-ordinates (speaker, addressee, place, time, etc.) as well as a set of possible worlds so that meanings could be defined as functions from a context-possible world pair to truth values. The context, according to this approach, is simply a specification of the identity of the speaker, the audience, time and place of utter-ance, the identification of any indicated objcts and anything else that is needed. What is needed, in this approach, is determined by the grammatical properties of the utterance. Thus the context for the interpretation of (6) consists of a speaker index, a place index and a time index, and the result of assigning values to these indices might result in an interpretation in which (6) is true iff Diane Blakemore arrived in Edinburgh on 22 March 2000.

(6)   I arrived here yesterday.

As Lewis himself recognized, the introduction of the context into the account raised the question of how the context is chosen for the interpretation of a particular context-dependent expression:

> Consider the sentence 'The door is open'. This does not mean that the one and only door that now exists is open; nor does it mean that the one and only door near the place of utterance is open. (1972:214)

The value of *the door*, claims Lewis, must be chosen from the objects that are somehow salient on a given occasion. And accordingly, he proposes to introduce a new contextual co-ordinate – a prominent objects co-ordinate.

However, judgements about the salience or prominence of objects are highly subjective, which suggests that the interpretation of a referring expression must depend on mental factors such as the expectations regarding the things that the speaker is likely to bring to the attention of the hearer. Morever, contextual prominence is not a sufficient condition for ensuring the correct choice of context for the assignment of reference. For example in (7) (from Blakemore 1987) the fact that both the entities referred to by *Periah's recording of the Moonlight Sonata* and *the Moonlight Sonata* are made accessible and hence salient to the hearer does not ensure that the correct reference is assigned to each of the two identical pronouns:

(7)   A: Have you heard Periah's recording of the Moonlight Sonata?
        B: Yes, *it* made me realize that I would never be able to play *it*.

In a later paper (Lewis 1979), Lewis acknowledges that the salience of objects and hence the value of a referring expression cannot be determined in advance but are adjusted in the course of interpretation so that the interpretation accommodates the assumption that the utterance of the sentence is acceptable.

In other words, the hearer uses that contextual information which yields an acceptable interpretation. However, this raises the question of what makes an utterance acceptable.

This question would seem to take us a long way from the concerns of formal semantics which, according to Lewis (1972), do not include the use of language by any person or population. It also seems to take us a long way from the concerns of generative grammarians as described by, for example, Radford (1997). For generative grammar is founded on the assumption that the grammar is an autonomous cognitive system, and that, in particular, the principles of grammar are autonomous from whatever principles constrain the use of language for communicative purposes. Indeed, according to this modular view of grammar, grammatical knowledge is qualitatively distinct and sealed off from the contextual knowledge which plays a role in, for example, reference assignment. Thus while I may be said to assign the correct referent to each of the instances of *he* in (8) on the basis of my belief that Prime Ministers are often called upon to open buildings, and do not usually work in libraries at universities, I would not be said to believe the grammatical principles which provide the basis for my judgement that (9) is ungrammatical.

(8)   My brother's going to meet the Prime Minister tomorrow. He's going to open the new library at the university where he works.

(9)   * Anna believes Ben to admire herself.

Moreover, grammatical principles cannot be said to be true or false in the way that a propositional representation is. As Chomsky says, 'the question of truth, conformity to an external reality, does not enter in the way that it does in connection with our knowledge of the properties of objects' (1980:27).

This would seem to suggest that the relations of truth and reference, which for logicians and philosophers are *the* relations in semantics, could have nothing to do with linguistic semantics as it is defined in generative grammar. Nevertheless, it has been argued that truth conditions do play a role in a linguistic theory of semantic representation. For example, Higginbotham (1988) argues for a level of semantic representation based on Davidson's (1967) version of truth conditional semantics. At this level, the speaker's knowledge of the meaning of the sentence in (10a) is represented in (10b), where the lexical entry for *walk* includes the information that the verb expresses a relation *walk (x,e)* which applies to a thing and an event if the event is an event of walking by that thing:

(10)   (a) John walks slowly.
          (b) Ee (walk, (j,e) & slow (e))

This representation, argues Higginbotham, captures the fact that our semantic competence includes the knowledge that (10a) entails both (11a) and (b).

(11)   (a) John walks.
       (b) Something slow takes place.

However, in contrast with Davidson, Higginbotham argues that truth conditions are not 'things that sentences of a language *have* or possible states of affairs they answer to' (1988:31). Rather they are things that speakers of a language come to know in virtue of knowing the semantic principles of their language. This suggests that semantic competence, which is mind-internal, determines truth conditions, which are mind-external. And indeed, it seems that according to Higginbotham, the things that do have truth conditions are *utterances* of sentences, which are, of course, outside the head. In other words, it seems that Higginbotham's approach is compatible with the *I-language* approach to language advocated by Chomsky, since he is not saying that semantic representations are representations of the external world, but rather that they are conditions on the truth conditions of utterances. Such a semantics, claims Higginbotham, can 'exploit the advantages of the usual truth-theoretic paradigm without running afoul of contextual entanglements' (1988: 29–30).

As we have seen, the fact that natural language sentences contain expressions whose reference depends on the context means that they cannot be said to directly encode anything that has truth conditions. Higginbotham's (1988) suggestion for getting us out of this 'contextual entanglement' is that we use a system of conditional normal forms (see Burge 1974) in order to capture speaker/hearers' knowledge of the meanings of sentences containing demonstratives and indexicals. While the antecedent of such a conditional contains the condition on truth conditions imposed by the linguistic properties of the context-dependent expression, the consequence contains the statement of truth conditions. Thus what the hearer knows when she knows the meaning of a sentence such as (12a) is represented in (12b).

(12)   (a) *She* is lazy.
       (b) If x is referred to by *she* in the course of an utterance of (12a) and
           x is female, then that utterance is true just in case *lazy (x)*.
                                                        (Higginbotham 1988: 35)

Since the truth value of the antecedent of (12b) depends on the context in which (12a) is interpreted, (12b) must be construed as a specification of particular conditions that must be satisfied by the context in order for the hearer to give a specification of the truth conditions for (12a). Thus contextual entanglements are avoided in the sense that (12b) gives no indication of whether or how these conditions are satisfied in a particular case.

If (12b) is part of linguistic competence, then, assuming the distinction between grammatical and world knowledge described above, we would not wish otherwise. However, then (12b) must be regarded as a specification of the contextual parameters whose values have to be set for the identification of the truth conditions of any utterance containing *she*, and one would expect at least an acknowledgement that there is a need for an explanation of how the hearer sets the values of these parameters in particular cases. Obviously, a hearer will not come to know anything about the truth conditions for a particular utterance of (12a) unless he knows something like the conditional in (12b). However, if coming to know the truth conditions for an utterance of (12a) is coming to know the truth conditions of the thought that is communicated by it, then the hearer must also know whether and how the antecedent of the conditional is satisfied, for the representation of this thought must contain a representation of the female who the speaker is taken to be referring to. In other words, the truth conditions for thoughts are *not* determined by what the hearer knows about the semantic principles governing language.

As Carston has shown in a series of publications (see for example, 1988, 1993, 1997a, 1997b), the linguistic under-determination of the propositional content of utterances is not exhausted by referential indeterminacy. Apart from the problem raised by lexical ambiguity (for example (13)) and the unspecified scope of quantifiers (for example (14)), we must also consider how hearers are able to recover the intended propositional content from utterances with missing constituents. The range of examples is not restricted to utterances which contain inherently elliptical expressions or constructions (for example, (15–17)), but also includes fully sentential utterances which are not generally classified as linguistically elliptical (for example (18)) and fragmentary utterances (for example (19–20)).

(13)   The coach left the stadium at midday.
(14)   Everyone has to go to the meeting.
(15)   We went out for Christmas. The meal was really nice. But it wasn't the same somehow. [same as having Christmas at home]
(16)   Don't sit on that rock. It'll fall. [if you sit on the rock]
(17)   He works too hard. [for what?]
(18)   Dogs must be carried. [if you are travelling on the London Underground with one]
(19)   On the table.
(20)   Lovely.

Moreover, there are utterances which, apart from their referential indeterminacy, have a meaning which determines a proposition with truth conditions, but not the proposition which is understood to have been expressed. For example, the hearer could recover a truth-evaluable proposition from (21) on the basis of its linguistic meaning and reference assignment. But this will not be a proposition which the speaker would have intended to communicate.

(21)   It'll take some time to get there.

It is not clear how one would capture the contribution made by linguistic meaning in these examples by means of conditional normal forms (cf. (12)). One would have to show that in each case there is a hidden indexical which imposes a constraint on the proposition expressed. While this may be feasible in cases of grammatical ellipsis, it is difficult to see how it would apply in cases such as (19), (20) or (21).[1] In other words, there are aspects of the truth conditional content of an utterance which cannot be determined by its linguistically determined semantic representation.

According to the standard versions of truth conditional semantics, the meaning of an expression is analysed in terms of the contribution it makes to the truth conditions of the sentence that contains it. However, when we shift our attention to the truth conditions of utterances, there is a further contextual entanglement not recognized by truth conditional semanticists. There are expressions which while they make a contribution to the truth conditions of the utterances which contain them, do not make the same contribution in every case. Thus as Carston (1997, 1998) shows, a speaker can use an expression to mean either something looser or something more restricted than the meaning it has taken out of context. For example, a child, angered by what he perceives as his mother's lack of maternal feeling, may produce the utterance in (22a):

(22)   (a) You're not a real mother.

On the other hand, the same child may well produce (22b) in order to clear up the confusion caused when his teacher addresses his childminder as his mother.

(22)   (b) She's not my mother, but only my childminder.

---

[1] See here the debate between Stainton (1994, 1997, forthcoming) who defends the idea that there are non-sentential assertions which have propositional content, and Stanley (2000, 2002) who argues that the phenomena Stainton calls non-sentential assertions are either grammatically elliptical and hence have a full sentential structure or are not genuine linguistic acts of communication at all and are more like winks or taps on the shoulder.

On the assumption that Higginbotham would give the conditional in (23b) as the linguistically determined semantic representation of (23a), it is difficult to see how he would capture the difference between the contribution made by *mother* to the truth conditions of (22a) and the contribution it makes to the truth conditions of (22b).

(23)   (a) She is a mother.
        (b) If x is referred to by *she* in the course of an utterance of (23a) and she is female, then that utterance will be true iff *adult female parent (x)*.

This chapter began with the question of whether truth conditional semantics could be regarded as a theory of semantic competence in the sense developed in the Chomskyan research programme. I have argued that a fundamental problem with grafting an externalist theory of truth conditional semantics on to an internalist theory of language is that the linguistic properties of an utterance do not fully determine a proposition with truth conditions – contextual entanglements are inevitable. This might be taken to suggest that alongside a theory of semantic competence we need a theory of pragmatic competence which would explain how we resolve these entanglements. In the next section I ask if there is any sense in which a notion of pragmatic competence is viable.

1.3   Pragmatic competence

Chomsky himself distinguishes *grammatical competence*, which he describes as the computational aspects of language that constitute knowledge of form and meaning, from *pragmatic competence*, which he defines as knowledge of the conditions for appropriate use, of how to use grammatical and conceptual resources to achieve certain ends or purposes (Chomsky 1980).

Unfortunately, Chomsky has said little further about the notion of pragmatic competence. But it is interesting to ask whether a system of knowledge about how to use language could solve the problems introduced in the last section. These are questions about how hearers recover the interpretations of utterances such as those in (12a) or (13–21) on the basis of the sometimes skeletal information provided by the grammar.

(12)   (a) She is lazy.
(13)   The coach left the stadium at midday.
(14)   Everyone has to go to the meeting.

(15)   We went out for Christmas. The meal was really nice. But it wasn't the same somehow. [same as having Christmas at home]
(16)   Don't sit on that rock. It'll fall. [if you sit on the rock]
(17)   He works too hard. [for what?]
(18)   Dogs must be carried. [if you are travelling on the London Underground with one]
(19)   On the table.
(20)   Lovely.
(21)   It'll take some time to get there.

A theory that explained how interpretations are recovered would have to actually integrate linguistic knowledge and non-linguistic knowledge. That is, it would have to provide a model of whatever does the interpretive work. It is difficult to see how this could be done by a system of knowledge.

It would seem then that a competence theory of pragmatic interpretation is impossible. And indeed Carston (1998, 1999) has argued that Kasher's (1991a, 1991b) attempts to develop Chomsky's brief remarks on pragmatic competence do not result in a theory of *competence* at all. Kasher (1991a,1991b) speaks of a number of different systems of pragmatic 'knowledge'. Of these it seems that only one is strictly language specific – the knowledge of basic speech act types, for example, assertions, questions and commands. The rest are domain-neutral or part of general knowledge. Thus in addition to a number of pragmatic 'modules', including one for basic speech acts and one for what he describes as 'talk-in-interaction', he proposes, first, a system called 'central pragmatics' which is defined as the knowledge of the general cognitive principles and general knowledge involved in the 'generation' of conversational implicatures, aspects of style and politeness, and, second, a system called 'interface pragmatics' which he defines as knowledge which is involved in integrating data from the language module and other sources (for example, in the assignment of reference to indexicals).

Carston (1998, 1999) argues that the principles which operate Kasher's central pragmatics are performance principles rather than principles which could be taken to constitute 'pragmatic knowledge' or 'competence'. For example, his general pragmatic principle which says 'Given a desired end, one is to choose that action which most effectively, and at least cost, attains that end' (1991b: 577) is a principle which guides behaviour. And his 'interface pragmatics', since it is a mechanism which integrates various inputs in accordance with a non-linguistic principle of best fit, must also be a performance mechanism.

For Carston this is not surprising for 'when it comes to internalist pragmatic theorising a shift from a competence to a performance perspective is virtually inevitable' (1999:93).

The performance perspective which Carston has in mind, and the one which informs this book, is not *linguistic* performance, but rather *cognitive* performance, or, more particularly, the inferential mechanisms which receive input from the linguistic performance mechanisms (the parser), perceptual sources (the senses) and conceptual sources (memory), and deliver interpretations (explicit and implicit content). In other words, according to this view, the point of contact between semantics and pragmatics is at the interface between the linguistic parser, which receives input from linguistic competence and delivers linguistically determined semantic representations, on the one hand, and the inferential mechanisms which take these semantic representations as input for the computations which deliver the representations which the hearer takes to be representations of the speaker's communicative intentions, on the other. These computations, like all performance mechanisms, are constrained by time and considerations of effort.

This is essentially the relevance theoretic picture of the relationship between linguistic form and pragmatic interpretation that I shall be outlining in chapter 3. Right now I wish to turn to a very different sort of case that has been made for a theory of pragmatic competence – a case which, as we shall see, has bearing on the sort of phenomena that are central to this book.

This case is made by Prince (1988). While she recognizes that there are aspects of interpretation, for example, conversational implicature, which fall outside the theory of linguistic competence, Prince draws attention to a range of phenomena which she argues are both pragmatic and linguistic. Consider, for example, the differences between the cleft structures in (24).

(24)   (a) It was Anna who played 'Summertime' at the Christmas concert.
        (b) It was 'Summertime' that Anna played at the Christmas concert.
        (c) It was at the Christmas concert that Anna played 'Summertime'.

These differences are pragmatic, according to Prince, because they are not differences in propositional content, but rather differences between the contexts in which the utterance of each sentence is felicitous. Thus (24a) but not (24b–d) is appropriate as an answer to (25a); (24b) but not (24a) or (24c–d) is appropriate as an answer to (25b); (24c) but not (24a–b) or (24d) is appropriate as an answer to either (25c) or (25d).

(25)   (a) Who played 'Summertime' at the Christmas concert?
        (b) What did Anna play at the Christmas concert?
        (c) At which concert did Anna play 'Summertime'?
        (d) Where did Anna play 'Summertime'?

Prince analyses these differences in terms of the distinction between focus and presupposition, so that 'the proposition conveyed is structured into two parts, one an open proposition [and the other] its instantiation' (1988:168). The felicitous use of one of these sentences 'requires that the open proposition be appropriately construed as shared knowledge' (1988:168). For example, the open proposition conveyed by (24a) is the one in (26).

(26)   x played 'Summertime' at the Christmas concert.

Prince suggests that this analysis of the pragmatic differences between these sentences could be unpacked along the lines suggested by Wilson and Sperber (1979). Thus the difference between (24a) and (24b) is that whereas the speaker of (24a) is communicating that (26) is the first 'background entailment' (Wilson and Sperber 1979), the speaker of (24b) would be communicating that (27) is the first background entailment.

(27)   Anna played x at the Christmas concert.

However, whereas Sperber and Wilson (1995) argue that the differences between (24a–c) are not linguistically determined, but the result of 'a natural linkage between linguistic structure and pragmatic effects' (1995:213), Prince argues that these pragmatic differences are arbitrary and language-specific and hence linguistically encoded. She argues against the view that they follow from an iconic property of *it*-cleft constructions by showing that the constructions used by other languages for performing the function performed by the English cleft may have 'a dramatically different' syntax (1988:168). For example, she compares English examples such as the ones in (28) with the corresponding Yiddish structures:

(28)   (a) ... zey hobn gefunen aykhmanen
           ... they have found Eichmann
        (b) ... *dos* hobn gefunen aykhmanen
           ... this they have found Eichmann
           ... it was they who found Eichmann
                              (Prince 1988: 169)

The English *it*-cleft involves syntactic subordination of the part of the sentence corresponding to the open proposition, and movement or isolation of the constituent corresponding to the instantiation of the variable in this proposition (together with marking of the variable's position, for example, with a trace). In contrast, in the Yiddish example, there is no subordination, no syntactic isolation of the focussed constituent and no trace. It consists of a single clause, has a post-verbal subject and has a dummy NP in first position that is not an argument of the verb. Moreover, as Prince points out, the *dos*-construction is syntactically equivalent to the *es*-construction in (29), which is used in a totally different context, namely, when the subject is non-thematic or, in other words, 'when the fewest assumptions about shared knowledge are warranted' (1988:169).

(29)   [Come to me, I've been away looking for you on twisted roads. I'm still young, inexperienced ...]

    (a) ... fremde mentshn kenen mikh farnarn
       ... strange people can me entice
       'Strange people can entice me'

    (b) ... *es* kenen fremde mentshn mikh farnarn (Shavaib: *Moyde ani*)
       ... it can strange people me entice
       'Strange people can entice me', 'It can happen that strange people entice me'

    (c) ?... *dos* kenen fremde mentshn mikh farnarn
       ... this can strange people me entice
       'It is strange people that can entice me'

Prince goes on to make the same kind of point about a range of other syntactic structures, for example, gapping, topicalization and VP preposing, as well as the referential options in examples such as (30).

(30)   (a) Last week I read a book and I met an author.
      (b) Last week I read a book and I met the author.

In each case she argues that cross-linguistic comparisons show that 'a significant part of a speaker-hearer's competence involves ... knowing which syntactic and referential forms trigger which nonlogical inferences' (1988:179).

The claim that these inferences are not due to the iconicity of the forms in question, while supported by cross-linguistic analysis, is controversial (see Sperber and Wilson 1995: 202–17). However, my aim here is not to enter into this controversy, but to locate Prince's work in the kind of theoretical picture that is being developed in this book. As interesting as this controversy may be, the question it raises about what we should do with linguistically encoded meaning which affects contextually determined aspects of interpretation must be addressed. For it seems clear that whatever we say about the nature of the phenomena discussed by Prince, there are linguistically encoded aspects of meaning which affect pragmatic interpretation – namely, many of the expressions which have been called discourse markers. For example, while it is uncontroversial that the differences between the following are due to the linguistically encoded meanings of *moreover* and *but*, it seems that these differences must be analysed in terms of the contexts in which they are appropriate. Note that both (a) and (b) are uttered by a single speaker.

(31)   (a) [I think you should accept this paper for the conference. It's well written and it's got wonderful examples.]
        Moreover, it's right on the conference theme.
        (b) [I think you should accept this paper. It's well written and it's got wonderful examples.]
        ? *But* it's right on the conference theme.

In other words, knowledge of the meanings of these expressions is knowledge of the contexts in which the utterances that contain them are appropriate.

Since this is knowledge about the linguistic properties of particular linguistic expressions, it must be regarded as part of linguistic competence. Since this knowledge is knowledge about the meanings of these expressions, we can also say that it must be regarded as part of semantic competence. At the same time, since this knowledge must be analysed as knowledge about the contexts in which utterances are appropriate, or knowledge about discourse functions, it would seem that it is in some sense pragmatic knowledge. Prince (1988) resolves this tension by proposing a sub-component of linguistic competence called 'discourse competence' or 'pragmatic competence'. A theory of pragmatic competence is, for Prince, distinct from that theory of pragmatics whose domain includes such matters as the identification of context-dependent aspects of propositional content and the recovery of implicatures. On these matters, Prince agrees with the view outlined above: they involve inferences which are constrained by general cognitive principles, and hence lie outside the domain of the grammar.

So the question is whether we really need Prince's extra component of the grammar? In chapters 3 and 4, I shall show that within a relevance theoretic framework there is no need for such a component, and that the contribution of expressions such as *moreover* and *but* can be analysed within a theory of linguistic semantics. However, as we shall see, the role of the semantic component is radically different from the one which I suspect Prince has assumed, for not only does it provide logical forms which are the input to those pragmatic processes which yield what is thought of as the propositional content of the utterance, but it also can provide information about the processes involved in using contextual assumptions for the recovery of the intended interpretation.

Such a semantic component would not, of course, be truth conditional, since it includes knowledge of the meanings of expressions and structures which do not play a role in the identification of truth conditions. The cleft constructions in (24a–c) and the utterances in (31a–b) are truth conditionally equivalent. However, as we have seen, the assumption that a sentence encodes a proposition with truth conditions cannot be maintained: there is a gap between what the sentence encodes and the interpretation that is recovered by the hearer. Moreover, there are aspects of what we think of as the propositional content of utterances in which the grammar seems to play no role at all (recall examples such as (19–21)). If linguistic semantics is not itself truth conditional, then the inclusion of so-called non-truth conditional meaning within its domain should not matter.

But can we abandon truth conditions like this? How can we divorce linguistic meaning from truth without abandoning the intuition that we use language to talk about the world?

1.4   Semantic retreat?

In fact, some theorists *have* abandoned this intuition, arguing that no expression of language should be analysed in terms of content. Thus although Anscombre and Ducrot's (1983, 1989) argumentation theory began simply as an attempt to accommodate non-truth conditional expressions (for example, *but*) by showing that meaning can have an argumentative component, it developed into a theory of radical argumentativism in which the function of language is argumentative rather than informative. As Iten (2000a, 2000b) has shown, while this approach has offered some important insights into the meanings of non-truth conditional expressions such as *but*,[2] it is not concerned with language or meaning as a cognitive phenomenon. Thus an utterance is not something produced by a particular speaker with particular intentions, but a collection of different points of view. And a point of view is not anchored in the mind of a particular person with particular thoughts. As Iten shows, this means that argumentation theory is unable to address the sort of questions raised in this chapter, namely, how

---

[2] For discussion of Anscombre and Ducrot's analysis of *but*, see chapter 4 below.

a hearer is able to recover the intended interpretation for context dependent expressions.

Anscombre and Ducrot's (1989) argument that language does not perform an informative function is based on the subjectivity of language. The fact that the meanings of some words involve subjective judgement is undeniable. And, as we have seen (in examples (22) and (23)), an expression can be used to make different contributions to the interpretation of an utterance in different contexts. However, as Iten (2000b) argues, this is not in itself a reason for saying that language is not used to represent the world *at all* – and, indeed Anscombre and Ducrot have admitted that there are some utterances which they cannot analyse in purely argumentative terms.

The arguments in the previous section were not arguments for abandoning the idea that language is used to describe the world or arguments for abandoning truth conditions altogether. The argument was simply that truth conditions cannot play a role within the semantic component of the grammar, or, in other words that the semantic representations generated by the grammar are sub-propositional and hence not bearers of truth values. Levinson (2000) describes this position as one of 'semantic retreat' (2000:240–2), arguing that a level of semantic representation which is not a representation of the world is extremely impoverished – so impoverished that it cannot even capture traditional sense relations (e.g. entailment, contradiction, hyponymy). Instead of pushing truth out of linguistic semantics, he recommends accommodating context dependence by letting pragmatics 'intrude into semantic representations and consequently into their interpretation' (2000:193) as, for example, in discourse representation theory (Kamp and Reyle 1993), or in file change semantics (Heim 1982). He tries to illuminate this point of view with the following metaphor:

> In these proposals [Kamp and Reyle, Heim] there is a common slate, a level of propositional representation, upon which both semantics and pragmatics can write – the contribution may be distinguished by the colour of the ink: semantics in blue, pragmatics in red! Semantics and pragmatics remain modular 'pens' as it were: they are separate devices making distinctively different contributions to a common level of representation. The slate represents the semantic and pragmatic content of accumulated utterances, and it is this representation that as a whole is assigned a model theoretic interpretation. (Levinson 2000:193)

Unfortunately, this metaphor confuses rather than illuminates. Having made it clear that anyone who does not agree that semantics is all about the business of assigning model theoretic interpretations is guilty of 'semantic retreat', Levinson uses the word 'semantics' in the above quotation to refer to the sub-propositional contribution made by linguistically determined meaning rather than the business of assigning model theoretic interpretations. That is, he seems to accept that we must distinguish between what the 'semantics' pen writes on the representation that is assigned truth conditions, on the one hand, and the assignment of truth conditions to the propositional slate where both pens have written, on the other. Levinson would, I believe, be right to distinguish the two enterprises. What the blue pen writes is one thing. Assigning truth conditions to a common propositional slate is quite another. However, he would have to say which one of these enterprises is semantics. He would also have to say something more about the common propositional slate. What kind of representation is it?

On the assumption that the grammar cannot have access to non-linguistic, contextual information, it is difficult to see how the propositional representation which is assigned truth conditions is a *linguistic* representation, as, I think, Levinson is arguing. For on this assumption, the red pragmatics pen cannot write on any level of representation in the grammar. But this is not to say that there is no mental representation at all that can be assigned truth conditions. Fodor (1998) has argued that thoughts are representations not just in the sense of being represented in the mind (in the same way as, say, grammatical representations), but also in the sense that their content is at least partly determined by their relationship with the external world. Indeed, he has argued that it is thoughts rather than English sentences which have truth conditions: 'English has no semantics. Learning English isn't learning a theory about what its sentences mean, it's learning how to associate sentences with the corresponding thoughts' (1998:9).

In other words, according to this view, there is no need to retreat from truth conditions *per se*. It is simply that the common propositional slate on which Levinson's two pens write is not a system defined by the grammar, but a representation defined by the cognitive system that delivers the contents of our thoughts, beliefs, assumptions, desires and intentions. As we will see, some of the thoughts communicated by an utterance are communicated explicitly, while others are communicated implicitly. For example, the utterance in (32B) explicitly communicates the assumption that Anna has a meeting and implicitly communicates that she is not here.

(32)   A: Is Anna here?
       B: She's got a meeting.

On Fodor's view both of these assumptions have truth conditions.

This is also the view of the relevance theoretic framework that I shall be arguing for in chapter 3. Thus Wilson and Sperber (1993) argue 'the primary bearers of truth conditions are not utterances but conceptual representations' (1993:23). However, although it is accepted that both explicitly communicated and implicitly communicated propositions have their own truth conditions, and 'are capable of being true or false in their own right' (Wilson and Sperber 1993:6), there is a tendency to single out a single explicitly communicated proposition – often referred to as the proposition expressed – as the one which carries the truth conditions of the utterance. The suggestion is that an utterance has truth conditions only in a derivative sense – that is, by virtue of expressing a proposition with truth conditions. As we shall see, within this framework the assumptions explicitly communicated by an utterance are not restricted to 'the proposition expressed'. So this raises the question of how we decide which of these propositions is the 'proposition expressed', and whether the notion of truth conditions need play any role in the answer.

As we shall see in the first section of chapter 2, a number of theorists have observed that our intuitions about the truth conditions of an utterance are variable and consequently unreliable. This observation will be borne out when we come to look more closely at so-called non-truth conditional phenomena. Bach (1999) and Neale (1999) have argued that the fact that our intuitions about the truth conditions of an utterance are so variable can be explained if we abandon the assumption that an utterance has a single set of truth conditions. This line of thought is, in fact, anticipated by Wilson and Sperber in the article cited above (1993). Thus although they assume throughout this paper that an utterance expresses a single proposition, they ask whether this approach is indeed justified, and speculate that the intuitions of an utterance as a whole are based on the assumption which makes the major contribution to relevance. As we shall see, their approach provides a cognitive framework in which these questions can be investigated. However, as Iten (2000b) has suggested, it also provides a framework for the exploration of the far more radical suggestion that there is no need, from a cognitive point of view, for the notion of 'the truth conditions of an utterance' at all.

This brings us back to Levinson's charge of 'semantic retreat'. As I hope I have made clear in this section, relevance theory is not retreating from semantics in the sense of retreating from truth conditions – not even if it adopts the radical view just described. Interpretations, according to relevance theory, are conceptual representations – conceptual representations of thoughts – and they have truth conditions. Nor is relevance theory retreating from semantics in the sense of retreating from the contribution of linguistically determined meaning (Levinson's blue pen). This contribution is, Levinson says, impoverished and schematic: it is a schema for the construction of a propositional representation rather than a proposition. At the same time, however, linguistically determined meaning makes a contribution to utterance interpretation which would be excluded from semantics if it were defined in terms of truth conditions. The blue pen does not just write on the 'propositional slate'.

The approach that I have just introduced is embedded in the view that language is a vehicle for thoughts and desires. That is, it views language in cognitive terms. However, non-truth conditional meaning is often viewed as the property of a theory which views language not as a vehicle for thought but as a vehicle for action. Speech act theory grew out of a dissatisfaction with the methods of formal logic as applied to ordinary natural language, and in particular, with what was perceived as an over-emphasis on the descriptive function of language. A theory which claimed to provide an alternative to formal semantics by focussing on ordinary language use might perhaps seem to provide a natural home for all those expressions which could not be accommodated within truth conditional semantics. In the next chapter, I shall explore speech act theoretic approaches to non-truth conditional expressions and ask whether they have in fact led to a unitary account of non-truth conditionality.

2 Non-truth conditional meaning

2.1 Varieties of non-truth conditional meaning

If 'meaning' is taken in its broadest sense to include both linguistically encoded meaning and meaning which is inferred from the context, then the term 'non-truth conditional meaning' can refer to two quite different aspects of the interpretation of an utterance. On the one hand, it can refer to the contribution made by expressions and structures which cannot be analysed as a contribution to the truth conditions of the utterances that contain them, for example, the contribution made by *but* in (1) and the cleft structure in (2a) and (b).

(1)   I've got the tomatoes and peppers but they didn't have any lemons.
(2)   (a) It was Anna who found the cat.
         (b) It was the cat that Anna found.

On the other hand, it can be taken to refer to meaning which cannot be attributed to the presence of any particular expression or structure but which is due to the particular context in which an utterance is made. Thus while the suggestion of contrast or incompatibility conveyed in (1) is due to the use of *but*, the suggestion that B did not manage to get everything is recovered from her utterance in (3) only because it is interpreted in the context triggered by A's question. In another context, for example, the one triggered by the utterance in (4), the suggestion would not arise.

(3)   A: Did you get everything?
         B: They didn't have any lemons.
(4)   What shall we make – chocolate mousse or lemon mousse?

In all of these cases, there is a suggestion which will not be regarded as a condition on the truth of the utterance that communicates it. Thus the truth or falsity of the suggestion that there is some kind of incompatibility between the two segments of (1) has no bearing on the truth value of (1) at all: it will be true iff (a) B got tomatoes and peppers and (b) the shop that B went to did not have any lemons. Similarly, B's utterance in (3) is true iff the shop B went to did not have any lemons: the fact that B did in fact obtain lemons or some suitable substitute would not turn her utterance into a falsehood.

As we have seen in the previous chapter, for some theorists this would be sufficient grounds for treating *all* of these suggestions within pragmatics. However, the result of this is to blur the distinction between linguistically encoded meaning on the one hand, and contextually determined meaning on the other. And in blurring this distinction one is denying oneself the opportunity of being able to explain the difference between what expressions such as *but* contribute to the interpretation of the utterances that contain them, on the one hand, and what expressions like *have* or *lemon* or *not* contribute, on the other. Contextually determined suggestions such as the one communicated by B's utterance in (3) are regarded as unproblematic in the sense that it is assumed that they can be explained in terms of inference and general purpose communicative principles. Linguistically encoded suggestions, however, do not sit comfortably in this picture. At the same time, however, they do not sit comfortably in semantics – on the assumption that semantics is a theory of the contribution that expressions and structures make to the truth conditions of the proposition expressed by the utterance that contains them. Accordingly, the emphasis in this chapter will be on linguistically encoded non-truth conditional meaning.

Perhaps the problem illustrated by *but* and cleft structures would not be such a worrying one, if it were restricted to these expressions. However, it is acknowledged that there is a wide range of expressions and constructions which raise the same problem. From the point of view of this book, the most important of these are the so-called discourse connectives or markers, some of which are illustrated below.

(5)   Ben is a New Zealander. *So* he loves rugby.
(6)   Ben is a New Zealander. *After all* he loves rugby.
(7)   Ben is a New Zealander. *Nevertheless* he loves rugby.
(8)   *Although* Ben is a New Zealander, he loves rugby.

While all of these utterances will be understood to have the same truth conditional content, they will not be understood in the same way. These differences must be attributed to the italicized words.

However, the phenomenon extends beyond the scope of this book. For example, there are expressions such as *too* and *even* whose meanings interact with focus.

(9)   *Even* Ben likes rugby.
(10)   Ben likes rugby *too*.

While (9) suggests that Ben's liking rugby is less likely than other people liking rugby, (10) suggests, depending on the focus, that Ben is not the only one to like rugby or that rugby is not the only sport Ben likes. However, both utterances will be true iff Ben likes rugby.

Similarly, while the sentence adverbials in (11–14) and the parentheticals in (15–17) clearly make a difference to the interpretation of the utterances that contain them, many theorists, for example, Bach and Harnish (1979), Nolke (1990) and Recanati (1987), would claim that all of these utterances are true under exactly the same conditions, namely, the situation in which they are not going to ask Tom.

(11)   *Fortunately*, they are not going to ask Tom.
(12)   *Sadly*, they are not going to ask Tom.
(13)   *Frankly*, they are not going to ask Tom.
(14)   *Regrettably*, they are not going to ask Tom.
(15)   They are, *I suppose*, not going to ask Tom.
(16)   They are not, *I warn you*, going to ask Tom.
(17)   They are not, *I bet*, going to ask Tom.

It should be pointed out at the outset that this view of sentence adverbials is not shared by other theorists. For example, Higginbotham (1988, 1989, 1994), who, as we have seen, aims to give a truth conditional semantics for natural language sentences, claims that it is possible to provide a truth conditional account of the meaning of a sentence adverbial such as *sadly*. As Carston (1999) points out, Higginbotham fails to distinguish between the question of whether a sentence adverbial can be given a truth conditional semantics *qua* semantics of the linguistic system, on the one hand, and the question of whether it encodes a meaning that contributes to the truth conditions of the utterance, on the other. Whatever the answer to the first question, it seems that the answer to the second – at least as far as *sadly* is concerned – is 'no'. Moreover, as Ifantidou-Trouki (1993) has shown, the answer to this second question does not seem to be the same for all sentence adverbials. Thus while the meanings of so-called illocutionary adverbials such as *sadly* do *not* seem to contribute to the truth conditions of the utterances that contain them, it seems that the meanings of so-called evidential or hearsay adverbials *do*. I shall discuss this problem in more detail in section 2.

As Wilson (1975) observed, truth conditionally equivalent expressions may communicate different attitudes or emotions. Thus for example, while (18) and (19) have the same truth conditions, the speaker's choice of *deprive of* in (18) suggests a positive attitude towards Tom which contrasts with the attitude communicated by *spare* in (19).

(18)   We were deprived of Tom's company tonight.
(19)   We were spared Tom's company tonight.

Much earlier Frege (1918) made similar observations about the differences in 'tone' created by the use of *cur* rather than *dog*. And more recently, Kaplan (1997) has discussed the differences in what he calls 'expressive content' created by the use of *the bastard* in examples such as (20) and the use in French of *te* rather than *vous* in examples such as (21).

(20)   Where's Stanley? Surely *the bastard* hasn't forgotten to come.
        Where's Stanley? Surely he hasn't forgotten to come.
(21)   Je t'aime.
        Je vous aime.

However we describe these differences, it is clear that they are not differences of truth conditional content.

The problem with all the expressions discussed so far is that although they occur in utterances which can be assumed to have truth conditions, they do not contribute to those truth conditions. However, there are also constructions and expressions whose use in an utterance means that it cannot be described as being true or false at all. Thus it is often claimed that imperatives such as the one in (22), interrogatives such as the one in (23) and exclamatives such as the one in (24) cannot be said to have truth conditions.

(22)   Turn off the computer.
(23)   Have you turned off the computer?
(24)   What a terrible noise!

This would suggest that the non-declarative syntax (the imperative, interrogative and exclamative word order) is non-truth conditional not in the sense that it contributes to a suggestion which is not a condition on the truth of the utterance that contains it, but rather in the sense that it makes talk of truth conditions irrelevant. The same kind of effect seems to be achieved by the use of certain particles, for example, *eh*.

(25)   He's a good cook, *eh*?

Not all particles have this effect, however. Thus while *eh* turns the host utterance into a question, the use of *huh* indicates that the host utterance is ironic and hence that the speaker is dissociating herself from the truth of the proposition expressed.[1]

(26)   He's a good cook, huh!

Other particles, for example, *oh*, seem to function more like an attitudinal adverbial – although it is much more difficult to pin down the exact attitude or emotion expressed.

(27)   Oh, this weather is awful.
(28)   Oh, you're here already.

It might be argued that these particles lie at the margins of linguistics.[2] However, if they are said to carry linguistic meaning at all, then it seems that this meaning cannot be analysed in terms of truth conditions.

In presenting these examples of non-truth conditional meaning I have simply assumed that you have intuitions about what the truth conditions of an utterance are, and, moreover, that these intuitions are the same as mine. This assumption is justified only to the extent that, first, we have pre-theoretic intuitions about truth conditions in the same way that we have intuitions about, say, grammaticality, and, second, that these intuitions are invariable from speaker to speaker. While it is possible that the examples that I have just cited have presented no difficulties for this assumption, it seems that the semantics literature is full of examples for which intuitions are not so clear-cut. Iten (2000b:230) gives the example made famous by Donnellan (1966):

(29)   The man drinking a martini is a famous philosopher.

The question is whether the utterance is true or false in a situation in which the man indicated is in fact a famous philosopher but is drinking from a martini glass containing iced water. The post-graduate students in my post-graduate summer school semantics class (Netherlands Graduate School of Linguistics, Utrecht 2001) were divided almost equally between 'true' and 'false', and there were some who were (understandably) reluctant to give a verdict.

Perhaps this simply shows that pre-theoretic intuitions cannot be relied on, and that we need a theoretical criterion for truth conditionality. The one that is

---

[1] See Blass (1990), for discussion of dissociative particles in Sissala. See also Wilson and Sperber (1993).

[2] For further discussion, see Wharton (2001).

usually invoked is based on the assumption that only truth conditional material can fall within the scope of a logical operator such as *if then*. Thus if we assume that *but* carries a suggestion of contrast, we can establish whether it is part of the truth conditional content of (30) by embedding (30) into a conditional, as in (31).

(30)   Tom is home but Ben is out.

(31)   If Tom is home but Ben is out, then we can have prawns for tea.

If the speaker is understood to be saying that we can have prawns for tea iff (32a, b and c) are true, then we would have to say *but* falls within the scope of the conditional and that it is truth conditional. If on the other hand, the speaker is understood to be saying that we can have prawns for tea iff (32a and b) are true, then the suggestion of contrast falls outside the scope of the conditional and *but* is non-truth conditional.

(32)   (a) Tom is home.
        (b) Ben is out.
        (c) There is a contrast between the fact that Tom is home and Ben is out.

The problem with this test is that it depends on our intuitions about the truth conditions of the conditional. In other words, it seems that in the end, we cannot avoid the appeal to intuitions – and it seems that intuitions may vary. Moreover, as Iten (2000b:213–14) has observed, it is not clear that the assumption that only truth conditional material can fall under the scope of a logical operator is correct. She asks us to consider Mary's utterance in (33) which will be understood to communicate the implicature in (34).

(33)   PETER: Would you like to go to the cinema?
        MARY: I'm tired.

(34)   Mary doesn't want to go to the cinema.

The problem is that even though (34) is clearly not part of the truth conditions of Mary's utterance in (33), it seems that it can fall within the scope of *if . . . then* in (35).

(35)   If Mary is tired, then Peter won't book cinema tickets.

Iten suggests that the explanation for this lies in the role that assumptions about causal connections play in a cognitive system: because establishing causal connections is so important to us, *if . . . . then* 'gets interpreted causally wherever possible' (Iten 2000b:214). Independent evidence for the centrality of causal connections can be found in the psycholinguistic literature (see Sanders and Noordman 2000).

In fact, as both Iten and Ifantidou-Trouki (1993, 1994) have discovered, it is not always grammatically possible to embed an utterance under a logical operator. However, the important point is that even when this is possible, intuitions are frequently divided. Indeed, one might want to say that the speaker of an utterance such as (29) produced in the context described has said something false and something true. How are we to account for this?

It is difficult to see how we can account for the variation in people's intuitions about truth conditions in a framework which assumes that every utterance expresses a single proposition which represents its truth conditions. By the same token, if we cannot assume that an utterance expresses a single proposition, there seems to be little justification for distinguishing between those linguistic expressions which contribute to the proposition expressed and those expressions which do not. As we shall see in the following two sections, those accounts which see meaning as either truth conditional or non-truth conditional have failed to provide a unitary account of the meanings of those expressions which are said to be non-truth conditional. This may not seem surprising, given the diversity of the range of the phenomena listed above. However, if the distinction between meaning which is truth conditional and meaning which is non-truth conditional is itself based on an assumption that cannot be maintained, then it would seem that the whole enterprise should never have got off the ground in the first place.

However, it did get off the ground. In sections 2 and 3 of this chapter we will look at the attempts that have been made to make sense of the truth conditional versus non-truth conditional distinction within a speech act theoretic framework. In section 4 we shall examine Bach's (1999) argument that once we abandon the assumption that each utterance expresses a single proposition, we can re-analyse some examples of expressions which have been treated as non-truth conditional as contributing to the truth conditional content of the utterances that contain them. However, as we shall see, not all of the expressions listed above are analysed by Bach in the same way, and Bach's proposals for accommodating the variations among intuitions about truth conditionality bring problems of their own.

2.2   Speech act theoretic approaches: indicating and describing

The aim of Bach's (1999) paper is to expose what he describes as the 'myth' of conventional implicature, a notion devised by Grice (1989) as part of his so-called theory of conversation. However, as we shall see, Bach only rejects Grice's account as it applies to a limited range of non-truth conditional expressions, and he maintains a Gricean-style analysis for a significant number of so-called discourse connectives, illocutionary adverbials, attitudinal adverbials, illocutionary and attitudinal particles. One of my aims in this chapter is to show that Grice's influential account of non-truth conditional meaning had its origins in speech act theory, and that in spite of his rejection of conventional implicature, Bach's (1999) analysis of illocutionary and attitudinal adverbials continues this tradition.

Speech act theory has provided a means of accommodating non-truth conditional meaning within a truth conditional framework. There is a sense in which this seems odd. Speech act theory originated as an alternative to truth conditional approaches to meaning and hence as a move away from what many philosophers perceived as an over-emphasis on the descriptive uses of language. Thus in *How to do things with words* Austin drew attention to the fact that language is not just used to describe the world, but also to change it. For Austin, language was a social phenomenon embedded in social institutions. To speak was to act – to make a prediction, to give an order, to make a promise, to declare war etc. – and to give the meaning of an utterance was to describe the act that it was used to perform.

However, although speech act theory and truth conditional semantics would appear to be irreconcilable, one can see why it might be thought that speech act theory should provide the natural home for many of our problematic expressions. Consider how someone would explain the meaning of *but*, or utterance initial *well*, or particles like *eh* to a non-native speaker of English. They are much more likely to give illustrations of their uses than attempt an analysis of the contributions they make to the meaning of the sentence that contains it. An approach to language which viewed meaning as use might seem to provide the appropriate theoretical framework for their analysis.

The problem, then, is how one could maintain a truth conditional approach to meaning by incorporating speech act theoretic machinery.[3] Originally, Austin saw the performative use of language as a complement to the descriptive use. Thus he distinguished between constative utterances, which truly or falsely described states of affairs, on the one hand, and performative utterances, which were used to perform felicitous or infelicitous speech acts. However, over the

---

[3] The following is a thumbnail sketch of the development of speech act theory, and I have skimmed over and skirted around a number of complex issues concerning the way in which Austin's original proposals were interpreted by speech act theorists such as Searle (1968, 1969) and Strawson (1973). I refer the reader to Levinson (1983) for a more detailed overview.

course of *How to do things with words* he abandons this approach so that even constative utterances have a performative element. They could be used to perform felicitous or infelicitous assertions. Austin's ideas were developed (and modified) by Searle (1969), who argued that utterances could have both an illocutionary component and a propositional component. This allows us to say that utterances may share their propositional content while differing in their illocutionary force. Thus although (36a–c) would be said to have the same propositional or descriptive content, they would be analysed as having different illocutionary forces or performing different speech acts.

(36)   (a) Tom rides his bike to school.
       (b) Does Tom ride his bike to school?
       (c) Tom, ride your bike to school.

This was taken to suggest that the role of the mood indicators in examples such as (36a–c) is not to contribute to the propositional content of the utterances that contain them, but is to indicate or show what speech act is being performed. In other words, they are indicators which encode illocutionary information.[4]

This idea has been applied to a range of phenomena which do not contribute to propositional content. Thus Austin (1962) proposes not only that performative verbs, such as the ones in (37), are indicators, but also that the functions of some of these constructions can be performed by expressions such as the ones in (38).[5]

(37)   (a) I conclude that Tom will not leave.
       (b) I bet that Tom will not leave.
       (c) I predict that Tom will not leave.
(38)   (a) Therefore Tom will not leave.
       (b) Probably Tom will not leave.

Urmson (1966) approaches so-called 'parenthetical verbs' such as the one in (39) in the same way, arguing that they are devices which 'prime the hearer to see the emotional significance, the logical relevance, and the reliability of our statements' (1966:197), and that they 'function with regard to a statement made rather as . . . the foot stamping and saluting can function in the Army to make it clear that one is making an official report' (1966:211–12).

(39)   They will, I suppose, arrive before 9.

---

[4] See Sperber and Wilson (1995), Wilson and Sperber (1988), Clark (1991), Clark (1993), for a critical examination of speech act theoretic accounts of mood and mood indicators.
[5] Recanati (1987) has argued that the analysis of performative verbs as indicators is mistaken, and that explicit performatives can be regarded as having descriptive (truth conditional) content. For discussion of Recanati's arguments, see Blakemore (1991).

Sperber and Wilson (1995) have drawn attention to a number of fundamental difficulties for the speech act approach to meaning (see also Wilson and Sperber 1988 and Clark 1991). Their critical assessment of the speech act theoretic analysis of non-declarative utterances has not only led to a re-analysis of mood and other so-called illocutionary force indicators, but also to a radically different approach to non-literal uses of language (see Sperber and Wilson 1995, 1985/6). However, most fundamentally, they have questioned the speech act theoretic assumption that language is a vehicle for social action and that the identification of speech acts is a prerequisite for understanding utterances, and have developed an alternative approach in which language is used for the communication of thoughts. From the point of view of this book, the importance of this move from language as action to language as a means of communicating thoughts lies in the way it allows us to abandon the speech act distinction between describing and indicating (outlined above) in favour of a cognitively grounded distinction between the ways in which linguistic form contributes to the inferential processes involved in utterance interpretation.

However, before we make this move, I would like to discuss the speech act distinction between describing and indicating as it has been applied to the analysis of sentence adverbials. As we shall see in the following chapter, sentence adverbials have played an important role in the argument that the speech act theoretic distinction between truth conditional meaning and non-truth conditional meaning is not co-extensive with the cognitive distinction just mentioned. However, their analysis is also central to the present chapter, for it contains ideas which are closely related to ones developed by Grice in his account of conventional implicature.

It is recognized that sentence adverbials do not perform the same function. Thus illocutionary adverbials such as the one in (40) are said to modify an illocutionary verb so that (40) is understood to communicate the proposition in (41).

(40)   Seriously, she is not here.
(41)   I am telling you seriously that she is not here.

Attitudinal adverbials such as *fortunately* are said to indicate the speaker's attitude to the proposition expressed, so that (42) is understood to communicate (43).

(42)   Fortunately, she is not here.
(43)   It is fortunate that she is not here.

Evidential adverbials are treated as indicators of the strength of the speaker's evidence for the proposition expressed, so that (44) is understood to communicate (45).

(44)   Obviously, she is not here.

(45)   It is obvious that she is not here.

And hearsay adverbials, which are sometimes treated as a sub-type of evidential adverbial, are said to indicate that the source of the information lies with
someone other than the speaker, so that (46) is regarded as communicating
(47).

(46)   Allegedly, she is not here.

(47)   It is alleged that she is not here.

In spite of these differences, all of these adverbials are analysed in the same
way within a speech act theoretic framework: that is, they are all regarded as non-
truth conditional and they are all analysed as indicators of the way in which the
utterance containing them is to be interpreted. Thus Recanati (1987) claims that
deleting an attitudinal adverb like *fortunately* 'would not change the proposition
expressed by the sentence . . . because the modification introduced by the adverb
is external to the proposition and concerns the speaker's emotional attitude to
the latter. This attitude is neither "stated" nor "described", but only "indicated"'
(1987:50). Similarly, Bach and Harnish (1979) analyse illocutionary adverbials
such as *seriously* as modifying the speech act that is performed. Urmson (1966)
describes evidential adverbials as indicators of the reliability of our statements.
And Palmer (1986) analyses hearsay adverbials as a sub-type of evidential,
arguing that they are a means of indicating diminished speaker commitment.

As Bach and Harnish (1979) have shown, one of the advantages of this sort
of analysis is that it enables us to explain the ambiguity of utterances such as
(48).

(48)   Seriously, is she here?

For according to their analysis, *seriously* could indicate either that the speaker
is asking seriously whether she is here or asking the hearer to tell him seriously
whether she is here. However, as we have seen, while non-illocutionary adverbials such as *fortunately* or *allegedly* might be analysed as contributing to a
higher-level description of some kind, they cannot be analysed as contributing
to a speech act description.

In fact, it has been argued that not all sentence adverbials can be analysed
as non-truth conditional indicators. Ifantidou-Trouki's (1993) investigation of
sentence adverbials is based on the test for truth conditionality which I discussed
in the first section of this chapter, namely, embedding the adverbial under the
scope of a logical operator such as *if. . . then*. Not only did she find that the

application of this test is not as straightforward as we are sometimes led to believe, but also she discovered that evidential adverbials (including hearsay adverbials) do in fact contribute to the truth conditions of the utterances containing them.

As Ifantidou-Trouki shows, the application of the standard truth conditionality test to attitudinal adverbials such as *fortunately* is unproblematic, and it seems to yield uncontroversial results. Thus she argues that the speaker of a conditional such as (49) would be understood to be saying that the circumstances under which they will play Monopoly do not include the state of affairs in (51), but only the state of affairs represented in (50).

(49)   If she has unfortunately lost the cards, then we will play Monopoly.
(50)   She has lost the cards.
(51)   It is unfortunate that she has lost the cards.

However, she argues that while this test can be applied straightforwardly to hearsay adverbials such as *allegedly*, the results do not accord with the standard speech act story. Thus the speaker of (52) will be understood to be saying that the truth of (53) is a sufficient reason to call the police.

(52)   If the cook has, allegedly, poisoned the soup, then the police should make an enquiry.
(53)   It is alleged that the cook has poisoned the soup.
                                                        (Ifantidou-Trouki 1993:76)

Allegedly, it seems, is truth conditional and cannot be analysed as an indicator.

The application of the test to illocutionary adverbials and evidential adverbials is, according to Ifantidou-Trouki, much less straightforward. She identifies two problems. First, when illocutionary adverbials are used in conditional utterances, they are interpreted as modifying the whole utterance rather than the embedded clause. For example (54) is interpreted as (55) rather than (56).

(54)   If Tom, frankly, continues to come home at 5 in the morning, then he will have to find somewhere else to live.
(55)   I tell you frankly that if Tom continues to come home at 5 in the morning, then he will have to find somewhere else to live.
(56)   If I tell you frankly that Tom continues to come home at 5 in the morning, then he will have to find somewhere else to live.

Second, there are some illocutionary and evidential adverbials which must be interpreted as VP adverbials when they are used in conditionals. For example,

Ifantidou-Trouki's example in (57) is interpreted as (58), which, as she says, is not the kind of interpretation we are interested in.

(57)   If Ben is evidently annoyed, then we will drop the subject.
(58)   If Ben is showing his annoyance in an evident way, then we will drop the subject.

Ifantidou-Trouki shows that the first problem can be solved by embedding illocutionary adverbials under the scope of factive connectives such as *because*. Since the speaker's use of *because* in (59) does not commit her to the truth of (60), the illocutionary adverbial *frankly* can be shown to be non-truth conditional as the speech act theoretic story predicts.

(59)   Anna should not be invited, because she frankly talks too much.
(60)   I tell you frankly that Anna talks too much.

Her solution to the second problem, however, shows that evidential adverbials do not conform to the speech act theoretic analysis. This solution hinges on the observation that manner adverbials and evidentials do not occur in the same kind of environments. For example, according to Jackendoff (1972), manner adverbials cannot occur before modals or aspect in US (and New Zealand) English. Thus in my (New Zealand) dialect, (61) can only be given an evidential interpretation.

(61)   The cook obviously will poison the soup.

Since *obviously* cannot be given a manner adverb interpretation in the conditional in (62), we can ask whether the speaker will be understood to be saying that the state of affairs in (63) is sufficient reason for going ahead with eating the meal.

(62)   If the cook obviously won't poison the soup, we can eat the meal without worrying.
(63)   It is obvious that the cook won't poison the soup.

Ifantidou-Trouki's verdict is that it is, and hence that, contrary to the speech act theoretic story, evidentials like *obviously* are truth conditional.

The final argument hinges on the distributional differences between an evidential adverbial such as *evidently* or *obviously* and their VP adverb analogues. While it is clear that there are environments in which, say, *evidently* cannot be given a manner adverb interpretation, it is not at all clear that the evidential *evidently* has a meaning which is completely unrelated to the meaning of the

VP adverb *evidently*. Similarly, it is not clear that the meaning of the VP adverb *frankly* is unrelated to the meaning of the illocutionary adverbial *frankly*. However, the speech act theorist is committed to saying that the meaning of the sentence adverbial is not equivalent to that of the corresponding VP adverb: the sentence adverbial is non-truth conditional while the VP adverb is truth conditional. If Ifantidou-Trouki is right, then sentence adverbials cannot be analysed uniformly in non-truth conditional terms in any case. However, apart from this, it simply seems counter-intuitive to say that *frankly* in (64) is not synonymous with *frankly* in (65).

(64)   Frankly, I don't give a damn.
(65)   She spoke to him frankly about his behaviour.

As we shall see in the following chapter, this problem can be solved in a framework which assumes that the bearers of truth conditions are not utterances but thoughts. However, we shall also see that within this framework, expressions such as sentence adverbials turn out to have nothing in common with other so-called non-truth conditional phenomena. In particular, they have nothing in common with the expressions which we turn to in the next section, namely, the ones Grice analysed in terms of conventional implicature.

2.3   Conventional implicature

In the last section we saw that the speech act theoretic distinction between describing and indicating has been applied to the analysis of a variety of non-truth conditional phenomena. Clearly, the validity of these analyses depends on the validity of the assumption which is central to the speech act theoretic programme, namely, that the interpretation of an utterance crucially involves the identification of the illocutionary act it performs. And as I have noted, this assumption has been questioned by Sperber and Wilson in their reassessment of the speech act theoretic approach to meaning. However, these analyses also depend on an understanding of what it means for an expression to indicate information rather than describe it. And as Rieber (1997:56) points out, writers who analyse expressions as indicators are much more concerned with what they communicate than how they communicate it.

The exception to this trend is Grice (1989). His answer to this question derives from his recognition that certain expressions presented a problem for his notion of saying and thus for his distinction between what is said and what is conversationally implicated. This distinction – between what is said and what is implicated – was itself a central component of Grice's attempt to salvage a minimal truth functional semantics for the natural language versions of the logical connectives in the face of the attempts by the ordinary language philosophers to show that the semantics for natural language could not be based on the semantics of artificial logical languages. In this sense, Grice was moving away from the speech act theoretic tradition. However, as the following discussion shows, his treatment of the expressions which posed a problem for his notion of saying turned out to follow the speech act theoretic tradition outlined in the preceding section.[6] In this section, I shall argue, first, that Grice's notion of conventional implicature fails to shed light on the question of what it means for an expression to indicate information, and, second, that Rieber's (1997) attempt to modify Grice's analysis within the speech act theoretic tradition only highlights the problems inherent in this approach.

Grice's most important contribution to the developments of modern pragmatics was to define a notion of speaker's meaning in terms of speaker intentions. Thus he claimed that: "'A meant$_{NN}$ something by x" is (roughly) equivalent to "A intended the utterance of x to produce some effect in an audience by means of the recognition of that intention"' and 'to ask what A meant is to ask for a specification of that effect' (1989:220). While it is clear that Grice wanted this notion of meaning to go beyond linguistically encoded or conventional meaning and that he saw inference as playing a key role in the identification of speaker meaning, it is equally clear that he intended the notion of conventional meaning as a special case of speaker's meaning. Hence his distinction between meaning something by *saying* it and meaning something by *implicating* it. While the identification of conversationally implicated meaning crucially involves inference and the assumption that the speaker is conforming to general conversational principles, his definition of 'what is said' (given below) circumscribes an area in which conventional meaning and speaker's meaning overlap.

(66)   An utterer U says that p iff:
         U did something x (1) by which U meant that p
                                (2) which is an occurrence of a type S which
                                    means 'p' in some linguistic system.
                                                        (Grice 1989:88)

However, as Grice recognized, this definition applies to the suggestions carried by words such as *but*, *therefore* and *so*, suggestions which he did *not* want to

---

[6] For an excellent outline of Grice's so-called theory of conversation and contribution to modern pragmatics, see Neale (1992).

count as part of what is said. Consider, for example, what he says about the suggestion carried by *therefore* in (67).

(67)   Bill is a philosopher and he is, therefore, brave.

> Now I do not wish to allow that, in my favoured sense of 'say', one who utters [67] will have *said* that Bill's being courageous follows from his being a philosopher, though he may well have said that Bill is courageous and that he is a philosopher. I would wish to maintain that the semantic function of the word 'therefore' is to enable a speaker to *indicate*, though not to *say*, that a certain consequence holds. (Grice 1989:21)

Accordingly, Grice suggests that we should describe this suggestion as a *conventional implicature*. Why is it so important for Grice to exclude the suggestion carried by *therefore* from what is said? In *The Lectures on Logic and Conversation* (Grice 1989) he simply says that this sense of 'what is said', which excludes the meanings of words such as *therefore* and *but,* has greater theoretical utility than other definitions. Neale (1992) takes this to mean that Grice wanted his notion of what is said to coincide with the truth conditional content of the utterance. The problem is that he also wanted it to coincide with the conventional meanings of the words uttered.

In fact, as Sperber and Wilson (1995) and Carston (1988, 1998, 2002) have shown, Grice failed to recognize the extent of the gap between linguistically encoded meaning and truth conditional content – a gap which is filled by inference and pragmatic principles. Given the role of pragmatically constrained inference in the recovery of truth conditional content, the existence of conventional meaning which does not contribute to truth conditions might not seem so problematic.

However, Grice did see this as a problem, and enlisted speech acts as a means of solving it. He begins by distinguishing between two kinds of speech acts: *central* or *ground-floor* speech acts, which include making assertions and telling people to do something, on the one hand, and *non-central* or *higher-order* speech acts, which are the speech acts indicated by expressions such as *therefore* and *but,* on the other. On the basis of this distinction, he modifies his definition of 'what is said' thus:

(68)   An utterer U says that p in uttering X iff U performs a central speech
        act with the content p and X contains some conventional device whose
        meaning is such that it indicates the performance of this central act.
        (Grice 1989:121–2)

Since expressions such as *therefore* and *but* indicate the performance of non-central acts rather than central acts, they are excluded from what is said.

Grice elaborates on the notion of a non-central speech act in his 'Retrospective epilogue' (Grice 1989:359–68). The speaker of an utterance such as (69), he argues, is performing two central speech acts of assertion and, at the same time, a higher-order speech act in which she is commenting on the performance of the central speech act. In this case, the effect of this comment is to indicate that there is a comment between the two assertions.

(69)   My brother-in-law lives on a peak in Darien; his great-aunt, on the other hand, was a nurse in World War I.

On this account, Grice claims, the fact that a hearer may find it impossible to establish a contrast between the two assertions does not mean that the speaker has *said* anything false. He would simply have committed a 'semantic offense' of misperforming the higher-order speech act. Similar analyses are suggested for *therefore*, which signals the performance of a higher-order speech act in which the speaker is commenting that one assertion is a conclusion derived from the other, and *moreover*, which signals that one assertion is additional to the other. In each case the misperformance of the higher-order speech act will never 'touch the truth value . . . of the speaker's words' (Grice 1989:362).

If an expression such as *on the other hand* or *but* signals the performance of a non-central speech act, then that speech act, like all speech acts, must have an illocutionary force and a propositional content. It seems that Grice would want to say that the speech act whose performance is signalled by *but* or *on the other hand* in an utterance such as (69) has the content in (70), and hence that this is the conventional implicature carried by *but*.

(70)   There is a contrast between the assertion that the speaker's brother-in-law lives on a peak in Darien and the assertion that his great-aunt was a nurse in World War I.

But if this is the case, then it is not clear what the force of the act is. It cannot be the act of contrasting since the fact that there is a contrast is represented by the propositional content of the act. More generally, it is not clear whether 'contrasting', 'adding' or 'explaining', which, according to Grice, are associated with *but*, *moreover* and *so* respectively, are speech acts in the sense made familiar by classical speech act theory (Austin 1962, Searle 1969). Perhaps one could say that this higher-order act is simply an act of commenting. But then one would have to say that acts signalled by the non-truth conditional discourse connectives – for example, *but*, *so*, *moreover* and *after all* – are individuated not by their illocutionary properties but by their propositional content. That would mean that these expressions are not after all being analysed as illocutionary force indicators, but are being treated as indicators of something propositional. And this would leave us with the task of specifying what exactly is the relationship between an expression such as *but* and the proposition in (70). For it is not clear that whatever is encoded by *but* appears in this proposition in the same way that, say, what is encoded by *great-aunt* or *lives* appears in the propositional content of the 'ground-floor' speech act performed by (69).

It seems that these questions might be answered by Rieber's (1997) modification of Grice's analysis of conventional implicature. According to his analysis, expressions such as *but* are *tacit performatives*. Thus he argues that (71) should be analysed as a conjoined proposition containing a parenthetical performative, that is, as (72):

(71)   Sheila is rich but she is unhappy.
(72)   Sheila is rich and (I suggest that this contrasts) she is unhappy.
                                            (Rieber 1997:54)

The classical speech act theoretic argument that performatives do not have truth values is no longer universally accepted. Thus according to Recanati (1987) they are self-verifying declarations and hence must be regarded as having a value 'true'. However, Rieber claims that his analysis is compatible with either analysis. Since, according to the classical approach, the performative in (72) has no truth value and simply 'indicates' that the propositional content has the force of a suggestion, the truth value of (71) does not depend on whether there is a contrast between wealth and unhappiness. At the same time, since according to Recanati's (1987) analysis the performative in (72) is a self-verifying declaration that the speaker is suggesting there is a contrast, its truth is not affected by whether there is a contrast. Thus it would seem that on either approach Rieber's analysis 'gets the truth conditions right' (1997:54).

However, the question is whether in getting the truth conditions right Rieber has also explained what expressions such as *but* communicate and how they do it. As I have argued (Blakemore 2000, Blakemore and Carston 1999), it is not clear that Rieber's assumption that all utterances containing *but* express a conjoined proposition can be maintained (see chapter 4, section 1, for further discussion). The question here, however, is not whether *but* should be analysed as *and* plus 'something else', but rather whether Rieber's re-analysis of Grice's notion of conventional implicature takes us any further towards an account of what it means for a linguistic expression to indicate or signal information.

According to Rieber, his analysis is one in which 'what is non-truth conditionally expressed by the discourse connective is part of their *conventional* meaning' (1997:55, my emphasis). At first sight it is not clear whether meaning can be both tacit and conventional. It might seem that in saying that the conventional meaning of *but* is analysed in terms of a performative of the form *I suggest that p*, Rieber is saying that there is a linguistically determined relation between *but* and the information that its utterance constitutes the performance of the act of suggesting that *p*. On the other hand, it would seem that in saying that this performative is tacit, Rieber is suggesting that the utterance does not actually contain an expression which identifies the act being performed.

It seems that the apparent contradiction here stems from the assumption that 'tacit' means 'implicit', and hence that in the absence of an actual performative verb, *I suggest*, the hearer must infer the information that the speaker is performing the act of suggesting on the basis of the context and pragmatic principles in the same way as a hearer would infer that the speaker of (73) is issuing a warning.

(73)   There's a bomb in that car.

In fact, it seems that Rieber does not intend 'tacit' to be construed in this sense, and that he is including *but* in that category of expressions which, according to speech act theoretic analyses, are conventionally performative, but which simply do not happen to contain a performative verb – for example, expressions such as *thanks* or *pardon*, which would be analysed as performatives *I thank you* and *I apologize* respectively.

From a speech act theoretic point of view, saying that *pardon* is equivalent to the explicit performative *I apologize* is illuminating only in the light of the constitutive rules for performing a successful act of apologizing. Analogously, saying that *but* is equivalent in meaning to a performative of the form *I suggest that p* is illuminating only to the extent that we understand what it means to perform the speech act of suggesting. Rieber does not give the constitutive rules for suggesting. Indeed, he is doubtful whether *suggest* is the most appropriate verb here, and proceeds instead to an account of what he means by signalling or showing or indicating.

According to this account, the act of showing consists of calling the hearer's attention to something 'that the hearer would believe were it brought to her awareness' (Rieber 1997:61). This sort of communication, he argues, is different from ordinary communication since 'the speaker does not need to stand behind her words; all he needs to do is to induce the hearer to notice something' (1997:61). This suggests that according to Rieber, the communicative act associated with the use of an expression such as *but* is analogous to the non-verbal act of, say, deliberately opening the fridge door in order to show someone how empty it is.

In his discussion of indicating, Rieber links his notion of showing to Sperber and Wilson's (1995) notion of ostension. However, Sperber and Wilson define ostensive communication as behaviour which makes it mutually manifest to the audience and communicator that the communicator intends, by means of that behaviour, to make a set of assumptions manifest or more manifest to the audience. Rieber, on the other hand, is thinking only of those cases in which some assumption(s) become manifest to the audience even if she does not recognize that the communicator had not intended to make them manifest. The assumption that the fridge is empty might have become manifest to the audience even if she had thought that the communicator was opening the fridge for the purpose of seeing whether there was any milk.

This might suggest that Rieber's distinction between 'ordinary communication' and showing is a distinction between cases in which the communicator provides indirect evidence for information, on the one hand, and cases in which the communicator provides direct evidence for information, on the other. For example, while the act of opening the fridge door may have provided direct evidence that it is empty, the act of producing the utterance in (74) can make the communicator's intention to make an assumption manifest only if the audience has first recognized the communicator's intention to make this assumption manifest.

(74)   There's nothing in the fridge.

For the relationship between the evidence produced (the utterance) and the assumptions conveyed is arbitrary, and it is only by discovering the communicator's intention to make particular assumptions manifest that the audience can discover, indirectly or inferentially, what these assumptions are.

However, Sperber and Wilson (1995:53) have argued that there is not a sharp dividing line between showing and saying that, but rather that there is a whole continuum of cases ranging from cases of showing to cases of saying that. *All* of these cases are cases of ostension in the sense that they involve making one's intention to convey information manifest, and they *all* involve inference. Thus even if the act of opening the door provides direct evidence for the information that the fridge is empty, there are other assumptions which are made manifest only indirectly – for example, that the communicator is trying to be relevant, that the communicator is aware that the fridge is empty. On this view, ostension is not just showing (to be contrasted with saying that), as Rieber seems to suggest, but a well-defined domain which covers all cases of human communication.

In this discussion it has been assumed that all ostensive communication consists in providing evidence (for example, opening the door of a fridge, producing an utterance) from which the audience is intended to derive assumptions by inference (for example, that the communicator is being relevant, that the fridge is empty). Moreover, it has been assumed that the key to the notion of showing or indicating lies in the nature of the relationship between the evidence provided and the assumptions that are derived. However, it seems that not all communication consists in providing evidence for assumptions. Consider the case in which a communicator taps the audience on the shoulder and points in the direction of an oncoming bus with the intention of getting the audience to form the assumptions in (75).

(75)   (a) A number 86 bus is approaching the communicator and audience.
         (b) We should get on the bus that is approaching.

In this case one would not say that the tap on the audience's shoulder or the pointing gesture are themselves evidence for (75a–b). Nor would one say that in making these gestures the communicator produces the evidence for (75a–b), as, say the act of opening the door could be described as producing the evidence for the assumption that the fridge is empty or the act of producing the utterance in (76) could be described as producing the evidence for the assumptions in (75).

(76)   An 86 is coming.

The evidence for (75a–b) is the sight of the approaching bus. On the other hand, one could say that these gestures alter the saliency of the bus so either it is accessible as a referent in the comprehension of a following utterance (for example (76)), or it is accessible as a referent in an assumption that the audience constructs for herself.

What distinguishes the act of pointing from the act of producing the utterance in (76) is not (*contra* Rieber) that it is designed to make the audience aware of information that she could have recovered for herself, but rather that it is not itself an act of producing the evidence from which information is derived. Pointing is, of course, a natural device rather than a linguistic one. The question is whether a linguistic expression such as *but* might be said to 'point' in this sense?

If using *but* is like pointing, then we have to be able to say, first, what information it makes salient, and second, what role this information plays in the derivation of communicated assumptions. Rieber's answer to the first question seems to be that it makes the information that there is a contrast between two statements more salient. However, Rieber does not show what role this information plays in the derivation of assumptions from utterances containing *but* – except, of course, that it is not part of their propositional (truth conditional) content.

2.4   Is conventional implicature a myth?

The assumption that whatever is encoded by *but* is not part of the truth conditional content of the utterances that contain it, was the starting point not only for Rieber's analysis, but for the first part of this book. However, Bach (1999) has argued that this assumption is mistaken and hence that there is no need for any account of non-truth conditional indicators or conventional implicature.

As Rieber has pointed out, a speaker who uses *but* in an attitude context such as the one in (77) will not necessarily be taken to be suggesting that there is a contrast.

(77)   Tom thinks that Sheila is rich but she is unhappy. However, I have always thought that all rich people are unhappy.

Rieber is, apparently, happy to live with this problem. However, it is not clear that he should be. As Wilson and Sperber have pointed out, it seems that no speech act theoretic analysis can accommodate the fact that expressions such as *but* and *so* can occur within indirect thought reports, since the speaker is neither performing the speech act supposed to be signalled by these expressions nor attributing any speech act to someone else.

I shall return to Wilson and Sperber's point in the following chapter. My aim in the final section of this chapter is to discuss Bach's (1999) argument that the fact that *but* can occur in the *that*-clauses of indirect quotations shows that *but* cannot be construed as carrying a conventional implicature, and that it contributes straightforwardly to what is said. As Bach says, while it is true that an expression such as *but* can be used to make 'an editorial comment on what he is reporting as being said', it can 'also contribute to *what* is being reported' (Bach 1999:339, my emphasis). Accordingly, he argues that an expression such as *but* functions as an operator which combines with the rest of the sentence to yield a proposition which, although it is not part of the truth conditional content of the utterance, is nevertheless something which has truth conditions.

As Bach recognizes, it is difficult to pin down the exact contribution *but* makes to the interpretation of the utterances that contain it because it interacts with the context. In the following chapter, I shall argue that this elusive quality of *but*, and, indeed, of many other expressions that have been analysed as discourse markers, can be explained in terms of the fact that it does not encode a concept. However, Bach is committed to an analysis in which *but* encodes conceptual information: according to him (and Grice 1989 and Rieber 1997), it encodes the information that there is some kind of contrast. The problem is that the nature of the contrastive relation seems to vary across contexts. Accordingly, his solution is to treat the information encoded by *but* as under-specifying the intended contrastive relation, or, in other words, as information which must be pragmatically completed or enriched by the hearer before she can identify the intended relation. This makes 'contrast' something like a blueprint for a concept, and Bach's treatment of *but* seems to follow the lines that he proposes for the analysis of indexicals. Unfortunately, Bach does not elaborate on this, and consequently, it is not clear either what the pragmatic processes which 'complete' the blueprint are or what the result of these processes is like in particular contexts.

Apart from this, there is a range of other expressions in English which have been treated as encoding a contrastive type of relation, but which are subtly different in meaning from each other and from *but* – for example, *however*, *nevertheless*, *although*, utterance-initial *yet* and *still*. Since Bach says very little, if anything, about these expressions, it is difficult to say how he would capture these subtle distinctions of meaning. He does note that *nevertheless* does not pass his indirect quotation test, and hence must be treated as a constituent of a higher-level speech act – that is, as a Gricean conventional implicature (see below). The effect of this, however, is not particularly illuminating: it simply amounts to saying that while *but* encodes a concept of contrast which is part of the propositional content of the utterance that contains it, *nevertheless* encodes a concept of contrast which is not part of the propositional content of the utterance that contains it. More generally, contrast seems to be just too crude for capturing the contributions of any of these expressions. Obviously, this is a problem not just for Bach, but for anyone who has analysed *but* in terms of contrast, and I will be returning to it in chapter 4 and in my discussion of coherence relations in chapter 5.

As Bach emphasizes, non-truth conditional analyses of *but* assume that its contrastive import is expressed in a proposition which is distinct from the conjoined proposition asserted. As we have seen, Grice's original suggestion was that *but conventionally implicates* the proposition that there is a contrast between the two statements. He then developed this analysis so that this extra proposition is a comment on the central speech act. Similarly, in Rieber's (1997) tacit performative account the contrastive import of *but* is expressed in a parenthetical performative which is comma'd off from the asserted conjunction. I believe Bach is right to say that there is something wrong with an approach in which a single expression encodes a proposition. However, it is not clear that he has in fact offered a real alternative to the conventional implicature account. His argument is that we do not need to treat *but* as contributing an extra proposition if we analyse it as an *operator* on the rest of the sentence: it preserves the original proposition(s) while yielding a new proposition. Bach does not provide a detailed account of the way in which *but* affects the two propositions it operates on. However, it seems that although he does not treat the contrastive import of *but* as something that is expressed in an implicated proposition, he does still treat it as a constituent of a proposition. That is, it seems that Bach assumes that the hearer of an utterance containing *but* recovers a proposition with something like the concept CONTRAST as a constituent.

Clearly, Bach's claim that *but* contributes to what is said conflicts with the generally held claim that *but* does not contribute to truth conditions. For example, it would generally be accepted that the fact that there is no identifiable contrast between the segments of utterances such as (78) does not affect its truth value. It is true provided that the roses are flowering and that the speaker has had breakfast.

(78)   The roses are flowering but I have had breakfast.

As we have seen in the first section of this chapter, intuitions about truth conditionality are not always straightforward. Not only do people's intuitions vary, but also the standard tests for truth conditionality are based on assumptions which cannot always be maintained. For Bach, this would not be surprising, since, according to him, these intuitions are the result of a forced choice. This choice, he argues, is based on the common misconception that every sentence expresses just one proposition. If we abandon the idea that a sentence can express one and only one proposition, then we can see how it could be partly true and partly false. Thus in (78) the 'primary propositions' that the roses are flowering and the speaker has had breakfast could be true, while the 'secondary proposition' that the fact that the roses are flowering contrasts with the fact that the speaker has had breakfast might be false (Bach 1999:328).

In fact, if Bach's claim that the information encoded by *but* does not fully determine the contrastive relation intended on a particular occasion, the 'secondary' proposition would not be the one given, but one derived by a process of pragmatic completion. Apart from this, it is clear that Bach's departure from the classical truth conditional position depends on the definition of a criterion for deciding on a particular occasion which of the propositions expressed by an utterance is primary and which is secondary. On the assumption that this can be done, it is worth asking what would be meant by 'the truth conditions of the utterance' on Bach's approach. As Iten (2000b) points out, it seems that this would have to mean the totality of the propositions expressed (primary and secondary). At the same time, the scope tests that are standardly used for testing for truth conditional content would be inapplicable, since logical operators and factive connectives only take a single proposition in their scope. As Iten says, this leaves those accounts which wish to maintain a distinction between truth conditional content and implicated content without a tool for drawing the distinction.

As we shall see, the idea that an utterance expresses more than one proposition has also been explored in relevance theoretic semantics (see Ifantidou-Trouki 1993, Blakemore 1990). However, paradoxically, this analysis was proposed for expressions such as illocutionary adverbials, apposition markers and parenthetical verbs, which according to Bach (1999) are *not* like *but* since they do not pass his indirect quotation test. According to him, all of these should be analysed as indicators of higher-order speech acts – that is, as Gricean conventional implicatures. In other words, it seems that for these expressions, Bach wishes to retain the notion of conventional implicature.

Since Bach does not apply his indirect quotation test to the entire range of non-truth conditional phenomena listed in section 1 of this chapter, it is difficult to know what he would say about syntactic devices such as cleft constructions, such as the ones in (79).

(79)   Tom said that it was Ben who ate the cake.

Since the construction can occur within the speech report, it would seem that it would, by Bach's criterion, be part of what is said. This would leave Bach with the problem of specifying the secondary proposition yielded by the cleft construction. However, before anyone begins this sort of task, perhaps we should look more closely at Bach's assumption that an element following the complementizer in an indirect quotation contributes to something propositional.

It is generally recognized that what Banfield (1982) calls represented speech and thought may include expressions and constructions which although they can be attributed to the person whose thought is being represented, cannot be easily analysed as contributing to something propositional. Consider for example, the uses of 'oh' and the repetition in (80), and the reformulations and repetition in (81).

(80)   She mustn't let her connexion with him go; oh, she mustn't let it go,
        or she was lost, lost utterly in this world of riff-raffy expensive people
        and joy-hogs. Oh, the joy-hogs.

(D. H. Lawrence, Lady Chatterley's Lover, 311)[7]

(81)   That was the way to live – *carelessly, recklessly*, spending oneself. He
        got to his feet and began to wade towards the shore, pressing his toes
        into the firm, wrinkled sand. *To take things easy, not to fight against
        the ebb and flow of life*, but to give way to it – that was what was
        needed. It was this tension that was all wrong. *To live – to live!*

(Katherine Mansfield, 'At the Bay', 206)[8]

It is true that the expressions and constructions which according to Banfield
characterize free indirect speech cannot be indirectly quoted in embedded
clauses as *but* can. However, the phenomenon of free indirect speech or thought
does raise the question of what is meant by saying that a writer or speaker is
representing a thought. If we say that *oh* in (80) or the repetition in (81) is
being used to represent a character's thought, then it seems we cannot construe
thoughts simply in terms of their (truth conditional) propositional content.

   Moreover, it seems that there are devices, such as emphatic stress, which are
generally considered not to contribute to propositional content and yet can be
indirectly quoted in an embedded construction. Thus while the marked stress
on *walking* in (82) would be understood as an editorial comment on the thought
being reported, it seems that (83a) can be interpreted in much the same way
as (83b) and hence that the emphasis on *needed* is being attributed to someone
other than the speaker/narrator.

(82)   She says she is WALKING to the station, for God's sake. It'll take at
        least an hour and the train leaves at 8.

(83)   (a) John pointed out that they couldn't really afford a holiday. But no,
            she said that she NEEDED to get away.
        (b) John pointed out that they couldn't really afford a holiday. But no,
            she NEEDED to get away.

These sort of phenomena suggest that Bach's argument that the use of *but* in
indirect quotations is evidence that it contributes to the (propositional) content
of utterances can be maintained only if either it can be shown that expressions
such as *oh* and devices such as repetition and emphasis do not encode any

---

[7] First published 1960; reprinted London: Penguin, 1961.
[8] From *Selected Stories*, chosen and introduced by D. M. Davin. First published 1953; reprinted
London: Oxford University Press, 1967.

aspect of a represented thought at all or or it can be shown that they contribute to something with truth conditions. It would seem that the first option is difficult to reconcile with the way that examples of represented thought and speech are interpreted, while the second is difficult to reconcile with the notoriously vague (and sometimes poetic) effects of these stylistic devices.

In the following chapter, I shall argue that the hearer of an utterance containing *but* does not recover an implicated proposition (see Grice) or a parenthetical proposition (see Rieber) or a proposition containing a contrast operator (see Bach). I shall argue that if we approach the question of what kind of information an expression such as *but* makes salient from a cognitive point of view rather than a speech act theoretic point of view, then not only will we have an account of how this information contributes to the interpretation of the utterances containing it, but also we will be able to explain exactly how *but* and the devices such as stress and repetition can be used in the representation of an attributed thought.

3 Relevance and meaning

3.1 Relevance and the semantics/pragmatics distinction

Relevance theory is known as a theory of pragmatics, and, indeed, Sperber and Wilson regard their book as a result of their different interests in the study of contextual factors in verbal communication – in Wilson's case, an interest which began with her work on presuppositions (Wilson 1975), and in Sperber's, an interest in rhetoric and symbolism (Sperber 1975); (see Sperber and Wilson 1995: vi). However, as we have seen, it is impossible to have a view of pragmatics without having a view of semantics, or vice versa, and it is not surprising that the relevance theoretic approach to pragmatics comes with a view of semantics attached. My aim in this chapter is not to give a complete survey of relevance theory,[1] but to outline those aspects which underlie the account of non-truth conditional meaning which I shall be giving in the next chapter. This will mean that the focus will be on the relevance theoretic view of the semantics/ pragmatics distinction, the distinction between explicit and implicit content and the relationship between linguistic form and relevance which derives, on the one hand, from the relevance theoretic commitment to a computational view of the mind, and on the other, from the principle which, according to relevance theory, constrains the inferences involved in understanding utterances.

Usually, pragmatics is defined after semantics. That is, its definition is thought of as being a consequence of the way one defines semantics. We have already seen an example of this – the view encapsulated in Gazdar's (1979) slogan 'PRAGMATICS = MEANING MINUS TRUTH CONDITIONS'. Let us instead start by looking at verbal communication as a whole.

As we have seen in the introduction to this book, there are different ways of looking at communication. According to the view advocated by, for example, Mey (1993), communication must be viewed as a social phenomenon, and a

---

[1] Sperber and Wilson have themselves published a number of paper-length outlines (see, for example, Sperber and Wilson 1987, Wilson 1994). In addition, there are encyclopaedia entries by Blakemore (1995) and Moeschler and Reboul (1994), and a textbook (Blakemore 1992).

theory of communication must say something about 'real communicative inter-action, as it happens in our society' (1993:81). However, Sperber and Wilson view communication from the point of view of the sub-personal cognitive processes which are involved in the human ability to entertain representations of other people's thoughts and desires and ideas on the basis of public stimuli such as utterances or gestures – for example, the cognitive processes which are involved in your ability to derive (1) as a representation of my thoughts in a situation in which I attract your attention to an approaching bus by pointing to it, or in the situation in which I produce the utterance in (2).

(1)   The bus which we are waiting for is approaching the bus-stop.

(2)   It's coming.

Notice that I say 'processes' rather than 'process' here. For Sperber and Wilson argue that communication is not a single process, and hence that there is not a single general answer to the question of how communication is achieved. In particular, they argue that neither decoding nor inference can provide the basis of a single model of communication:

> We maintain that communication can be achieved in ways which are as different from one another as walking is from plane flight. In particular, communication can be achieved by coding and decoding messages, and it can be achieved by providing evidence for an intended inference. The code model and the inferential model are each adequate to a different mode of communication; hence upgrading either to the status of a general theory of communication is a mistake. (Sperber and Wilson 1995:3)

This distinction – between the process of decoding messages and the process of making inferences from evidence – is the basis of their distinction between semantics and pragmatics. The first kind of process is performed by an autonomous linguistic system – the grammar – which is dedicated to the performance of mappings between a linguistic stimulus (utterance) and a semantic representation for that utterance. The other kind of process – the inferential process – integrates the output of the decoding process with contextual information in order to deliver a hypothesis about the speaker's informative intention.

The question of what drives an audience's search for the interpretation of an utterance or any example of communicative behaviour is, according to Sperber and Wilson, a special instance of the question of what drives our search for the explanation of *any* human behaviour. Consider, for example, a bus-driver who is preparing to leave from a bus stop and sees in his rear mirror the reflection of an anxious-looking woman holding a bus pass, making ineffectual attempts to cross the busy road behind him. If he is prepared to invest effort in processing this behaviour at all, he will use contextual assumptions to derive inferences about the woman's beliefs (for example, that his bus is about to leave), desires (for example, that she wants to cross the road) and intentions (for example, that she intends boarding a bus – preferably his). In other words, his explanation will involve the attribution of beliefs and intentions.

According to Sperber and Wilson, the bus-driver's search for such an explanation is governed by the fact that the human cognitive system is geared towards the *maximization of relevance*. That is, it is a consequence of the fact that he is looking for the maximal improvement to his overall representation of the world. Sperber and Wilson identify three ways in which new information *P* yields an improvement to a person's representation of the world, or, in other words, three types of *cognitive effect*:

(i)   It may yield a *contextual implication*, or in other words, an assumption which is the result of a deduction that crucially involves the synthesis of *P* and the context *C*.
Example: in a context which includes the assumption that if a person is carrying a bus pass, then they intend to travel on a bus, the bus-driver in the situation described above will derive the contextual implication that the woman carrying the bus pass intends travelling on a bus.

(ii)   It may *strengthen* an existing assumption. This is the effect derived when an assumption in the context is independently derived from a new set of premises that includes *P*.
Example: The bus-driver's assumption that the woman is crossing the road in order to travel on his bus may be strengthened by the assumption that she is holding a bus pass.

(iii)   It may contradict and lead to the elimination of an existing assumption.
Example: The bus-driver's assumption that the woman intends travelling on his bus is contradicted and eliminated when he sees the woman give the bus pass to someone standing by the bus stop and walk off in the opposite direction.

Sperber and Wilson's claim is that the more cognitive effects derived the greater the relevance of the input. However, relevance is also a function of the processing effort required for the derivation of cognitive effects, and this means that the greater the processing effort the less relevant the information. Thus for example, although most of the travellers on the Manchester bus just mentioned may derive *some* cognitive effects from the headline in the newspapers they are reading – 'TORNADO ABOUT TO HIT FLORIDA COAST' – this information will be considerably less relevant to them than it will be for a reader whose family lives on the coast of Florida.

This principle, which Sperber and Wilson (1995) call the *cognitive principle of relevance,* applies to the explanation of behaviour which does not involve communication – for example, the behaviour of the anxious woman described above. However, suppose that the woman on seeing the bus had waved her weekly bus pass above her head in such a way that the bus-driver was bound to see it in his mirror. In this case, the driver would not simply infer that she wanted to catch his bus, but he would attribute to her a higher-order intention, namely, the intention to make evident her intention to inform him of something (her desire to catch the bus). Sperber and Wilson call this intention a *communicative intention*, and the behaviour which gives rise to the attribution of such an intention is known as *ostensive communication*. Their point is that in contrast with non-communicative human behaviour, this kind of behaviour gives rise to a specific expectation of relevance simply by virtue of the fact that it is an overt demand for attention.

Their first point is that a hearer who recognizes that someone has a communicative intention is justified in expecting enough cognitive effects for the information to be worth processing. It is simply not in a rational communicator's interests to demand the effort that recovering cognitive effects requires if there is no reward at the end. However, Sperber and Wilson argue that the audience's expectation goes further than this. It is true that they cannot expect maximal relevance – either from the point of view of effects (rewards) or effort (cost). Even if a communicator has the most relevant information, he may be prevented from communicating it by other considerations (for example, tact, politeness, the law). At the same time, it may not be within his capabilities to produce the most audience-friendly communicative behaviour possible. On the other hand, while it may not be possible for the communicator to achieve maximal relevance, it is clearly within his interests to achieve the greatest degree of relevance possible. After all, genuine communicators do want to hold their audience's attention, and they have a greater chance of doing this if their utterances are the most relevant ones given their abilities and interests. Sperber and Wilson call this level of relevance *optimal relevance*:

> *Optimal relevance* (Sperber and Wilson 1995)
> An ostensive stimulus is optimally relevant iff:
>
> (i) it is relevant enough for it to be worth the audience's effort to process it (it achieves adequate cognitive effects);

(ii) it is the most relevant stimulus compatible with the communicator's abilities and preferences.

And they capture the generalization about what hearers can expect from ostensively communicated information in what they call the *communicative principle of relevance*:

> *The communicative principle of relevance* (Sperber and Wilson 1995)
> Every act of overt communication communicates a presumption of its own optimal relevance.

This principle should not be construed as a suggestion that every act of overt communication is in fact optimally relevant: communicators can be mistaken about the relevance of the information they communicate, and the presumption of relevance they communicate can be false. The point is simply that every act of overt communication is evidence of the communicator's belief that the information they want to communicate is relevant. Nor should the principle be construed as a claim that communicators always succeed in being optimally relevant. Communicators can be mistaken about the contextual and processing resources of their audiences.

It seems that these last two points have led some critics to claim that Sperber and Wilson's principle cannot be an empirical claim since it is irrefutable (for example, Mey 1993). As we have just seen, the communicative principle of relevance is grounded in the claim that human cognition is geared towards the maximization of relevance, which, as Sperber and Wilson point out, is not irrefutable and far from a truism. This means that the communicative principle must itself be an empirical claim. At the same time, in contrast with Grice's (1989) maxims of conversation or Horn's Q and R principles (Horn 1984), the communicative principle of relevance is not a default principle that can be over-ridden in certain contexts. If it is true, it is true for every case of communication (including the cases in which the presumption of relevance communicated is false and the cases where communication fails).

It may be thought that the case for the role of inference in communication rests on the non-verbal nature of the example used. It is true that for Sperber and Wilson, the communicative intention can be made manifest by any kind of ostensive behaviour – waving, rolling one's eyes, sniffing, grunting, sighing, groaning or even the use of silence. And it is true that inferential processes do all the work in such cases for the recovery of the communicator's informative intention. However, Sperber and Wilson's contribution to pragmatics is to demonstrate that the inferential processes involved in these kinds of examples are also involved in the interpretation of utterances, and hence that all aspects of utterance interpretation are constrained by the communicative principle of relevance. Utterances are, of course, distinguished from non-verbal ostensive stimuli, by the fact that they have coded linguistic properties. As Sperber and Wilson have pointed out, the possession of a shared linguistic code enables communicators to produce much more subtle and more determinate evidence for their intentions than they can in the absence of such a code (Sperber and Wilson 1995:27–8). However, they have also pointed out that the linguistically encoded properties of utterances are never enough on their own for the identification of the speaker's intended message. There is inevitably a gap between what the grammar delivers – the linguistically determined semantic representation – and the interpretation intended. And this gap is filled by pragmatically constrained inference. Indeed, it seems that in some cases – slips of the tongue, contradictions, for example – the linguistic system is overridden by the inferential system. For example, consider the slip of the tongue in (3) (taken from Blakemore (1992)) and the contradiction in (4).

(3)   Obviously, in the outer islands nobody speaks English. So brush up your English [utterance produced by presenter of a television holiday programme on the Greek islands].

(4)   I know it's a job that takes forever. But it doesn't take *that* long [produced in response to claim about the time that a particular task would take].

Given the appropriate contextual assumptions, the hearer of both these utterances would be able to recover an interpretation which matches the speaker's informative intention in spite of the linguistic evidence produced rather than because of it.

I do not wish to suggest here a picture in which the linguistic system is responsible for the delivery of interpretations except in certain cases, for example (3) and (4), where it is overridden. As we shall see, this *is* the picture suggested by other approaches. However, it is not a picture that is compatible with an approach in which the interpretation of communicative behaviour is governed by the communicative principle of relevance (above). Recall that according to this principle, the hearer of an utterance is entitled to expect that the speaker has aimed for a level of optimal relevance. This means that she is entitled to expect that the speaker has aimed to produce an utterance whose processing requires the lowest amount of processing effort that is compatible with his interests and abilities. In other words, according to the communicative principle of relevance, the hearer is entitled to expect that the interpretation of an utterance does not call for any unnecessary processing effort. A speaker who produced an utterance whose interpretation required contextual assumptions which were not accessible to the hearer at all or who could have achieved the same effects by producing an utterance whose interpretation required more easily accessed assumptions would, of course, fail to meet the level of optimal relevance communicated by his utterance. (Speakers whose desire to show off their extensive vocabulary, technical knowledge or their political correctness outweighs their desire to communicate the informational content of their utterances may spring to mind here.) However, equally, the presumption of optimal relevance would be false in cases where the speaker causes unnecessary processing by requiring the hearer to process concepts which are already highly accessible. Such speakers run the risk of being classed as patronising or even of not being listened to. It follows from this that a speaker who aims at a high degree of explicitness will not necessarily produce an optimally relevant utterance. Consider the following dialogue between two friends who live in different parts of the country:

(5)   A: What's the weather like up there?
        B: Terrible. It's been raining for hours.

B could have achieved the same cognitive effects by producing the utterance in (6):

(6)   The weather up in Manchester is terrible. It has been raining outside in Manchester for hours.

However, this utterance would not be consistent with the communicative principle of relevance: since it encodes concepts which are already accessible to A it entails processing effort which does not result in cognitive effects.

  More generally, the communicative principle of relevance implies that the most appropriate means for communicating a proposition is not necessarily one which fully encodes all of its constituents. Hence the use of fragmentary or subsentential utterances or of fully sentential utterances with missing constituents. Recall the examples given in chapter 1.3, repeated here as (7–12).

(7)   We went out for Christmas. The meal was really nice. But it wasn't the same somehow. [same as having Christmas dinner at home]
(8)   Don't sit on that rock. It'll fall. [if you sit on the rock]
(9)   He works too hard. [for what?]
(10)   Dogs must be carried. [if you are travelling on the London Underground with one]
(11)   On the table.
(12)   Lovely.

As Carston (1988, 1998, 1999) has shown, such examples show that the gap between linguistically encoded information and the explicit content of utterances is not simply one that is bridged by the process of reference assignment and disambiguation.[2] This point has been appreciated for some time within the relevance theoretic framework. Thus Wilson and Sperber (1981) claimed that while reference assignment and disambiguation yield (14) as an interpretation for (13), most hearers will interpret it as expressing something much more specific, for example (15).

(13)   [produced in a situation in which John Smith is playing the violin] He plays well.

(14)   John Smith plays some musical instrument well.

(15)   John Smith plays the violin well.

Wilson and Sperber's point has been developed by Carston into what she calls the semantic under-determinacy thesis (Carston 1988,1998,1999). She has shown that the gap between the linguistically encoded properties of an utterance and the explicit content recovered is not only demonstrated by cases in which the hearer uses inferential processing to enrich or build on the linguistically encoded representation, but is also evident in utterances in which speakers use expressions to mean either something more restricted or something looser than their encoded meanings. In addition to the examples repeated from chapter 1.2 as (16) and (17), we may add (4) (repeated below) and Carston's (1999) examples in (18–21).

(16)   [produced by child angered by her mother's lack of maternal feeling] You are not a real mother.

(17)   [produced by child after teacher has mistaken her childminder for her mother] She's not my mother, she's my childminder.

 (4)   [produced in response to claim about the time needed for a particular task] It takes forever. But it doesn't take *that* long.

(18)   The steak is raw.

(19)   Holland is flat.

(20)   Jane is a bulldozer.

(21)   Bill isn't a human being.

As Carston says, all of these cases involve what Sperber and Wilson (1997) have called *ad hoc* concept formation. That is, they are understood to communicate a proposition which includes a concept that is derived by narrowing

---

[2] For further discussion of non-sentential utterances, see Stainton (1994).

and/or loosening a concept encoded by a lexical item. For example, although (4) is a contradiction from a linguistic point of view, it is not understood this way because the concept encoded by *forever* is replaced by a weaker concept of A LONG TIME, which shares some but not all of the implications of the stronger one. The same kind of loosening process is involved in (16, 18, 19, 20). In contrast, the speaker of (21) intends the concept encoded by *human being* to be replaced by a narrower concept than the one it encodes, that is, one that denotes only a subset of the species of human beings. For further discussion, see Carston (1998), (1999) and Sperber and Wilson (1985/6), (1997).

As we shall see in the following section, cases such as these have important implications for the way in which the distinction between explicit and implicit content is drawn. However, I would like to end this section by underlining what the semantic under-determinacy thesis implies for the relationship between semantics and pragmatics. According to this thesis, the fact that the linguistically determined semantic representations of utterances such as (7–12) and (16–21) do not fully determine the propositions they are understood to express is an inevitable consequence of the fact that 'natural language sentences do not encode full propositions but merely schemas for the construction of (truth-evaluable) propositional forms' (Carston 1999:105).

This thesis is in direct conflict with the view that while linguistically semantics does under-determine the proposition expressed in many cases, this is simply a consequence of the fact that this happens to be the most convenient means of communication for speakers and hearers. It is always possible to supply a sentence which *does* fully encode the proposition expressed independently of the context. Thus Katz (1977) argued that pragmatics saves us from the 'wasteful verbosity' of having to spell out everything explicitly in the grammar of our sentences, so that instead of having to use sentences such as (22), we can in the appropriate context use sentences such as (23).

(22)   The man who has just asked the stupid question about the relation between the mental and the physical has, thank God, left the room.

(23)   Thank God, he is gone.

(Katz 1977:19–20)

According to this view, semantics is viewed as bearing the real responsibility in communication, and pragmatics is simply called in as a sort of convenient auxiliary support system.

However, as Sperber and Wilson (1995) have pointed out, Katz's explicit version of (23) is not in fact referentially determinate: its interpretation still requires inference based on contextual information. This raises the question of whether it is at all possible to eliminate referential indeterminacy in the linguistic form of an utterance. Sperber and Wilson suggest that the only context-invariant representation would be something like (24), where references to time and space are provided by universal co-ordinates.

(24)   Thank God, the man x who at time t was in location l has at time t', left the room which the man x was in at time t.

(Sperber and Wilson 1995:192)

However, as Carston (1999) points out, such universal co-ordinates cannot themselves be encoded by natural language expressions. Moreover, as Sperber and Wilson say, we can never be certain that (24) does express the same thought as the speaker's utterance in (23) since it is possible that in our internal language of thought we fix reference in terms of private time and space co-ordinates rather than universal co-ordinates.

This last point might be worrying for those who see the aim of utterance interpretation in terms of the identification of an assumption which is an exact duplication of the thought the speaker intended to communicate, for it implies that it is never possible to know whether the thought the speaker has when he produces the utterance in (23) is the same as the thought that the hearer recovers when she interprets it. The problem seems even more serious when one considers the cases of *ad hoc* concept formation discussed by Carston (2000b:36) (illustrated in (16–21) above). Consider her example in (25):

(25)   A: Are you going to the party?
        B: I'm tired.

As Carston says, tiredness is a matter of degree, and the level of tiredness communicated by the predicate *tired* varies from context to context. In this case, she argues, it communicates something paraphrasable as 'tired to an extent that makes going to a party undesirable to B' (Carston 2000b:36). Since the exact extent depends on specific contextual information (how tired would B have to be before he turns down a party invitation, how much does B like parties?), and since this *ad hoc* concept cannot be fully encoded by a natural language expression, there seems to be no way of knowing whether the concept the hearer recovers is exactly the same concept that the speaker had in mind.

Should this really worry us? If communication is, as is sometimes suggested, a matter of inducing a hearer to entertain specific thoughts, the answer would seem to be 'yes'. For then its success would depend on whether or not the hearer recovered those particular thoughts. But in fact, it is not at all clear that anyone can have a controllable effect on someone's actual thoughts, that is, on the assumptions that they actually represent, and it would not be rational for a speaker to have an intention over which he has no control. Accordingly, Sperber and Wilson have defined their notion of an informative intention in terms of the intention to alter the *cognitive environment* of the audience.

A person's *cognitive environment* is the set of assumptions which she is capable of constructing and as accepting as true, or in other words, the set of assumptions which are *manifest* to her. Manifestness is a matter of degree, and which assumptions are more manifest to someone at a particular time will depend on her physical environment and cognitive abilities. Since manifestness is a dispositional notion, it is possible for an assumption to be manifest to someone even if they do not actually represent it: it will be manifest provided that it is capable of being non-demonstratively inferred. To use Sperber and Wilson's example, while it is unlikely that someone who had not read pages 40–1 of their book (1995) had actually entertained the thought that Noam Chomsky has never played billiards with Ronald Reagan, this assumption would have been manifest to them, since they were capable of inferring it from what they did know or believe.

Since the hearer's cognitive environment does not consist of the assumptions she actually entertains, it is possible for the communicator to have some controllable effect on it. Thus Sperber and Wilson define their notion of an informative intention as follows:

> *Informative intention:* the intention to make manifest or more manifest in an audience a set of assumptions *I* (1995:58)

Given this definition of the informative intention, the question of whether the assumption that the hearer recovers from examples such as (23) or (25) duplicates the thought that was originally entertained by the speaker does not arise: 'It seems to us neither paradoxical nor counter-intuitive to say that there are thoughts which we cannot exactly share, and that communication can be successful without resulting in an exact duplication of thoughts in communicator and audience' (Sperber and Wilson 1995:193).

However, while Sperber and Wilson do not define the communicator's informative intention as an intention to induce specific thoughts in the audience, they do recognize that communicators do expect to alter the audience's actual thoughts, and moreover, that they can form assumptions about which thoughts an audience is most likely to entertain as a result of their utterances. Indeed, the relevance theoretic approach to pragmatics is an exploration of the way in which they do this.

The main thrust of this section has been that they do *not* do this by encoding their thoughts, that is, by finding an utterance which fully encodes the information they want to communicate. We have seen that the possibility of finding such an utterance appears to be non-existent. Moreover, as Sperber and Wilson remind us, we do not entertain semantic representations in the sense that we entertain thoughts. Semantic representations are recovered by unconscious, automatic decoding processes and can only be used as an input to the inferential processes which yield representations which can be entertained as thoughts by the hearer. The question is, then, given that the gap between the encoded semantic representation and the interpretation that is recovered by the hearer is filled by non-demonstrative inference processes which take contextual assumptions as premises, how can the speaker identify the contextual assumptions which the hearer will actually entertain?

The answer, according to Sperber and Wilson, lies in the cognitive principle of relevance, and the special role that relevance plays in ostensive communication captured in the communicative principle of relevance (see above, p. 63). Since the speaker knows that the hearer is looking for relevance, and since the speaker knows that the hearer approaches ostensively communicated information on the assumption that the speaker has aimed at optimal relevance, the speaker has reason to believe that the hearer will adopt a comprehension strategy which allows her to arrive at the level of relevance which is consistent with her expectations for the least processing effort.

This might seem to suggest that it is the speaker's responsibility to produce the utterance which is most likely to meet the hearer's expectations of relevance for the least amount of processing effort. However, as we have seen, speakers can make slips of the tongue. Recall the example in (3):

(3)   Obviously, in the outer islands nobody speaks English. So brush up your English [utterance produced by presenter of a television holiday programme on the Greek islands].

How does a hearer who assumes that (3) is consistent with the principle of relevance deal with this? Sperber (1994) suggests that the answer depends on the level of the hearer's metarepresentational abilities. A hearer at the lowest level adopts a strategy which does not involve metarepresenting the speaker's thoughts: restricting herself to the linguistically encoded meaning of *English*, she simply looks for an interpretation that is relevant enough, and on finding it assumes that it is the intended one. The adoption of this strategy would result in communication failure in (3), since the hearer would not find an acceptable interpretation. However, as Sperber points out, most hearers are capable of adopting a strategy which involves metarepresenting the speaker's thoughts: by asking herself on what interpretation of *English* the speaker might have thought his utterance was relevant, the hearer may be able to infer that he meant 'Greek' instead of 'English'. In fact, most hearers can go further than this, and metarepresent the speaker's thoughts about what he would think was relevant enough. By adopting this strategy, hearers can deal not only with incompetent speakers such as the speaker of (3), but also speakers who lie (non-benevolent speakers).

In the picture I have been trying to draw here, the fundamental ability in communication is not linguistic encoding and decoding, but the ability to derive inferences which result in assumptions which are entertained as metarepresentations of other people's thoughts, desires and intentions. Pragmatics does not simply enter when linguistic decoding fails: on the contrary, the linguistic system is subservient to pragmatic inference in the sense that it functions as an aid to the inferential system – as an input to independently functioning inferential systems. If this view is right, then it justifies the order which I have adopted in this chapter, that is, pragmatics first, *then* semantics. However, we are not ready for semantics yet. In the next section, I turn to the distinction between the two ways in which assumptions may be communicated by an utterance.

3.2   Implicit and explicit verbal communication

The distinction between implicitly communicated information and explicitly communicated information is usually discussed from the point of view of Grice's distinction between what is said and what is implicated (see chapter 2). Associated with this view is the assumption that it corresponds to the distinction between semantics and pragmatics, so that explicitly communicated information is regarded as being within the domain of semantics, while implicitly communicated information is said to fall within the domain of pragmatics. My aim in this section is to show that the distinction that has been developed in relevance theory is not compatible with the Gricean one. The question of how the distinction should be drawn has attracted a great deal of controversy (see, for example, Bach 1994, Carston 1988, 1998, 1999, 2002, Recanati 1989). I do not plan to enter this controversy here: I simply intend to outline how the relevance theoretic distinction between explicit communication and implicit communication is different from the Gricean one, and thereby set the stage for the discussion of the ways in which linguistic form can provide an input to pragmatic inference.

The intuition is a strong one in cases such as (26). Most people would agree that B has explicitly communicated that he and the hearer are in Manchester, and only indirectly communicated that they should take umbrellas.

(26)   A: Should we take umbrellas?
       B: We're in Manchester.

The problems only start to emerge when one asks how the distinction is drawn. In fact, Grice's distinction between what is said and what is conversationally implicated did not derive from an interest in cases such as this. As has been well documented, his primary concern was to maintain a minimalist truth functional analysis of the natural language counterparts of the logical connectives in the face of examples in which they appeared to carry suggestions over and above their truth functional meanings. The notion of conversational implicature seemed to allow Grice to say that at the level of what is said, these expressions could be given the same meanings as their logical counterparts. Thus for example, in (27) he could say that the suggestion that she turned the computer on before she started to type is a conversational implicature derived on the basis of the assumption that the speaker is presenting the events described in the order in which they happened and is thus conforming to the maxim of manner. This would allow him to maintain an analysis of *and* in which it is equivalent to the logical connective &.

(27)   She turned on the computer and began to type.

The underlying assumption is that what is said is restricted to the truth conditional content of the utterance, while the implicature is information that has no bearing on what is assessed for truth. Thus (27) is true if and only if she turned on the computer and she began to type, and its truth value would not be affected by the fact that the events actually took place in a different order.[3]

As we have seen in the previous chapter, it seems that Grice's aim was to define what is said so that it overlapped with the notion of conventional or linguistically encoded meaning. We have already seen how the phenomenon he called *conventional implicature* – expressions such as *but* and *therefore*, for example – made it difficult for Grice to maintain this definition. However, apart from this, Carston (1988, 1998, 1999, 2002) has shown that Grice's distinction cannot be reconciled with the fact that the propositional content of utterances is not fully determined by their linguistically encoded meanings. It is true that Grice did recognize that the context plays a role in the assignment of reference and in disambiguation. However, as Carston's work has demonstrated, the extent of the gap between linguistically encoded meaning and propositional

---

[3] For critical discussion of Grice's analysis of conjoined utterances, see Blakemore and Carston (1999), Carston (1993), Carston (2002).

content extends much further than this. Moreover, while Grice may have recognized the importance of context in reference assignment and disambiguation, he did not acknowledge that its role was constrained by the same sort of general pragmatic principles that he claimed were involved in the recovery of implicatures. Consider the example given by Wilson and Sperber in an early critique of Grice's theory of conversation (Wilson and Sperber 1981).

(28)   I refuse to admit them.

Interpreted in the context of the question in (29a), reference assignment and disambiguation will yield the assumption in (29b), while interpreted in the context of (30a), it will yield (30b).

(29)   (a) What do you do when you make mistakes?
        (b) The speaker refuses to confess to the mistakes he makes.
(30)   (a) What do you do with gate-crashers?
        (b) The speaker refuses to let gate-crashers in.

As Sperber and Wilson (1995:183) say, explicit content is much more inferential and much more worthy of pragmatic investigation than Grice envisaged.

Carston has undertaken such a pragmatic investigation, showing not only that the suggestions Grice analysed as generalized conversational implicatures (for example, the suggestion of temporal sequence in (27)) should be re-analysed as pragmatically determined elements of explicit content, but also that pragmatically constrained inference is involved in the interpretation of negative utterances and non-literal utterances (for example, (16–21); (see Carston 1988, 1993, 1995, 1997a, 1997b, 1999, 2002) The distinction between explicit and implicit communication that emerges from this work departs from Grice's distinction (or the distinctions that are based on this distinction) in the sense that it does not equate explicitly communicated information with conventionally encoded information and allows for the contribution of pragmatic inference in its identification. However, as we shall see, it departs from the Gricean distinction in another sense as well – one which has implications for the role of truth conditions in a cognitive theory of communication.

Let us consider B's utterance in (31), which is a dialogue between myself and a colleague:

(31)   A: Are you going away this summer?
        B: I have to finish my book.

A will have understood B to have implied that she is not going away (on holiday) this summer. But what is B explicitly communicating here? First, let us consider what B means by *book*. She does not intend to refer to the sort of book that you are reading now, one whose pages are densely covered in print and are bound between covers, with the title and author's name emblazoned on the front. This may be the book that she dreams about as she sits at her computer, but it is not what she is referring to in (31). *Book* must be understood as 'book that B is writing' and only exists (in its completed state) in B's imagination. Given this interpretation of *book*, *my book* cannot be interpreted as the book she owns, the book that she has ordered, the book that she has borrowed from the library, the book that she has given to someone else as a gift, or even the book that she has published. These are all possible interpretations of the possessive pronoun, but the one which will be recovered in this instance is 'the book she is in the process of writing'. If this is the interpretation of *my book*, then *finish* will be interpreted not as 'finish reading' but as 'finish writing', where the concept understood to be communicated by *write* will not be 'make marks on paper with a pen', or even 'tap the keys of a computer keyboard', but something considerably wider, involving planning, thinking, revising, researching – in other words, everything that is involved in authoring a book intended for publication.

The point is that none of this is *encoded* in the semantic representation of B's utterance. It is recovered by pragmatically constrained inferences which develop the linguistically encoded semantic representation of B's utterance using (non-linguistic) contextual information. The result of this inferential development of the linguistically encoded semantic representation – the *explicature* – will be a premise in the inferential processes which yield the *implicatures* communicated by the utterance, in this case, the implicated assumption that the speaker is not going away on holiday this summer.

I hope that this one example is sufficient to show how the relevance theoretic distinction between explicatures and implicatures differs from the one derived from Grice's distinction between explicit and implicit content. In contrast with Grice's distinction, the relevance theoretic one is drawn according to the way in which an assumption is derived: if an assumption is derived by inference processes that develop the linguistically encoded semantic representation of an utterance, then it is an explicature. If it is derived in an inference in which the explicature is one of the premises, then it is an implicature.

It might be argued that Grice's distinction was an equally derivational distinction in that while what is implicated was defined as an assumption whose derivation crucially involved the maxims of conversation, what is said was defined as an assumption whose identification never involved the maxims. However, as Sperber and Wilson showed, it is not possible to maintain this sort of distinction, since the maxims are as much involved in the recovery of what is said as they are in the recovery of implicatures (see above). Moreover, it seems clear that Grice's attempts to develop an account of conventional implicature were motivated by his desire to defend a notion of what is said in which truth conditional content of an utterance departs only minimally from its linguistically encoded meaning. In other words, the tool for distinguishing explicitly communicated assumptions from explicitly communicated assumptions is in the final analysis one which sorts truth conditional content from non-truth conditional content.

This is not the tool used by relevance theory: truth conditions do not play a role in distinguishing the explicit content of an utterance from its implicit content. Indeed, Sperber and Wilson have extended the notion of explicit content as it has been presented here to include *higher-level explicatures* or assumptions which are derived by developing the semantic representation of an utterance such as (31B) so that an explicature such as (32) is recovered and embedding it under a propositional attitude or speech act description, say, (33a) or (33b).

(32)   The speaker must finish the processes involved in preparing the book she is authoring for publication.

(33)   (a) The speaker regrets that she must finish the processes involved in preparing the book she is authoring for publication.

      (b) The speaker says that she must finish the processes involved in preparing the book that she is authoring for publication.

Neither (33a) nor (33b) would standardly be regarded as being part of the truth conditional content of B's utterance in (31). As we have seen in the previous chapter, sentence adverbials which encode information about the speaker's propositional attitude, for example, *regrettably* or *sadly*, are not regarded as contributing to the truth conditions of the utterances that contain them. However, in a relevance theoretic framework both (33a) and (33b) are part of the explicit content of the utterance, since they are derived by developing the linguistically encoded semantic representation, and sentence adverbs such as *regrettably* are regarded as contributing to the explicit content – that is, the higher-level explicatures – of the utterances that contain them. We will be turning to the question of how these adverbs contribute to explicit content in the following section.

However, while Wilson and Sperber (1993) see assumptions such as (33a,b) as explicitly communicated rather than implicitly communicated, they nevertheless make a distinction between explicatures such as the one in (32), which they call the *proposition expressed*, and the higher-level explicatures in (33), on the grounds that higher-level explicatures 'are not normally seen as contributing to the truth conditions of the associated utterance' (1993:6). In other words, while all explicatures and all implicatures are conceptual or propositional representations and can represent states of affairs in the world truly or falsely, only the proposition expressed can be a truth condition. By the same token, while sentence adverbs such as *regrettably* contribute to a propositional representation, they do not contribute to the truth conditions of the utterance, and hence do not contribute to the proposition expressed. This would seem to suggest that there is a role for truth conditions at the level of explicit content after all.

As Wilson and Sperber recognize, this is in line with the traditional account. However, in the course of their paper they mention examples of illocutionary adverbials which do seem to contribute to the truth conditional content of the utterances that contain them. For example, Mary's utterance in (34) would be a contradiction if *on the record* and *off the record* did not contribute to its truth conditional content.

(34)   PETER: What can I tell our readers about your private life?
        MARY: On the record, I'm happily married. Off the record, I'm about to divorce.

Examples such as this lead Wilson and Sperber (1993:23) to question the assumption underlying their distinction between the proposition expressed and higher-level explicatures, namely, that we have a consistent, coherent set of intuitions about the truth conditions of utterances.

Within the cognitive framework of relevance theory, where the bearers of truth conditions are not utterances but conceptual representations, it might seem that there is no reason to maintain this assumption. On the other hand, if we abandon it, we are left with the problem of explaining the intuition that there *is* a difference between the role that (32) plays in the interpretation of B's utterance in (31) and the role played by (33a).

(31)   A: Are you going away this summer?
        B: I have to finish my book.
(32)   The speaker must finish the processes involved in preparing the book she is authoring for publication.
(33)   (a) The speaker regrets that she must finish the processes involved in preparing the book she is authoring for publication.

A possible way forward here is suggested by an exercise in Blakemore (1992:95). The reader is asked to consider a situation in which a speaker finally utters (35) after strenuously denying the hearer's repeated accusation that he has eaten her chocolates.

(35)   OK, I ate them. [uttered in a weary tone of voice]

The proposition expressed by this utterance is (36a), while (36b) is a higher-level explicature.

(36)   (a) The speaker ate the hearer's chocolates.

        (b) The speaker admits that he ate the hearer's chocolates.

However, the speaker does not expect to achieve optimal relevance by communicating (36a), since the hearer has made it clear that she believes this already. If the utterance is relevant, it is relevant by virtue of the cognitive effects the hearer derives from (36b). In other words, the suggestion is that we may distinguish between the assumptions explicitly communicated by an utterance according to their relative contributions to relevance.

Clearly, this suggestion is inconsistent with the traditional view that every utterance expresses a single proposition. However, as we have seen in the previous chapter (2.1), this view is no longer universally accepted. In particular, Bach (1999) has argued that an utterance should be regarded as expressing multiple propositions. As Iten (2000b) has observed, his solution to the problem has left us with the question of how we should distinguish between the explicit and the implicit content of utterances. Her point is that since logical operators such as *if... then* can only take one proposition in their scope, Bach's claim would mean that we cannot use the traditional scope test to test for truth conditionality. However, as Iten recognizes, this is only a problem if testing for truth conditionality were an essential part of the process of determining which propositions communicated by an utterance were explicitly communicated and which propositions were implicitly communicated: as we have seen, the relevance theoretic distinction between explicit and implicit content does not mention truth conditions at all. The key question is not whether an assumption contributes to truth conditions, but whether it is derived by developing the linguistically encoded semantic representation. In other words, the recovery of explicatures involves both decoding and inference, while the recovery of implicatures involves just inference.

3.3   Conceptual and procedural encoding

According to the picture painted so far, linguistic semantics does not deliver truth evaluable propositional representations, but rather schematic logical forms which are taken as input by pragmatic inferences constrained by the principle of relevance. The result is a set of communicated assumptions which, as we have seen in the previous section, may either be the product of encoding and inference – that is, explicatures – or be the product of inferential processing alone – that is, implicatures. In this picture, the question for linguistic semantics is not what contribution an expression makes to truth conditions, but rather what kind of contribution it makes to pragmatic inference, or, in other words, what kind of cognitive information it encodes.

The question I would like to address in this section is whether we should be looking for one answer to this. Should we expect linguistic semantics to provide only one kind of input to pragmatic inference? From a purely theoretical point of view, there is every reason to expect the answer to be 'no'. The picture I have drawn is based, first, on the assumption that there are two distinct processes involved in utterance interpretation – decoding and inference, the first being an input to the second, and, second, that the inferential phase of utterance comprehension involves the construction of conceptual (or propositional) representations which enter into inferential computations. This means that, in principle, linguistic form could encode not only the constituents of the conceptual representations that enter into inferential computations but also information which constrains the computations in which these computations are involved. In other words, it is possible for linguistic form to encode either *conceptual* information or *procedural* information.

Bach (1999) has argued that this distinction is in fact vacuous since after all, in some way or other anything one utters 'constrains the inferential phrase of comprehension' (1999:361). It is true that the inferences a hearer derives from an utterance depend on its conceptual content in the sense that this is what interacts with the context in the derivation of its explicit and implicit content. However, the interpretation the hearer derives also depends on the contextual assumptions which she uses in their derivation and on the type of inferential computations she performs.

Consider, for example, the sequence in (37) (adapted from Hobbs 1979):

(37)   (a) Tom can open Ben's safe. (b) He knows the combination.

There are two ways in which this sequence might be interpreted, depending on whether the (b) segment is understood as evidence for the proposition expressed by (a) or as a conclusion derived from (a). In the first interpretation, the proposition expressed by (b) is functioning as a premise which has the proposition expressed by (a) as a conclusion, while in the second interpretation, it is a conclusion in an inference that has the proposition expressed by (a) as a premise. The claim that linguistic meaning can encode information about the inferential phase of comprehension means that there are linguistic expressions (*so* and *after all*, for instance) which encode information about which of these inferential procedures yields the intended interpretation. Hence the difference between (38) and (39).

(38)   Tom can open Ben's safe. So he knows the combination.
(39)   Tom can open Ben's safe. After all, he knows the combination.

As I showed in Blakemore (1987), the fact that there *are* linguistic expressions and constructions which constrain inferential procedures can be explained within relevance theory in terms of the communicative principle of relevance. Recall that according to this principle, a hearer who recognizes that a speaker has made his intention to communicate manifest is entitled to assume that that speaker is being optimally relevant. In other words, in making his communicative intention manifest, the speaker is communicating his belief, first, that his utterance will achieve a level of relevance high enough to be worth processing, and, second, that this level of relevance is the highest level that he is capable of, given his abilities and preferences. Since the degree of relevance increases with the number of cognitive effects derived and decreases with the amount of processing effort required for their derivation, the use of an expression which encodes a procedure for identifying the intended cognitive effects would be consistent with the speaker's aim of achieving relevance for a minimum cost in processing.

Since the distinction between conceptual encoding and procedural encoding is the result of a move away from the assumptions underlying the speech act theoretic distinction between describing and indicating, there is no reason to expect the two distinctions to be co-extensive. However, the story of the development of the notion of procedural encoding began with my (1987) attempt to provide a relevance theoretic analysis of Grice's notion of conventional implicature, and my concern with a limited range of non-truth conditional constructions led me to the hypothesis that the distinction I was drawing might simply be a cognitively grounded version of the speech act theoretic one. If this hypothesis was right, then all non-truth conditional constructions would be examples of procedural encoding and all examples of procedural encoding would be examples of non-truth conditional meaning.

Subsequent research showed that this was not in fact the case. While the notion of a procedural constraint on implicatures has been applied to the analysis of a range of non-truth conditional discourse markers,[4] the investigation of

---

[4] See, for example, Blass (1990), Higashimori (1994), Itani (1993), Iten (2000b), Jucker (1993), Unger (1996).

the role of inference in the recovery of explicit content has suggested that the notion of procedural meaning can be extended to expressions and constructions which encode constraints on the recovery of explicatures. Some of these constructions – mood indicators, illocutionary particles and attitudinal particles, for example – are analysed as encoding constraints on the inferential processes involved in the recovery of higher-level explicatures (see Wilson and Sperber 1988, 1993, Clark 1991, 1993). Thus Wilson and Sperber (1993) have suggested that the use of the particle *huh* in (40) encourages the hearer to construct the higher-level explicature in (41).[5]

(40)   Peter's a genius, huh!
(41)   The speaker of (40) doesn't think that Peter is a genius.
                                    (Wilson and Sperber 1993:22)

In such cases, the equation between procedural meaning and non-truth conditional meaning is maintained, since higher-level explicatures are not regarded as contributing to the truth conditional content of utterances (but see the discussion above). However, it has also been suggested there are expressions, notably, pronouns, which should be analysed as constraints on what Wilson and Sperber (1993) call the proposition expressed (see section 2 above). As we have seen, the pronouns *she* and *him* in (42) cannot be analysed as encoding their referents. Given the role of the context in the interpretation of these expressions, one might want to say that linguistic decoding yields a skeletal conceptual representation such as the one in (43).

(42)   She saw him.
(43)   Some female saw some male.

However, following Kaplan (1989), Wilson and Sperber (1993) have argued that pronouns do not encode constituents of a conceptual representation, but only procedures for constructing such a representation. In other words, they contribute to truth conditional content only in the sense that they constrain the hearer's search for the representations of their referents. If this is right, it would seem that there are expressions which encode procedures but which contribute to what is traditionally regarded as truth conditional content. In other words, it would seem that it is not the case that all procedural meaning is non-truth conditional.

It may nevertheless be true that all cases of non-truth conditional meaning are instances of procedural encoding. However, Wilson and Sperber (1993) and

---

[5] See also Blass' (1990) analysis of hearsay particles in Sissala.

Ifantidou-Trouki (1993) have argued that sentence adverbials such as the one in (44) encode a constituent of a propositional representation such as the one in (45).

(44)   Unfortunately, Tom is not hungry.
(45)   It is unfortunate that Tom is not hungry.

If (45) is not a condition on the truth of (44), then this would amount to saying that there are examples of non-truth conditional meaning which are not procedural.

One might conclude at this point that we should abandon the distinction between conceptual and procedural meaning because it does not provide us with a cognitively grounded account of the distinction between truth conditional meaning and non-truth conditional meaning. However, this would be to assume that the traditional distinction between truth conditional and non-truth conditional meaning is *the* fundamental distinction in a theory of semantics. Let us take stock of the arguments so far:

> *First*, we have seen (in chapter 1) that the gap between linguistic encoding and the propositional content of utterances means that semantic representations do not encode truth conditions. The domain of truth conditional semantics is not natural language semantics but propositional thoughts or conceptual representations.
>
> *Second*, it has been argued (in this chapter) that the gap between linguistically encoded representations and conceptual representations is filled by inference. This suggests that the output of linguistic semantics is the input to inferential processes, and hence that the question for linguistic semantics is what kind of information does semantic encoding provide for pragmatic inferential processes. The conceptual–procedural distinction has emerged from the attempt to answer this question.
>
> *Third*, it has been argued (in chapter 2) that attempts to explain what expressions and constructions that do not contribute to truth conditions *do* contribute to have appealed to the notion of indicating, which has been explicated in conceptual terms. As we have seen, this has raised more questions than answers.
>
> *Fourth*, it has been argued that we do not seem to have consistent or uniform intuitions about truth conditionality. Indeed, it has been suggested (in the previous section) that knowing what the truth conditions of the utterance are may not be part of utterance understanding at all.

Taken together, these arguments suggest that the distinction between conceptual and procedural encoding should not be judged according to whether it provides a relevance theoretic re-analysis of the distinction between truth conditional and non-truth conditional meaning (or, indeed, the distinction between describing and indicating). The question is whether it yields a cognitively justified account of the contribution made by semantic encoding to pragmatic processing. We have seen that within relevance theory, the distinction can be justified in both cognitive and communicative terms. However, before we can say that it provides a framework for the analysis of those expressions which have been classified as non-truth conditional (or as indicators), we need to say a great deal more about what it means to say that a given expression encodes procedural meaning. In particular, we need to know how we would recognize that an expression encodes procedural information rather than conceptual information.

Clearly, this question does not arise in those studies which take non-truth conditionality to be an essential property of discourse markers (see for example Fraser 1990, 1996). However, the move away from the assumptions underlying the speech act theoretic distinction between describing and indicating has not only yielded a different semantic distinction: it has also created the possibility that the expressions classified as discourse markers do not fall into a single class from a semantic point of view. For as we have seen, not all cases of non-truth conditional meaning are cases of procedural encoding. In principle, it is possible for an expression classified as a discourse marker to encode either a concept or a procedure. Accordingly, it is essential for any study of these expressions conducted within the relevance theoretic programme to include tests for distinguishing conceptual meaning from procedural meaning.

If we recall what has been said about procedural encoding so far, we will see that we seem to know more about what procedural meaning is not than what it is. Specifically, an expression which encodes procedural information encodes information which is not a constituent of the conceptual representations over which inferential computations are performed. However, it seems that from this negative characterization we can draw certain conclusions about what properties we can expect an expression which encodes procedural meaning to have. The remainder of this chapter will be an exploration of these properties.

It is well known that some words are easier to paraphrase than others. For instance, it is easier to find a universally acceptable paraphrase for words such as *tree* or *lecture* than it is for words such as *love* or *freedom*. Nevertheless we do feel that we should be able to provide paraphrases for all of these words, whether we agree on them or not, and we can discuss whether one paraphrase is better than another. That is, even when the definition of a concept proves controversial, there is a sense in which each speaker can bring it to consciousness and say whether two expressions encode the same concept without having to actually test whether they can be substituted for each other in all contexts. As anyone who has tried to analyse them will know, the situation is very different with expressions such as *but* and utterance initial *well*. Ask a native speaker what these mean, and you are much more likely to receive a description or illustration of their use than a straightforward paraphrase. Moreover, native speakers are unable to judge whether two of these expressions – say, *but* and *however* – are synonymous without testing their inter-substitutability in all contexts. As I have said in the introduction of this book, it is the elusiveness of these expressions which is the source of their fascination.

If it is difficult for native speakers to make synonymy judgements, then it is not surprising that the translation of these expressions is notoriously difficult. Nor is it surprising that they are challenging for second language learners. According to Wilson and Sperber (1993), the elusiveness of these expressions can be explained if they are analysed as encoding procedures rather than concepts: 'Conceptual representations can be brought to consciousness; procedures cannot. We have direct access neither to grammatical computations nor to the inferential computations used in comprehension. A procedural analysis would explain our lack of direct access to the information they encode' (Wilson and Sperber 1993:16).

Applying this to so-called discourse markers, we might expect to find discourse markers whose analysis provides considerably less of a challenge to the theorist than others. And indeed, this does seem to be the case. For example, while the analysis of *but* has proven extremely controversial – almost to the extent that it has created an industry amongst semanticists – one does not find the same controversy surrounding the analysis of *in contrast*. I shall be returning to the difficulties of analysing *but* (and some of its less notorious relatives) in the following chapter. In the meantime let us continue with the question of how we can recognize procedural encoding.

As we have seen, it has been argued that not all non-truth conditional meaning is procedural. For example, it has been argued (by Wilson and Sperber 1993 and Ifantidou-Trouki 1993) that sentence adverbs such as *seriously* or *in confidence* encode constituents of conceptual representations even though they do not contribute to the truth conditions of the utterances that contain them. Why are these expressions not analysed in the framework I suggested for expressions such as *but* or *so*? According to Wilson and Sperber (1993), there are important differences between these expressions which provide indirect support for the distinction between conceptual and procedural encoding.

First, while sentence adverbials such as *seriously* have synonymous VP adverbial counterparts, it is not the case for expressions such as *but*, *after all* or *well*. Thus while the sentence adverbial *seriously* in (46) encodes the same concept as the truth conditional VP adverbial in (47), it is not the case that the discourse connective *well* in (48) is synonymous with its truth conditional counterpart in (49).

(46)   Seriously, you will have to leave.

(47)   He looked at me very seriously.

(48)   A: What time should we leave?
         B: Well, the train leaves at 11.23.

(49)   You haven't ironed this very well.

As I have argued (Blakemore 1996), it seems that some expressions analysed as discourse connectives behave more like sentence adverbials in this respect. Thus it seems likely that *in other words* as it is used in (50) encodes the same concept as *in other words* as it is used in (51).

(50)   In other words, you're banned.

(51)   She asked me to try and put it in other words.

Second, while sentence adverbials can be semantically complex, it does not seem that expressions such as *but* or *so* can combine with other expressions to produce semantically complex expressions. Thus the meanings of the complex sentence adverbials in the following examples are compositional in the sense familiar to semanticists.

(52)   In total, absolute confidence, she has been promoted.

(53)   Speaking quite frankly, I don't think people ever ask themselves those kind of questions.

(54)   Putting it more brutally, you're sacked.

As Wilson and Sperber (1993) say, this semantic compositionality is not surprising if we analyse these expressions as constituents of conceptual representations that undergo regular semantic interpretation rules. By the same token, one would not expect expressions which encoded procedures to combine to be a constituent of a complex expression. Hence the unacceptability of (55).

(55)   ?Tom likes pop art. Totally however, Anna prefers Renaissance art.

Notice that some discourse connectives – including so-called 'contrastive' ones – can occur in complex constructions. Compare (55) with (56).

(56)   Tom likes pop art. In total contrast, Anna prefers Renaissance art.

As Rouchota (1998) has shown, while expressions that have been analysed as encoding procedures can combine in some way, it does not seem that they combine in the same way as the conceptual expressions in (52–4) or (56). Consider (57–8).

(57)   The cat left footprints all over the manuscript of my book. But after all, he can't read.

(58)   The exam scripts are covered in mud. So he must have walked over them too.

To say that an expression does not encode a concept is to say that it does not encode a constituent which undergoes the inferential processes involved in developing logical forms into explicatures. This means, amongst other things, that it does not encode a constituent of a representation that undergoes the inferential processes involved in the development of highly fragmentary utterances such as (59).

(59)   Coffee.

However, as I have shown (Blakemore 1997a), it seems that there are some expressions which are analysed as encoding procedural information which can be used as fragmentary utterances. For example, consider (60), produced following a rambling account of the trials and tribulations of having to spend the entire summer vacation finishing writing a book.

(60)   But still.

Similarly, consider (61), produced by a university professor after hearing the secretary's summary of the explanation given by a student for the failure to submit her assessed work.

(61)   Nevertheless.
        (from Blakemore 1997a)

It should be noted that neither of these utterances was produced with the rising intonation characteristic of an unfinished utterance. They were intended as complete utterances – in the same way as (59) was.

In fact, there is an important difference between the fragmentary utterance in (59) and the fragmentary utterances in (60) and (61). Moreover, this difference helps clarify the distinction between conceptual and procedural encoding, and accordingly, it is worth spending a little time on it.

If (60–1) were like (59), then we would have to say that the hearer is expected to use contextual assumptions and pragmatically constrained inference to develop their linguistically encoded semantic representations into an enriched propositional representation that can be assessed for relevance. For example, given certain contextual assumptions, the hearer might derive the explicature in (62), while in another context she might derive the explicature in (63).

(62)　It is time to have a coffee break.
(63)　The speaker believes that we need to buy coffee.

Since the construction of the explicature is the responsibility of the hearer, there is no way for the speaker to predict exactly how his utterance will be interpreted. Thus even in a particular context, for example, the one in which the speaker and hearer are checking the contents of their cupboards before they go to the supermarket, there is a range of explicatures that the hearer might construct. For instance:

(64)　(a) The speaker believes that coffee should be included on the shopping list.
　　　(b) The speaker believes that there is not enough coffee for the rest of the week.
　　　(c) The speaker is telling the hearer to buy coffee at the supermarket.

and so on. Any of these assumptions could be consistent with the principle of relevance in the circumstances.

At first sight this might seem to be what goes on in the interpretation of (60–1). Thus according to my (1987) analysis of (61), there is a range of assumptions which the hearer might have recovered, for instance:

(65)　(a) The student could have handed in some of the work.
　　　(b) The student's circumstances do not justify bending the rules.
　　　(c) There are other students whose circumstances have been difficult.
　　　(d) The student has not tried hard enough.

and so on.

However, whereas the assumptions in (64) are all a development of the concept encoded by *coffee*, none of the assumptions in (65) can be regarded as a development of a concept encoded by *nevertheless*. The role played by *nevertheless* in the recovery of these assumptions is quite different. Although there is a whole range of assumptions that the hearer of (61) might have justifiably constructed, this range is constrained: it does not matter what assumption the hearer constructs as long as it gives rise to the right sort of cognitive effects. More specifically, it does not matter what assumption the hearer constructs provided that it achieves relevance in the way that is prescribed by the meaning of *nevertheless*. In other words, the speaker's intention in (61) is simply that a hearer construct an assumption which gives rise to the cognitive effects consistent with the constraint encoded by *nevertheless*. We shall see exactly what this constraint is in the following chapter. My aim here is simply to underline the difference between the role played by an expression which encodes a concept in the interpretation of fragmentary utterances and the one played by an expression which encodes a procedure. The point is that in an utterance such as (60) or (61) it does not matter what assumption the hearer constructs as long as she recovers the cognitive effects consistent with the constraint encoded by the expression or construction used by the speaker. Indeed, as Deirdre Wilson (personal communication) has pointed out, it is conceivable that the speaker's intention in such utterances might not include the construction of an assumption at all, in which case the discourse connective simply serves as a means of activating the right kind of cognitive effects. This would seem to be the case in an example such as the following:

(66)   [speaker and hearer(s) are subjected to a long and angry speech by someone who then leaves the room slamming the door. There is a brief and stunned silence] Well.

Once again, the nature of the constraint imposed by *well* will be discussed in the following chapter. The point is that while it is difficult to identify any proposition that the speaker might have intended to express, knowing the meaning of the expression *well* enables us to say something relatively specific about the range of cognitive effects that he intended to achieve.

This is not the case in (59). Here the hearer is simply expected to construct an assumption which has the concept encoded by *coffee* as a constituent and which yields the intended cognitive effects. However, which cognitive effects are recovered by the hearer depends entirely on the context and his assumption that the utterance is optimally relevant. There is no linguistically encoded constraint on these cognitive effects, and in particular, one cannot say that knowing the meaning of *coffee* helps us say what they might be.

As I observed in Blakemore (1997a), non-truth conditional sentence adverbials may be used as fragmentary utterances. For example, a child may produce (67) in response to her mother's question whether she has much homework:

(67)   Unfortunately.

However, this example is much more like the *Coffee* example in (59), since the hearer is expected to construct explicatures which include one which has the concept encoded by *unfortunately*, for example (68):

(68)   It is unfortunate that the speaker of (67) has a lot of homework.

As in (59), the meaning of *unfortunate* plays no role in determining how the proposition that the daughter has a lot of homework is relevant: this is determined by the context and the principle of relevance. In this way, fragmentary utterances may be used as evidence for the distinction I have drawn between two different types of non-truth conditional meaning, or in other words, for the claim that there cannot be a unitary account of the expressions that have been identified as non-truth conditional.

If this claim is right, then there cannot be a unitary account of the semantics of expressions which have been classified as discourse markers or discourse connectives. Some turn out to encode concepts, and can be treated – from a semantic point of view – alongside expressions such as *coffee* or, perhaps more accurately, alongside expressions such as *unfortunately*. This makes the analysis of their meanings relatively unproblematic, although like sentence adverbials, they raise interesting and important questions about truth conditionality and the distinction Wilson and Sperber (1993) have drawn between the proposition expressed and higher-level explicatures (cf. Ifantidou-Trouki 1993). Others turn out to encode procedures, and as a result resist straightforward analysis. The complexity and elusiveness of the meanings encoded by these expressions provide part of the justification for the content of the chapter that follows: not only does it include yet another attempt to provide an analysis of *but*, but it will be restricted to the analysis of relatively few expressions, namely, a selection of the so-called *contrastive* or *adversative* expressions, *but*, *nevertheless*, *however* and perhaps the most slippery of all the English discourse markers, *well*. However, my primary objective in this chapter is not so much to provide the definitive analysis of these expressions, but rather to develop a better understanding of the notion of procedural encoding. For while I might have given some theoretical and empirical justification for the existence of procedural meaning, we still have no real idea of what procedural information is.

4 *Procedural meaning*

4.1 Constraints on relevance: new questions

According to the arguments of the previous chapter, the distinction between conceptual and procedural encoding cross-cuts the speech act theoretic distinction between describing and indicating: not all of the expressions defined within the speech act theoretic framework as indicators can be analysed as encoding procedures, and not all expressions which encode procedures are analysed within the speech act theoretic framework as indicators. In view of the fact that the two distinctions are not co-extensive, the decision to take the relevance theoretic distinction as the fundamental one in a theory of linguistic semantics could be construed as a recommendation to simply forget the speech act theoretic distinction, and in particular, as a recommendation to drop the notion of indicating or signalling or pointing altogether. After all, it seems that we now have something less metaphorical to work with, namely, coded means for constraining the inferential tasks involved in utterance interpretation. However, in this section I shall show that we still have much to learn about what it means for an expression to encode a procedure. Moreover, it seems that it may be illuminating to compare such expressions with natural or non-coded means for pointing to something.

Let us recall my (1987) analysis of the role of *after all* in (1):

(1)   Ben can open Tom's safe. After all, he knows the combination.

A hearer who interprets (1) will take the conceptual representation in (2a) together with the conceptual representation in (2b) and derive the conceptual representation in (2c). The effect of this inference will be a strengthened assumption, or, in other words, a conceptual representation which is held with a degree of strength that is higher than it would have been prior to the interpretation of the second segment.

(2)   (a) Ben knows the combination of Tom's safe.
       (b) If Ben knows the combination of Tom's safe, then he can open Tom's safe.
       (c) Ben can open Tom's safe.

I have described the interpretation of (1) in this way in order to underline, first, the point that the hearer performs an inference in order to recover the intended interpretation, and, second, the point that what the hearer ends up with is a conceptual representation. My (1987) argument was that while *after all* plays a role in the recovery of this conceptual representation, it does not do this by encoding anything that is a constituent of it. Rather it encodes information about the inferential process that the hearer should use.

Wharton (2001) has suggested that this distinction is a particular instance of a more general distinction between *translational* encoding, where concepts are activated by the use of expressions which translate them, and *non-translational* encoding, where concepts are activated by leading the audience to an inferential route that results in a conceptual representation. In order to explicate this distinction, Wharton uses examples which do not involve a coded signal: for instance, a person points at a cloud, intending to communicate 'It's going to rain'; or a person deliberately and openly shows someone their shiver, intending to communicate 'I feel cold.' In these cases, he argues, the audience is expected to work out the communicator's intended interpretation inferentially. However, she is guided in this process by the communicator's communicative behaviour.

These examples should recall our discussion of Rieber's (1997) attempts to unpack the notion of indicating (chapter 2.3). In particular, it could be argued that in both of Wharton's examples the communicator is indicating something that the audience might have noticed for herself. However, notice that in contrast with Rieber, Wharton is not proposing that the communicator is indicating the fact that it is raining: he is proposing that the communicator is providing a signal which guides the audience towards an inferential route that will result in the conceptual representation 'It's going to rain.'

By the same token, Wharton is not proposing that non-translational coding involves pointing to or signalling a concept in the way that Rieber proposes that, for example, *but* signals the concept of contrast. He is proposing that it involves producing a signal which 'automatically guides the inferential route a hearer should take, a route they would not reliably take unless they knew the code' (2001:144). This is what I mean by procedural encoding in this section: expressions such as *after all*, *but* or *so* do not encode a constituent of a conceptual representation (or even indicate a concept), but guide the comprehension process so that the hearer ends up with a conceptual representation.[1]

With this in mind, let us return to Bach's (1999) objections to Rieber's (1997) re-analysis of Grice's (1989) account of conventional implicature. It will be recalled that Bach's argument was that since an expression such as *but* can feature in indirect thought reports such as (3), it must be analysed as contributing to what is said, and cannot, therefore, be treated as a conventional implicature (*contra* Grice 1989, Rieber 1997).

(3)   Tom thinks that Sheila is rich but unhappy. But I have always thought that all rich people are unhappy.

This sort of example is clearly a problem for any speech act theoretic analysis: since the speaker is reporting thoughts rather than words, he cannot be attributing any speech act to Tom. The question is whether it is a problem for an approach which treats *but* as encoding procedural information. As we have seen in chapter 2, the fact that an expression can appear in an indirect report of someone's thoughts does not in itself show that it is not procedural: pronouns and mood indicators, for example, go unremarked in reports of thoughts. If this sort of example is a problem, then it can only be a problem for the claim that *but* constrains, and hence contributes to, the recovery of implicit content rather than explicit content.

Wilson and Sperber (1993) have argued that within the relevance theoretic approach the speaker of an utterance such as (3) is reporting thoughts rather than words. However, it seems that by 'thought' they do not simply mean thought content, but something which could encompass the attribution of a particular inferential process. Thus they argue that where (4a) is understood as an indirect speech report of (4b) the speaker is 'not drawing an inference herself', but 'attributing a certain inference to Peter' (Wilson and Sperber 1993:15).

(4)   (a) Peter thought that Mary had a holiday, so he should have one too.
       (b) Peter thinks, 'Mary had a holiday, so I should have one too.'
                                                    (Wilson and Sperber 1993:15)

As we have seen in my discussion of Bach's (1999) arguments against conventional implicature accounts (chapter 2.4), it seems that free indirect speech (or thought) and, indeed, indirect speech reports, can include expressions and

---

[1] Note that Wharton's notion of non-translational coding is more general than the notion of procedural meaning in the sense that it can refer to coded expressions which are not part of the linguistic code, e.g. interjections such as *aha* or *wow*.

devices which are not regarded as contributing to propositional content. Recall the examples of free indirect speech in (5) and indirect speech in (6).

(5)   That was the way to live – *carelessly, recklessly, spending oneself.* He got to his feet and began to wade towards the shore, pressing his toes into the firm, wrinkled sand. *To take things easy, not to fight against the ebb and flow of life*, but to give way to it – that was what was needed. It was this tension that was all wrong. *To live – to live!*

     (Mansfield, 'At the Bay', 206).

(6)   John pointed out that they couldn't really afford a holiday. But no, she said that she NEEDED to get away. [capitals indicate stress]

These examples demonstrate that attributed thought does not necessarily mean attributed thought content. Clearly, the study of free indirect style will shed light on exactly what is being attributed in examples involving devices such as repetition and emphatic stress. However, it seems that whatever we say about the interpretation of so-called stylistic devices in free indirect (and indirect) speech, we cannot say that a speaker of an utterance such as (3) or (4a) can be said to be attributing an inference to someone in the sense that she is meta-representing that inference. As I have argued in the previous chapter, we do not have direct access to inferential procedures, or, indeed, any kind of computational process. If this is right, then it is not clear how we could represent – or meta-represent – such a process, for it would have to be represented in conceptual terms. Obviously, it is not impossible for people to represent inferential computations in conceptual terms: teachers of logic do this for a living. Nor is it necessarily impossible to provide a conceptual representation of the inferential procedure encoded by *but*: this is what I shall be attempting to do in the next section. However, I do not believe this is what happens when someone attributes the inferential procedure encoded by *but* to someone else in utterances such as (3).

Let us look at what goes on in a non-attributive example involving *but*:

(7)   Sheila is rich but she is unhappy.

The hearer is intended to perform an inferential computation involving the explicit content of the utterance and accessible contextual assumptions which results in a conceptual representation. In Wharton's (2001) terms, this conceptual representation is not encoded by *but*, but is *activated* by it in the sense that it encodes information about the inferential route the hearer should take in order to arrive at the intended conceptual representation. We shall be examining the meaning of *but* in more detail below. For the moment, let us just say that this inferential route is such that the hearer of (7) arrives at a conceptual representation which contradicts the assumption in (8).

(8)   Sheila is happy.

However, the speaker can assume that her utterance will achieve relevance in this way only if she assumes that (8) is manifest to the hearer. And so it will be – provided that the hearer can derive it from the first segment of the utterance and accept it as true (or probably true).[2] Since (8) is only deducible from the first segment of (7) given the contextual assumption in (9), the speaker's use of *but* makes it mutually manifest that she believes that (9) is amongst the assumptions manifest to the hearer.

(9)   All rich people are happy.

Notice that the hearer will not construe the speaker to be communicating that (9) and (8) are assumptions she takes to be true. As Rieber (1997) has pointed out, it would be very strange for a speaker to communicate that she believes a proposition to be true only for the purpose of denying it.[3]

In some cases, it seems, a speaker may produce an utterance containing *but* even when it is mutually manifest that the hearer does not hold the contextual assumption(s) necessary for the deduction of the assumption being contradicted. Consider, for example, 'jokey' or ironic utterances such as (10) (produced at a linguistics conference).

(10)   This is Paul. He's a syntactician, but he's quite intelligent.

Here the hearer will recognize that the segment introduced by *but* is intended to achieve relevance by virtue of contradicting (11) which is deducible from the assumption in (12) only given the contextual assumption in (13).

(11)   Paul is not intelligent.
(12)   Paul is a syntactician.
(13)   No syntactician is intelligent.

---

[2] See the definition of manifestness in chapter 3, section 3, or Sperber and Wilson (1995:39).

[3] This is Rieber's (incorrect) construal of my earlier (1987, 1989) analyses of the interpretation of utterances containing *but*. The speaker's use of *but* does not provide evidence of the speaker's beliefs about rich people, but rather evidence of the speaker's beliefs about what the hearer thinks about rich people. These beliefs may, of course, be mistaken. However, as we have seen in the previous chapter, even when a speaker fails to produce an utterance which is consistent with the presumption of optimal relevance, a hearer is able to consider how the speaker might have intended his utterance to achieve optimal relevance. The point is that in this case, the hearer is guided in her considerations by the meaning of *but*.

However, since it is manifest to the hearer of (10) (in the context described) that the speaker has not attributed the assumptions in (11) or (13) to her, she will not assume that the *but* segment was intended to achieve relevance by contradicting and eliminating an assumption which is assumed to be manifest to her. On the other hand, the hearer may take the speaker to be contradicting and eliminating an assumption which is assumed to be manifest to somebody. In this way, the speaker's use of *but* encourages the hearer to make an inference that would be made by a person (or the sort of person) who did hold the assumptions in (11) and (13), or in other words, to derive the cognitive effects that would be derived by this sort of person.

In this example, the point of activating the attributed assumptions in (11) and (13) is to communicate the speaker's attitude towards those assumptions. In the context described, we may assume that this attitude is one of dissociation; hence the ironic effect (see Sperber and Wilson 1995:237–43, Wilson and Sperber 1992). This is not the case in Rieber's (1997) example in (3) above or in Wilson and Sperber's (1993) example in (4a), where the speaker has made it explicit that he is attributing certain assumptions to someone (Tom in (3) and Peter in (4a)), and the relevance of the utterance simply lies in the information it communicates about what Tom and Peter believe. Thus in (3) the speaker's use of *but* activates the attributed assumption in (9) and the contradiction and elimination of the attributed assumption in (8). In other words, examples such as these arise because it is possible for assumptions to be manifest as attributed assumptions, and the speaker will be understood to be using *but* or *so* in order to attribute an inference to someone in the sense that the use of these expressions encourages the hearer to make use of these attributed assumptions in a particular kind of inference.[4]

In the last chapter, I argued that the notion of procedural meaning can be justified within the relevance theoretic framework in both cognitive and communicative terms. However, according to my original account of semantic constraints on relevance (Blakemore 1987), relevance theory provided not only an explanation for why languages have linguistically encoded constraints on relevance at all, but also an explanation for why there are expressions with particular types of functions. Thus in Blakemore (1992) I suggested a classification of discourse markers corresponding to the three types of cognitive effects summarized below:

---

[4] In section 4.2.3 I shall show that the phenomenon I have been discussing here has implications for the way in which the assumption eliminated as the result of the procedure encoded by *but* is characterized.

An input achieves a cognitive effect if:

(i)   it allows the derivation contextual implications;

         or

(ii)   it strengthens an existing assumption;

         or

(iii)   it leads to the contradiction and elimination of an existing assumption.

It does seem that one can identify discourse connectives whose meanings are linked to these cognitive effects. Consider, for example, the functions of *after all* in (1) (repeated below) and *so* in (14).

(1)   (a) Ben can open Tom's safe. (b) After all, he knows the combination.
(14)   (a) Ben can open Tom's safe. (b) So he knows the combination.

As we have seen, by indicating that the hearer is expected to follow an inferential route in which the proposition expressed by segment (b) is a premise for the deduction of the proposition expressed by segment (a), the speaker of (1) is indicating that segment (b) is relevant by virtue of strengthening an existing assumption. In contrast, by indicating that the hearer is expected to follow an inferential route in which the proposition expressed by segment (b) is a conclusion derived in an inference in which the proposition expressed by (a) is a premise, the speaker of (14) is indicating that segment (b) is relevant by virtue of being a contextual implication.

Similarly, the discussion of the examples in (3) and (10) assumed that we can link the function of *but* to the cognitive effect of contradiction and elimination (see above). Consider, for example, the sequence in (15), where the relevance of the second segment lies in the fact that it contradicts and eliminates an assumption presumed to have been made manifest by the first, namely (16).

(15)   There's a pizza in the fridge, but leave some for tomorrow.
(16)   You can eat all the pizza in the fridge.

I shall return to the analysis of *but* in the next section. My aim here is to raise the general theoretical questions about my original account of procedural meaning which I shall be addressing in the more detailed discussion that follows.

The analyses just sketched suggest not only that the meanings of discourse markers or connectives are linked to cognitive effects, but more particularly, that they directly encode the type of cognitive effect intended. Thus *but* is analysed as encoding the information that the hearer is intended to follow an inferential route which ends in the elimination of a contextual assumption, while *after all* is analysed as encoding the information that the intended inferential route is one which results in the strengthening of an existing assumption. As I pointed out (Blakemore 1987), the hearer of an utterance containing, for example, *after all,* is intended to recognize that she is expected to access a particular set of contextual assumptions for its interpretation. Thus the hearer of (1) will recognize that she is intended to access the assumption in (2b).

(2)   (b) If Ben knows the combination of Tom's safe, then he can open Ben's safe.

However, this is a consequence of the constraint *after all* imposes on the intended cognitive effect and the communicative principle of relevance: the hearer is expected to access the smallest and most accessible set of contextual assumptions that enable her to interpret the (b) segment so that it strengthens an assumption made accessible by the (a) segment. In other words, according to this analysis, *after all* imposes a constraint on the hearer's selection of context only derivatively.

While this notion of a constraint on relevance allows us to distinguish three broad categories of discourse connectives, it does not, however, allow us to draw more finely grained distinctions between the meanings of the different expressions which fall into a particular category. Thus for example, while there is a whole range of expressions whose use seems to be connected to contradiction and elimination, these are not always interchangeable with *but* or, indeed, with each other. For instance, it seems that while examples such as (17) suggest that the function of *nevertheless* is similar to that of *but*, there are other cases, for example (18), in which the substitution of *but* by *nevertheless* yields an odd if not unacceptable result.

(17)   Anna is a wonderful pianist but/nevertheless she can't sing.

(18)   A: Did you get my article?
           B: Yes, but/? nevertheless the last page is missing.

Similarly, while there are contexts in which *but* and *however* are interchangeable, the fact that there are other contexts in which *but* cannot be substituted by *however* suggests that *however* does not encode exactly the same constraint on interpretation as *but*. Compare, for example, (19) and (20):

(19)   A: I suppose that it's summer in New Zealand now.
           B: Yes it is. But/However, the weather is not much better than here at the moment.

(20)   A: Come on, we've got time for another coffee.
           B: But/?However, I've got a meeting at 2.00.

Clearly, an account in which these expressions constrain relevance by encoding the cognitive effect of denial and elimination would not capture the differences between them.

As Blass (1990) has pointed out, the range of expressions whose meanings can be analysed in terms of strengthening include a number of expressions which are either not interchangeable at all or are only interchangeable in certain contexts. Thus although one might say that the second segment of both of the sequences in (21) and (22) has the effect of strengthening an assumption communicated by the first, it is clear that *indeed* and *after all* do not make the same kind of contribution to the interpretation of the utterances which contain them.

(21) I think Verity should be player of the match. After all/?Indeed, she scored all the goals.

(22) Verity played well today. Indeed/?After all, she was brilliant.

The situation is complicated further by the fact that *indeed* can be used to play a role which, although it seems to have something to do with strengthening, is not exactly the same as the one in (22). As (23) shows, this role is shared by *too*.

(23) A: Verity is playing well today
      B: She is indeed/too.

However, the use of *too* is inappropriate in (24) .

(24) ?Verity played well today. She was brilliant too.

As Blass (1990) observes, in some dialects *too* has a use which is connected not with strengthening but with contradiction:

(25) TOM: Anna isn't coming with us.
      BEN: She is too.

Moreover, it has a further role, shared by *also*, which, it seems, cannot be analysed in terms of any of the three cognitive effects at all.

(26) (a) Anna plays the PIANO. She ALSO plays the trumpet.
      (b) Anna plays the PIANO. She plays the TRUMPET too.

In this role, *too* interacts with the focus phenomena discussed by Prince (1988), which I analysed along the lines suggested by Wilson and Sperber (1979) and Sperber and Wilson (1995) as constraints on the contextual assumptions used in the derivation of cognitive effects (Blakemore 1987). I do not plan to revisit this particular discussion here. The point of (re-) introducing these focus-related phenomena was to suggest that there are discourse markers which, although they can be analysed as encoding inferential procedures, cannot be analysed as encoding a particular cognitive effect at all. In other words, not only is an analysis of procedural meaning based on the three cognitive effects of contextual implication, strengthening and elimination not fine-grained enough to capture the differences between expressions such as *but* and *nevertheless* and *however*, but also it is not broad enough to capture all the ways in which linguistic expressions and structures can encode information about the computations involved in the interpretation of the utterances that contain them.

My aim in this chapter will not be to give an exhaustive account of the non-truth conditional discourse markers which encode constraints on relevance. Apart from the fact that this would either be frustratingly superficial or impossibly long, it is not clear that it would contribute to a better understanding of the theory of meaning which deals with the way in which elements of linguistic structure map directly on to the computations involved in utterance interpretation (see Blakemore 1987:144). Accordingly, I shall focus on the analysis of *but* (4.2) and its less notorious relatives *nevertheless* and *however* (4.3) in order to show how a more precise account of procedural meaning can capture the (often very subtle) differences between apparently similar discourse markers, and then turn to the analysis of (discourse-initial) *well* in order to show that the explanation of how procedural meaning works must go beyond the encoding of cognitive effects (4.4).

4.2   A procedural analysis of *but*

The discussion that follows will not be a repeat of my earlier discussions of this problematic expression (Blakemore 1987, 1989, 2000). While the resulting analysis represents a return to my original 1987 position that all uses of *but* in English can be accommodated in terms of a single procedure, I reach this conclusion via a different (and, I believe, more straightforward) route. At the same time, I shall argue that there are uses of *but* which suggest that my 1987 definition of the procedure encoded by *but* requires modification if we wish to maintain Sperber and Wilson's (1995) definition of manifestness.[5]

4.2.1   but *and contrast*
For both Rieber (1997) and Bach (1999), the problem of accounting for the meaning of *but* is a matter of accounting for what they call its contrastive

---

[5] Iten (2000b) gives an excellent critical discussion of a wide range of literature on *but* which includes an account of the discrepancies between my 1987 and 1989 analyses.

import. Similarly, Fraser (1990) concludes that 'the core meaning of *but* is to signal simple contrast, nothing more' (1990:309). As students in introductory semantics classes quickly find out, there is nothing 'simple' about contrast. While each of the following pairs is said to exhibit contrast or antonymy, the relationship must be analysed differently in each case:

(27) dead   alive
       hot   cold
       north   south
       buy   sell

Contrasts are not always determined by the linguistically encoded meanings of the words used. Thus in (28) the contrast between (a) and (b) must be derived inferentially on the basis of contextual assumptions, or, in other words, as contrasting contextual implications, for example, (29a) and (b).

(28) (a) Anna likes to read.
      (b) Tom likes to play sports.
(29) (a) Anna likes intellectual activities.
      (b) Tom likes physical activities.

The contrasting contextual implications in (29) may also be recovered from an *and* conjunction in which the speaker provides no lexical indication of contrast. Alternatively, the speaker may lead the hearer towards this interpretation by using the subordinators *while* and *whereas* – or, according to Fraser, *but*. In other words, according to Fraser, *but* is simply a linguistic means of indicating the contrasts in symmetric utterances such as the following:

(30) (a) Ben is rich and Verity is poor.
      (b) Verity is poor and Ben is rich. ($\equiv$ 30a)
      (c) Anna likes reading and Tom likes tennis.
      (d) Tom likes tennis and Anna likes reading. ($\equiv$ 30c)

And, indeed, it would seem that *but* can be substituted for *and* in these examples. For example:

(31) Anna likes reading but Tom likes tennis.
(32) Tom likes tennis but Anna likes reading.

My first task in this section is to show that the inter-substitutability of *and* and *but* in utterances such as (30) and (31–2) is an illusion. The contexts in which it is acceptable to use *and* in order to communicate what we might think of as a symmetric contrast are not contexts in which the use of *but* is acceptable. I shall argue that the unacceptability of *but* in these contexts is a consequence of its role in activating an inference which results in the contradiction and elimination of an assumption, and that uses of *but* which may look like (symmetric) contrastive uses out of context turn out to have a different (non-symmetric) function when examined in contexts that yield an acceptable interpretation.

It will be recalled that according to Lakoff (1971), the apparently contrastive use of *but* in (31) must be distinguished from its use in (33), where the speaker's use of *but* appears to indicate the unexpectedness of the expectation presumed to have been derived from the first segment, namely, that John is dishonest.

(33)   John is a Republican but he is honest.

This would seem to suggest that *but* should be analysed in terms of *concession*, where this is defined along the lines suggested by Quirk *et al.* (1972): 'Concessive conjuncts signal the unexpected, surprising nature of what is being said in view of what was said before that' (1972:674). As Iten (2000b) points out, there is a range of English expressions which might seem to indicate concessivity, and these are not always inter-substitutable. I shall take this point up in the following section. Here my aim is to show that acceptable uses of *but* do not always conform to Quirk *et al.*'s definition of concessivity. Moreover there are utterances containing *and* which would appear to be concessive on Quirk *et al.*'s definition, but where the use of *but* is unacceptable. Once again, my argument will be that the unacceptability of *but* is a consequence of its role in activating an inference that is linked to the cognitive effect of contradiction and elimination.

First, then, let us consider a contextualized example of an *and* conjunction which can be interpreted as communicating a symmetric contrast. The utterance in (34) was heard as part of a BBC weather report in which the speaker was reviewing the week's weather in Britain.

(34)   The wettest weather has been in Preston where they have had 15mm of rain and the driest weather has been in Ashford where there has been only 3mm of rain.

The substitution of *and* by *but* in this example would have been odd even though the speaker could be described as drawing a contrast between the wettest place and the driest place. The point seems to be that since there is, by definition, only one place which can be described as the wettest, no listener would have expected Ashford to be like Preston with respect to the amount of rainfall it received. It is simply assumed that listeners realize that there will be one place that is the wettest and one place that is the driest and that they want to know what they are. In other words, while the information explicitly communicated by the conjoined utterance is assumed by the speaker to be relevant to the listeners, it is not assumed that its relevance lies in the denial and elimination of an assumption that Ashford and Preston are alike with respect to the rainfall they received during the week.

It is not difficult to identify similar examples. For instance, the speaker of the following utterance has been sent from the kitchen to find out what everyone would like to drink.

(35)   Larry, Sue and Simon want coffee and Bob, Jane and Tom want wine.

The substitution of *but* would only be acceptable here if there was something surprising either about the fact that Bob, Jane and Tom did not want the same drink as the others or about the fact that they wanted wine. Of course, it is not difficult to think of a context in which this might be the case. If it was assumed that Sue never drank wine or that Sue habitually did everything that her husband Larry did, then (36) would be acceptable.

(36)   Larry wants tea but Sue wants wine.

Similarly, there are contexts in which utterances that look like the weather report example in (34) are acceptable. Consider B's utterance in (37):

(37)   A: What has the weather been like this winter?
         B: Well, it was really wet before Christmas, but since then it's been
         quite dry.

Here B's use of *but* can be taken as evidence of his (possibly mistaken) assumption that A believes that the weather has been uniform throughout the winter and hence that there is a single answer to his question. Thus the hearer is expected to perform the inference in (38).

(38)   The post-Christmas weather would be the same as the pre-Christmas
         weather only if it was really wet.
         The post-Christmas weather was not extremely wet.
         Therefore, the post-Christmas weather was not the same as the pre-
         Christmas weather.

This suggests that the only sense in which *but* has anything to do with contrast in this example is that it introduces a segment which plays a role in the elimination of the assumption that there is no contrast to be drawn. However, there are other examples involving *but* which although they may *look* like the weather report example in (34), have nothing to do with contrast at all. For example, while the hearer of a British weather report would find the use of *but* unacceptable in (34) on the grounds that there is no reason to expect the rainfall in the two places to be the same, the use of *but* in the (constructed) weather report in (39) will be acceptable to a hearer who knows that Chicago is notorious for its wind.[6]

(39)   New York was the windiest city in the United States today, but Chicago had light winds.

In this case, the assumption being contradicted is not an assumption that New York and Chicago are alike, as in (37), but rather an assumption (presumed to have been derived on the basis of the hearer's encyclopaedic knowledge) that Chicago is invariably the windiest city in the country. This difference should not, however, obscure the fact that in *both* examples the hearer is expected to perform an inference which results in the contradiction and elimination of an assumption. That is, *but* encodes the same procedure in each case, and the only difference is that whereas in (37) the eliminated assumption which the speaker attributes to the hearer is on the basis of the question she has asked (namely, that the weather was uniform throughout winter and hence that there is a single answer to her question), in (39) the eliminated assumption is one which the speaker presumes is held by the hearer on the basis of assumptions he holds about the hearer's encyclopaedic knowledge (namely, that Chicago is an extremely windy city).

The use of *and* in these utterances would not have yielded the same sort of interpretation. Nor, it seems, would the use of *whereas* or *in contrast*. For example, neither of the utterances in (40) could be interpreted as suggesting that the hearer's assumption that she could expect a simple, homogeneous description of the weather was mistaken. Similarly neither of the utterances in (41) would be interpreted as suggesting that the assumption that Chicago had strong winds is incorrect.

(40)   (a) It was really wet before Christmas and after Christmas it was quite dry.
        (b) It was really wet before Christmas, whereas after Christmas it was quite dry.

---

[6] I am grateful to Wiebke Brockhaus for drawing my attention to this sort of example.

(41)   (a) New York was the windiest city in the United States today and Chicago had light winds.

        (b) New York was the windiest city in the United States today. In contrast Chicago had light winds.

I do not want to suggest here that *in contrast* and *whereas* encode the same kind of information. On the contrary, it seems that *in contrast* exhibits behaviour which is symptomatic of conceptual encoding, while *whereas* would seem to have the properties which suggest procedural encoding. In particular, while it is possible to form a complex adverbial by qualifying *in contrast* by, for example, *complete* or *total*, it is not possible to form a complex expression containing *whereas*. At the same time, the procedure which is encoded by *whereas* cannot be the same as the one encoded by *but* since, as we have just seen, its use does not lead to the same sort of cognitive effect. If my analysis of (37B) is right, then *but* encodes a procedure which can be defined in terms of the cognitive effect of contradiction and elimination. The use of *whereas*, on the other hand, seems to indicate that the relevance of the utterance lies in the derivation of a set of parallel and contrasting contextual implications, for example, the ones in (42):

(42)   (a) We were unhappy with the weather before Christmas.

        (a') We were happy with the weather after Christmas.

        (b) We couldn't go outside much before Christmas.

        (b') We could go outside often after Christmas.

etc.

The suggestion, then, is that utterances containing *and* (for example (34)), can be understood as communicating a contrast in this sense: they achieve relevance by virtue of yielding parallel and contrasting contextual implications, and the substitution of *and* by *but* is appropriate only if it is possible to recover an interpretation in which the speaker is understood to be contradicting and eliminating an assumption (which may be an assumption that there is a respect in which the two states of affairs described are the same).

If this is right, then there is no need to distinguish between a contrast *but* and a denial of expectation *but* (see Lakoff 1971, Blakemore 1989, 2000). As Foolen (1991) has suggested, the similarities between examples such as (31) and (32) are superficial, and disappear as soon as we consider the contexts in which they are appropriate.

(31)   Anna likes reading but Tom likes tennis.

(32)   Tom likes tennis but Anna likes reading.

4.2.2   but *and concessivity*

Does this mean that all uses of *but* are concessive? Recall that Quirk *et al.*'s (1972) definition of a concessive expression requires the unexpectedness of what is being said, given what has been said before that. In the same vein, Dascal and Katriel (1977) suggest that the role of *but* in cancelling expectations or assumptions is restricted to those cases such as Lakoff's example in (33) in which the cancelled assumption is one derived inferentially from the interpretation of the segment preceding the one introduced by *but*. However, as we have just seen in example (39), the assumption which the speaker cancels through his use of *but* is not always one which may be derived inferentially from the preceding segment. It is simply an assumption derived from the hearer's encyclopaedic knowledge about Chicago which will be triggered by the mention of Chicago. It is possible that the first segment of (39) may trigger the encyclopaedic information that the hearer has about windy cities in the United States, which may include the assumption that Chicago is one of the windiest cities in the United States. Given this contextual assumption, the hearer may derive the assumption that is contradicted by the second segment, namely, that Chicago was very windy that day. However, this is not to say that the assumption that Chicago was very windy is derived as part of the interpretation of the first segment.

Similarly, although B's reply in (43) may be understood to contradict the assumption in (44), this assumption is not one which is derived from the first segment of the utterance. Indeed, uttered with the appropriate intonation, this segment would be understood to suggest the assumption in (45a) which contextually implies the falsity of (44) given the contextual assumption in (45b).

(43)   A: Do all the buses from this stop go to Piccadilly Gardens?
        B: The 85 and the 86 do, but the 84 and 87 go to Cross Street.
(44)   The 84 and 87 buses go to Piccadilly Gardens.
(45)   (a) All the other buses from this stop do not go to Piccadilly Gardens.
        (b) The 84 and 87 buses go from this stop.

The assumption in (44) would of course follow from the information that the 85 and the 86 buses go to Piccadilly on the assumption which is underlying A's question, namely, that all buses from the stop are alike in respect of whether they go to Piccadilly Gardens, and hence that there is a single 'yes' or 'no' answer to her question. However, uttered with the appropriate intonation, the first segment will suggest that there are other buses from the stop which are not like the 85 and the 86 in this respect, which, given the contextual assumption in (45b), contextually implies that the 84 and the 87 do not go to Piccadilly Gardens. In the absence of the contextual assumption in (45b), the hearer may find it relevant to know which buses do not go to Piccadilly Gardens (and hence which ones to avoid should she wish to go there), and the speaker would thus be provided with a reason for encouraging the hearer to see the relevance of the second segment as lying in the contradiction and elimination of (44). However, it seems that the *but* segment could also be relevant in a context which included the assumption in (45b). In this case, the falsity of (44) would provide the context for the interpretation of the second segment so that the speaker would be understood to be informing the hearer not just where the 84 and 87 buses go, but where they go given that they do not go to Piccadilly Gardens.

If this is right, then it seems that the cancelled assumption is not necessarily an assumption derived, or even derivable, from an act of communication at all (*contra* Bell 1998:527). And indeed, it is possible for a speaker to use *but* as a means of activating the procedure of contradiction and elimination in utterances which are not preceded by any discourse or act of communication at all (for further discussion, see Blakemore 1998).

(46)   [A gives B, who has just received a shock, a glass of whisky]
         But I don't drink.

Even if one could modify the definition of concessivity so that examples such as (39) and (43) are accommodated, it is extremely difficult to see how one could analyse this use of *but* as concessive, for, intuitively, the speaker is not conceding anything. As a number of authors have pointed out (notably, Anscombre and Ducrot 1977, Horn 1989) this non-concessive use of *but* is not restricted to discourse initial uses of *but*, but is found in utterances such as the one you are reading now. I shall turn to these so-called correction uses of *but* below. My point here is simply to underline the point that concessivity is too narrow for a definition of *but* that can accommodate all its uses.

If concessivity is too narrow, it is also too broad. Kitis (1995) has drawn attention to a use of *and* which seems to conform to Quirk's definition of concessivity, but which cannot be substituted by *but*. Thus she argues that whereas in her example given in (47) the speaker can be understood to be suggesting that the fact that the woman is seeing other men is surprising (and perhaps outrageous) given that her husband is in hospital, the utterance in (48) must have a 'back-tracking' interpretation in which the hearer is denying an assumption presumed to have been derived from the first segment (for example, that the woman is having an unpleasant time).

(47)   Her husband is in hospital and she is seeing other men.

(48)   Her husband is in hospital but she's seeing other men.

(from Kitis 1995)

There is a similar contrast between the utterance in (49), produced with stress on *honest*, and Lakoff's original example in (33) (repeated below).

(49)   John is a Republican and he is HONEST.

(33)   John is a Republican but he is honest.[7]

Kitis cites the example in (47) as evidence for her argument that *and* can function as an emotional device signalling the speaker's involvement. Her aim is to explain not only why *and* has this function, but also why it is used in preference to *but*, which is 'the prototypical adversative or contrastive connective' (Kitis 1995). As I have argued elsewhere (Blakemore 2000, Blakemore and Carston 1999), the fact that the speaker of (47) or (49) can be interpreted as communicating an emotional attitude (for example, of surprise or outrage) does not mean that *and encodes* emotional involvement. It is possible to account for the interpretation of these utterances without having to abandon a minimal truth functional semantics for *and*. According to this argument, the use of *and* is justified according to the principle of relevance only if the relevance of the conjoined proposition expressed has cognitive effects over and above the relevance of each of its conjuncts taken individually. In other words, the speaker is understood to be communicating a guarantee of optimal relevance for the *conjoined* proposition. In some cases, this may involve mapping the utterance on to a stereotypical scenario or schema in which one event is a necessary precursor for another. This will result in the sort of narrative interpretations that Grice (1989) analysed in terms of conversational implicatures but which in relevance theory are analysed in terms of the inferential development of linguistically encoded semantic representations (see chapter 3). For example, according to Carston (1993, 2002), the utterance in (50) is interpreted as communicating an explicature of the form in (51).

(50)   She got on her horse and rode into the sunset.

(51)   [She]$_i$ got on [her horse]$_j$ at t_n and [she]$_i$ rode [her horse]$_j$ into the sunset at t_{n+1}

---

[7] Iten (2000b) seems to mistake the interpretation of (49) for the so-called denial of expectation interpretation recovered from (33) and cites it as evidence that the latter interpretation can be recovered from an *and*-conjunction.

However, the aim of Blakemore and Carston's paper (1999) is to show that an *and* conjunction does not always achieve relevance as a narrative sequence. One of the non-narrative interpretations they mention is the one recovered from (52) produced with stress on the pronoun *he*.

(52)   John is a Republican and HE is honest.

This utterance would be acceptable if produced as an argument against the assertion that all Republicans are dishonest. However, notice that the validity of this argument depends on the truth of the conjunction of the two propositions expressed. Neither conjunct taken on its own would constitute proof of the falsity of the proposition that all Republicans are dishonest. In contrast, the use of *but* in (33) indicates that the segment it introduces is relevant by virtue of contradicting an assumption which the hearer is presumed to have derived from the first segment.

   The utterances in (47) and (49) illustrate another way in which *and* conjunctions can be relevant: the speaker can be taken to be expressing an attitude to the truth of the conjoined proposition expressed. While it is not the case that the speaker's attitude is encoded by *and*, it seems that there is an expression whose meaning can be analysed in terms of the way it activates this sort of interpretation, namely *yet*. Thus (53) will be interpreted in the same way as (47).

(53)   Her husband is in hospital (and) yet she is seeing other men.

The recovery of this interpretation will depend on the hearer's ability to access something like the contextual assumption in (54).

(54)   It is normally the case that a woman whose husband is in hospital will
         devote herself to his care.

Notice that although the hearer is expected to be surprised that the woman is not devoting herself to her husband's care, she is not expected to abandon the assumption in (54). On the contrary, the speaker's assumption that the hearer will share his attitude of moral outrage is based on the (possibly mistaken) assumption that the hearer believes assumptions such as (54) are legitimate. Similar remarks can be made about (49).

   In contrast, the use of *but* in (48) and (33) activates an inferential process which results in the contradiction and elimination of an assumption. For example, on one interpretation (suggested to me by the audience of a lecture at Osaka University), the speaker of (48) may intend the hearer to abandon the assumption in (55c) which is presumed to be the result of the following inference:

(55)   (a) If the woman's husband is in hospital, she will not be having a very good time.

(b) The woman's husband is in hospital. (first segment of (48))

(c) The woman isn't having a very good time.

In this case, the identification of the contradiction would depend on the contextual premise that a woman who sees other men is having a good time. This is not the only interpretation of (48), of course. However, in using an expression which activates the cognitive effect of contradiction and elimination, the speaker is signalling that he presumes the hearer to have derived an assumption from the first segment of (48), which is in fact false, or in other words, that he presumes the hearer to have made an inference (for example, the one in (55)) which is illegitimate. This raises the question of why a speaker should utter the first segment of (48) when he has reason to believe that the hearer will use the proposition it expresses in what he considers to be an illegitimate inference. The point is that a hearer who recognizes that she is expected to abandon (55c) will also recognize that she is expected to abandon the contextual premise(s) used in its derivation, in this case (55a). This means that the speaker's intention in producing (48) could be to get the hearer to abandon this assumption and as a result form new assumptions about the woman in question (for example, that she flouts social conventions). A parallel analysis can be given for (33).

This account of (48) (and (33)) follows straightforwardly from the claim that *but* encodes the information that the relevance of the segment it introduces lies in the cognitive effect of contradiction and elimination. By the same token, the fact that *but* activates this cognitive effect means that it cannot be used to achieve the effects which can be achieved by the conjoined utterances in (47) and (49) or by the use of *yet* in (53), for these do not involve contradiction and elimination. *All* of these utterances, including the *but* utterances, might be described as concessive in the sense that they involve unexpectedness. However, this does not help us explain the interpretive differences noted by Kitis (1995). In other words, the answer to Kitis' question (why can't *but* have the same function as *and* in (47)?) lies in its analysis in terms of the cognitive effect of contradiction and elimination.

4.2.3   but *and manifestness*
If the use of *but* is linked to the cognitive effect of contradiction and elimination, then it will be acceptable only in those contexts in which the hearer is able to

derive a contradiction, or in other words, only in those contexts in which the interpretation of the utterance prefaced by *but* includes an assumption which is contradictory to an assumption presumed to be manifest to the hearer. As we have seen, a speaker may be mistaken about the contextual resources of the hearer, and may use *but* to indicate that the hearer is expected to eliminate an assumption which she does not in fact hold. Thus, for example, the hearer of (56) may not have had any intention of eating the whole pizza.

(56)   There's a pizza in the fridge, but leave some for tomorrow.

However, we have also seen that people are able to form assumptions about what others believe will be relevant to them, and hence that they are able to form assumptions about what others believe will be manifest to them. Thus the hearer of (56) is able to recognize that the speaker's use of *but* is based on the belief that the assumption in (57) is manifest to her even if she is not capable of deriving it given her contextual resources.

(57)   I can eat the whole pizza.

In this case, the speaker's (possibly mistaken) assumption is based on the assumption that the hearer is capable of deriving (57) from the first segment of (56). However, we have seen that in many cases the assumption which the speaker intends the hearer to eliminate is not derived from the interpretation of the first segment of the *but* utterance at all, but is simply an assumption which the speaker has reason to believe is manifest to the hearer. Thus the speaker's evidence for assuming that the eliminated assumption is manifest to the hearer may be provided by an utterance made by the hearer herself. Or it may be provided by a state of affairs which is mutually manifest to speaker and hearer. For example, in (46) (repeated below), the speaker will have evidence for the assumption that the assumption that the hearer is expected to drink the whisky will be mutually manifest to them.

(46)   [A gives B, who has just received a shock, a glass of whisky]
       But I don't drink.

However, Iten (2000b) has argued that the requirement that the eliminated assumption is *manifest* to the hearer is too strong, since there are uses of *but* where the speaker has reason to believe that the hearer is not capable of accepting this assumption as true or as probably true. The cases she has in mind involve the so-called 'correction' use of *but*, for example (58).

(58)   He's not clever, but hardworking.

It has been claimed (for example, by Anscombre and Ducrot 1977 and Horn 1989) that there is a semantic distinction between *but* as used in (58) and *but* as used in examples such as (56) and (46), or in other words, that *but* is ambiguous between two meanings: a denial of expectation meaning and a correction meaning. As these authors point out, these two meanings are encoded by different lexical items in some languages, for example, Spanish, German, Hebrew and Swedish. Moreover, the two *but*s are claimed to have different distributional properties: first, while the first clause of an utterance containing correction *but* must contain an explicit, unincorporated negation, this is not the case in utterances involving denial *but*; and second, while the second clause of an utterance containing correction *but* undergoes conjunction reduction when it shares material with the first clause, this is not the case in utterances involving denial *but*. Thus while the (a) examples in (59–61) can be interpreted as involving correction *but*, the (b) examples must be interpreted as involving denial *but*.

(59)   (a) He isn't clever, but hardworking.

        (b) He's clever, but not hardworking.

(60)   (a) It's not ambiguous, but vague.

        (b) It's unambiguous, but vague.

(61)   (a) He's not my grandson, but my nephew.

        (b) He's not my grandson, but he is my nephew.

However, Iten (2000a,b) has shown that none of the arguments for the ambiguity of *but* are compelling, and hence that it would be worth looking for a unitary semantic analysis which could accommodate all of its uses, including the so-called correction ones. At the same time, she argues that in order to accommodate these uses within a single constraint on implicit content, we must modify my 1987 analysis so that the assumption eliminated as a result of the use of *but* is simply *accessible* in the context. Since an assumption is accessible provided that it is entertainable and hence does not have to be accepted as true or probably true, it is possible to analyse the use of *but* in an example such as (58) in terms of the contradiction and elimination of the assumption in (62), even though this assumption is deemed to be false.

(58)   He's not clever, but hardworking.

(62)   He is clever.

While there may be a case for modifying the analysis of *but* in this way, it is not, I believe, made by so-called correction uses of *but*. Iten seems to assume that the assumption eliminated by the *but* segment in (58) on its correction interpretation must be one that is made manifest by the first segment of the sequence. Since the first segment of (58) is denying the truth of (62), either (62) cannot be understood as the assumption eliminated by the *but* segment, which it clearly is, or we must re-analyse *but* so that the inferential procedure it activates does not necessarily have to result in the elimination of a manifest assumption. Iten's solution is based on the generally accepted view that negative sentences make accessible their positive counterparts. While this may be the case, it is not clear that this solution fully accounts for the role that *but* plays in the interpretation of a sequence such as (58).

Like any utterance, a negative utterance such as (63) may achieve relevance in any of the three ways summarized in the first section of this chapter: that is, it may yield contextual implications, or it may strengthen an existing assumption, or it may lead to the contradiction and elimination of an existing assumption.

(63)   He's not clever. (− first segment of (58))

In some cases, the actual interpretation of (63) will depend on the principle of relevance and the contextual assumptions which are accessible to the hearer. However, in other cases the hearer will be given linguistic clues as to the direction in which relevance is to be sought. Intonation is one means of guiding the interpretation process. However, my concern here is with the role played by *but* in utterances such as (58).

For an utterance to achieve relevance as a contradiction, it must communicate an assumption which is contradictory to an assumption which the hearer believes to be true. This means that a speaker who indicates that the hearer is expected to derive this kind of cognitive effect from an utterance, is communicating his (possibly mistaken) assumption that a given assumption is manifest to the hearer. Thus a speaker who intends (63) to achieve relevance as a contradiction is communicating his assumption that the assumption in (62) is manifest to her. Now, let us consider (63) as a part of the utterance in (58). If *but* is, as I have argued, a means of activating an inference which results in the contradiction and elimination of an assumption, then its use will indicate that the speaker believes there is an assumption manifest to the hearer which is contradictory to an assumption he is communicating. What is this assumption? Since being hardworking is not in itself incompatible with being clever, there would seem to be no reason for the hearer to opt for (62). On the other hand, this is an assumption which would be presumed to be manifest to the hearer provided that the first segment (that is, (63)) is itself relevant as a contradiction.

In making this interpretation salient for the interpretation of the segment it introduces, *but* is also making it salient for the first segment. This effect is to make (62) manifest to the hearer for the interpretation of *both* segments.

In other words, what distinguishes utterances such as (58) from other utterances involving *but* is that the interpretation of each of its segments involves an inferential procedure that results in the contradiction and elimination of the same assumption.

The fact that *but* sends the hearer on this inferential route for the interpretation of the segment it introduces does not always mean that it makes this route salient for the interpretation of the first segment. For example, while it is not impossible to think of a scenario in which the speaker of (64) might wish to contradict the hearer's assumption that he had homework and replace it with the assumption that the teachers want the pupils to cover their books, the sequence will not receive a correction interpretation analogous to the interpretation recovered from (58).

(64)   I haven't got any homework, but the teachers want us to cover our books.

This raises the question of why the speaker of an example such as (58) can be understood to be communicating that the relevance of both segments lies in the contradiction and elimination of the same assumption and why he cannot be understood in this way in examples such as (64). The answer, or at least the key to an answer, seems to lie in the formal (or linguistic properties) of the utterances in question. In the first place, the intonation of the first segment of (64) may be inconsistent with its interpretation as a denial: imagine, for example, how this segment would be uttered by a child who has been asked by a friend whether he will have time to go to the park for a game of football. However, apart from this, it seems that the correction interpretation is ruled out by the fact that the two clauses share no linguistic material at all, and hence that there is not an appropriate linguistic environment for the conjunction reduction, which, as we have seen, characterizes correction uses of *but* in English. By the same token, the conjunction reduction in the second clause of (58) suggests a correction interpretation in which each segment achieves relevance by contradicting and eliminating the same assumption.

This suggestion would seem to be supported by Iten's (2000b:144) observation that whereas (65) cannot receive a correction interpretation, its German translation with *sondern* in (66) must be interpreted in this way (in spite of the fact that the two segments share no linguistic material at all).

(65)   John didn't make a salad, but Jack bought a cake.

(66)   John hat keinen Salat gemacht, sondern Jack hat einen Kuchen gekauft.

In other words, whereas English *but* encodes a single constraint linked to the cognitive effect of contradiction and elimination, and the way in which a hearer will interpret an utterance in accordance with this constraint depends on the linguistic environment in which *but* occurs, in German the information that the hearer is expected to recover an interpretation in which each segment is relevant as a contradiction of the same assumption is encoded in the meaning of *sondern*.

If my analysis of so-called correction uses of *but* is correct, then they do not show the requirement that the eliminated assumption must be accessible rather than manifest. However, there are other types of examples mentioned by Iten (2000b) which do seem to suggest that the requirement that the eliminated assumption be manifest cannot be met. Consider, for example, the utterances in (67) and (68):

(67)   Tom was meant to be here, but his car broke down.

(68)   I would have liked to go on holiday this year, but I couldn't afford it.

The use of *but* in (67) will be understood to indicate that the hearer should abandon the assumption in (69). However, this assumption is manifestly false. Similarly, the use of *but* in (68) will be understood to activate an inferential process which results in the elimination of the assumption in (70) whose falsity is made manifest by the first segment of the sequence.

(69)   Tom is here.

(70)   I can come.

In these cases, it seems, there is a case for saying that while the speaker presumes the eliminated assumption to be manifestly false, he will assume that it will be accessible to the hearer in the sense that the speaker will judge it to be one which is 'likely to occur to the hearer for consideration in the context' (Iten 2000b:160). In particular, it seems that the speaker of, for example (67), expects the hearer to speculate on the consequences of (69) should it have been true, or in other words, that the hearer is expected to consider the consequences of (69) being true in a possible world which is in all other respects the actual world. For instance, in such a world it may be possible to make the inference in (71):

(71)   (a) If Tom is here, we will have a quorum for the meeting. (contextual premise)
       (b) Tom is here. (= 69)
       (c) We will have a quorum for the meeting. (conclusion)

In this case, the point of the *but* segment is to activate an inferential process which results in the elimination of (69) and thus encourage the hearer to recognize that the conclusion in (71c) is not actually valid. A similar kind of analysis could be given for (68).

The claim that *but* always activates an inferential procedure which results in the elimination of an assumption which is manifest to the hearer would also seem to be undermined by the attributive uses of *but* discussed in 4.1. According to my analysis of Rieber's (1997) example in (3), the speaker is explicitly attributing the inference which is activated by the use of *but* to Tom and thereby indicates that the hearer is expected to derive the cognitive effects which would be derived by a person who held the assumption in (9), namely the elimination of (8).

(3)   Tom thinks that Sheila is rich but unhappy. But I have always thought that all rich people are unhappy.

(9)   All rich people are happy.

(8)   Sheila is happy.

Similarly, according to my analysis of the ironic utterance in (10), the speaker is using *but* in order to lead the hearer to the cognitive effects that would be derived by the sort of person who held the assumption in (13), namely the elimination of (11).

(10)   This is Paul. He's a syntactician, but he's quite intelligent.

(13)   No syntactician is intelligent.

(11)   Paul is not intelligent.

If this is right, then the speaker's use of *but* does not indicate that he presumes the assumptions in (8) and (11) to be manifest to the hearer – at least not as assumptions which she is capable of accepting as true (or probably true) – but only that they are manifest as attributed assumptions. In other words, it seems that what the speaker is assuming in each of these cases is that (72) and (73) are manifest to the hearer.

(72)   Tom believes that Sheila is happy.

(73)   There are people who believe that Paul is not intelligent.

It might be argued that the manifestness of an assumption like (72) might be sufficient for the manifestness of (8). And indeed, the fact that someone believes something to be the case would in some cases be regarded as sufficient evidence for accepting it as true or probably true. However, as we have seen, in an example such as (10) the speaker intends the hearer to recognize that he has dissociated himself from the use of *but* and hence the inference made on the basis of (13). Moreover, as Sperber and Wilson's (1995) account of irony shows, the success of the irony will depend on whether this attitude of dissociation is one which is shared by the hearer. Hence the speaker of the ironic utterance in (10) cannot be said to presume that the conclusion that would be derived on the basis of (13), namely (11), is manifest to the hearer. On the other hand, it seems that the hearer could be said to presume that (11) is accessible to the hearer in the sense proposed by Iten (2000b). That is, the speaker's use of *but* in this example is based on his assumption that (13), and, therefore (11), are available to the hearer for consideration in the context. As in the examples in (67) and (68), the hearer is expected to be able to consider what kind of inference would be made if a given assumption were true. In other words, she can be expected to recognize (13) as the conclusion that would be derived by someone who accepted the truth of (11).

4.3   *However* and *nevertheless*

4.3.1   *The* but, however, nevertheless *hierarchy*

As Fraser (1990) suggests, the more general the constraint imposed by a discourse connective, the more difficult it is to analyse. Fraser has described *but* as the most general of the contrastive discourse markers in the sense that it 'imposes the least restrictions on the relationship between S2 and the S1 with which it is contrasted' (1990:308). The fact that the already extensive literature on *but* continues to grow would seem to bear this out, as does the fact that my analysis of *but* proposed in 4.2 is the result of many previous attempts. However, if this analysis is right, we can at least link *but* to a specific cognitive effect. Moreover, if this analysis is right, *but* does not encode contrast, as suggested by Fraser. On the other hand, there does seem to be something in the claim that there is a cluster of expressions which are somehow related to *but*, and that of these *but* has the most general meaning. In fact, it seems that one can order at least some of the members of this family of expressions according to their inter-substitutability. Thus it seems that while *but* has the most general meaning in the sense that it can always be used in utterances in which *however* and *nevertheless* are acceptable, *however* and *nevertheless* must be more restrictive since they cannot always be used in utterances in which *but* is acceptable. Moreover, it seems that *nevertheless* must be more restrictive than *however*, since while there are utterances in which both *nevertheless* and *however* are acceptable, there are also utterances in which *however* is acceptable but not *nevertheless*. This is illustrated in the examples in (74–6). While (74) shows utterances in which all three expressions are equally acceptable, (75) contains examples of utterances in which *but* and *however* are acceptable, but not *nevertheless*, and (76) has examples of utterances in which only *but* is acceptable.

(74)   (a) I am sure she is honest. Nevertheless, the papers are missing.
        (b) I am sure she is honest. But the papers are missing.
        (c) I am sure she is honest. However the papers are missing.

(75)   [in response to: Have you got my article?]
        (a) Yes, but the last page is missing.
        (b) Yes. However, the last page is missing.
        (c) Yes. ?Nevertheless, the last page is missing.

(76)   [speaker, who is in shock, has been given a whisky]
        (a) But I don't drink.
        (b) ?However, I don't drink.
        (c) ?Nevertheless I don't drink.

I do not want to suggest that the aim of anybody analysing the family of so-called contrastive discourse connectives should be to produce a hierarchy such as this. It is not at all clear that the full range of such expressions could be accommodated in this way. Nor is it clear what this exercise would contribute to the understanding of the roles that these expressions play in the interpretation of the utterances that contain them. However, it does seem that an analysis of the expressions I have mentioned here must account for the sort of facts in (74–6), and that an account of *however*, for example, must explain why it can be used in utterances such as (74c) and (75b) but not in (76b).

As I explained in the first section of the chapter, it is difficult to see how such an explanation could be provided by the analysis of these expressions as semantic constraints on relevance, where these are understood along the lines suggested in Blakemore (1987). For according to this account, expressions which constrain relevance perform this role by encoding constraints on cognitive effects. Thus *so* was analysed as encoding the cognitive effect of contextual implication, *after all* was analysed as encoding the cognitive effect of strengthening, and *but* was analysed as encoding the cognitive effect of contradiction and elimination. However, while this notion may allow us to distinguish between three broad categories of discourse connectives, it does not enable us to capture the fine-grained distinctions in meaning between the range of expressions that fall into each category. If we are to provide an explanation of the facts illustrated in (74–6) within the semantic framework I have proposed, then clearly we must take another look at the notion of a semantic constraint on relevance and ask whether it can be extended to include other information about inferential processes.

4.3.2   however

Fraser (1990) claims that the difference between *but* and *however* lies in the fact that 'whereas *but* signals a simple contrast between S1 and S2 with no particular emphasis on S1 or S2, hence the interchangeability of the segments when the target [of the contrast] is the direct message conveyed by S1', *however* 'signals that S1 is being emphasized, placing the S2 message in a more subordinate role' (1990:313). He goes on to argue that although *but* can be used in all *however* contexts, it will 'be interpreted as emphasizing S2 when it does so' (1990:313).

Since Fraser does not explain what he means by 'emphasis' or 'subordinate' or, indeed, 'simple contrast', it is difficult to say how it enables us to account for the discrepancies between *however* and *but*. As we have seen in 4.2.1, the claim that *but* encodes a symmetric relation of contrast is based on the assumption that it is based on its apparent inter-substitutability with *and* in utterances such as (30c) and (d).

(30)   (c) Anna likes reading and Tom likes tennis. $\neq$
         (d) Tom likes tennis and Anna likes reading.

However, once these utterances are contextualized it becomes evident that the substitution of *but* results in a different non-symmetric interpretation in which the speaker is signalling that the segment introduced by *but* is relevant by virtue of contradicting an assumption presumed to be manifest (or accessible) to the hearer. In other words, according to this argument, these uses of *but* are as asymmetric as those uses which are generally recognized as asymmetric uses of *but*, namely, the use known as denial of expectation *but* illustrated by Lakoff's (1971) example in (33) (repeated below), and the so-called correction use illustrated in (58) (repeated below).

(33)   John is a Republican but he is honest. $\neq$
(33′)   John is honest but he is a Republican.
(58)   He's not clever, but hardworking. $\neq$
(58′)   He's hardworking, but not clever.

Fraser might want to say that *however* can be substituted for *but* only in its asymmetric uses, thus maintaining his claim that *however* is always asymmetric. However, this would not explain why *however* can be substituted for *but* in its denial of expectation use in (33) but cannot be substituted for *but* in its correction use. Compare, for example (58) and (77).

(77)   ?He is not clever; however, not hardworking.

The fact that (77) cannot be given a correction interpretation might be attributed to the fact that *however*, in contrast with *but*, does not form a co-ordinated structure and hence cannot introduce a clause which has undergone conjunction reduction. However, it seems that it is possible to recover an interpretation from (78), where the absence of an explicit negation rules out a correction reading, and hence that the problem in (77) is that the meaning of *however* is not compatible with a correction interpretation.

(78)   He is clever; however, not hardworking.

It will be recalled that there is another use of *but* where it cannot be replaced by *however*, namely, the use which Fraser (1998) calls the protest use, illustrated in (76b) (repeated below).

(76)   [speaker, who is in shock, has been given a whisky]
        (a) But I don't drink.
        (b) ?However, I don't drink.

If it is indeed the case that *but* is a co-ordinator and *however* is not, as suggested above, then this discrepancy might appear odd. However, as Schiffrin (1987) has pointed out, the fact that an expression is classified as a co-ordinator from a syntactic point of view, does not mean that it cannot be used discourse-initially. For instance, neither of the utterances below would be regarded as continuations or interruptions of another speaker's utterance.

(79)   [the speaker (a young child) triumphantly presents her mother with flowers] AND I've got you a present.
(80)   [speaker finds bunch of flowers and birthday card on doorstep] And I thought she'd forgotten.

Moreover, as I have pointed out elsewhere (Blakemore 1987, 1998), there are other discourse connectives which cannot function as co-ordinators but which are unacceptable if used discourse-initially. For example, while *so* is acceptable in a sequence such as (81), the use of *therefore* is unacceptable.

(81)   [driver takes a right turn at an intersection]
        PASSENGER: So we're not going past the post office.
        PASSENGER: ?Therefore we're not going past the post office.

This would suggest that the discrepancy between (76a) and (b) must be explained in terms of the meanings of *but* and *however*.

It might be argued that the problem in (76b) is not so much that *however* cannot be used discourse-initially, as that it cannot be used to preface an objection or protest. And indeed, it would seem that its use would be odd in an example such as (82) (adapted from Iten 2000b).

(82)   A: We had a very nice lunch. I had an excellent lobster.
        B: But what about the money?
        B': ?However, what about the money?

However, as (83) shows, it seems that there are acceptable uses of *however* in which it is understood to preface an objection.

(83)   A: She's had a very difficult time this semester.
        B: However, I think she should hand in at least some of the work.

As we have seen, the fact that *but* can be used in correction utterances such as (58) and objections such as (76a) and (82) can be explained in terms of its analysis as an expression which encodes the information that the speaker is expected to perform an inference which results in the elimination of an accessible assumption. The question is, then, what information does *however* encode that is inconsistent with its use in these cases but is consistent with its uses in examples such as (83) (above), (84) (the *however* counterpart of (33)), (85) (the *however* counterpart of (39)), or the partial answer in (86) (the *however* counterpart of (43)).

(84)   John is a Republican; however, he's honest.
(33)   John is a Republican, but he's honest.
(85)   New York was the windiest city in the United States today; however, Chicago had light winds.
(39)   New York was the windiest city in the United States today, but Chicago had light winds.
(86)   A: Do all the buses from this stop go to Piccadilly Gardens?
        B: The 85 and the 86 do; however, the 84 and 87 go to Cross Street.
(43)   A: Do all the buses from this stop go to Piccadilly Gardens?
        B: The 85 and the 86 do, but the 84 and 87 go to Cross Street.

As we have seen, the speaker's use of *but* in (33), (39) and (43) activates the procedure of contradiction and elimination so that the relevance of the segment it introduces is understood to lie in the elimination of an accessible assumption, that is, in the elimination of (87) and (88) and (89) respectively.

(87)   John is honest.
(88)   Chicago had strong winds.
(89)   The 84 and 87 buses go to Piccadilly Gardens.

However, in all of these utterances the speaker can also be understood to be communicating information which yields cognitive effects which do *not* involve the elimination of these assumptions. Let us consider them each in turn.

According to the analysis generally given for (33) (for example, Lakoff 1971, Blakemore 1987), the assumption eliminated by the use of *but* is one which is made manifest by the interpretation of the first segment. In other words, the use of *but* in this example is based on the speaker's (possibly mistaken) assumption that the hearer will derive (87) as an implicature from the first segment. However, in contradicting this assumption, the speaker will not be understood to be suggesting that the first segment has no relevance at all. On the contrary, the hearer is encouraged to seek relevance in a different direction, and in this sense receives the speaker's guarantee that the information that John is a Republican is relevant in some other way.

As we have seen in 4.2.1, the interpretation of (39) is slightly different in that the eliminated assumption in (88) is not one that is presumed to have been derived as an implicature from the first segment. It is simply an assumption that is presumed to be part of the hearer's encyclopaedic knowledge, perhaps triggered by the mention of winds in the first segment or simply by the mention of Chicago (in the context of a weather report). However, while it cannot be assumed that the hearer will have derived (88) as an implicature from the first segment, it can be assumed that she will have derived other information from it and on this basis judge it to be relevant. In other words, the speaker can be understood to be communicating her assumption that this segment will have relevance that does not involve the elimination of (88).

According to the analysis given in 4.2.2, the point of the *but* segment in (43) is to indicate that the assumption underlying the hearer's enquiry, namely, that all the buses leaving from the bus stop are headed for the same destination, is mistaken, and hence that there is not a single 'yes' or 'no' answer to her question. However, as I observed, it could be argued that the elimination of (89) could be achieved simply by the utterance of the first segment, particularly if this were uttered with a contrastive intonation. In this case, then it would seem that the second segment does not achieve relevance in a way that is not already achieved by the first. However, even if this were the case, the relevance of the first segment is not exhausted by the elimination of (89). On the contrary, the speaker may believe it is relevant by virtue of the fact that the hearer will now know that there are two buses which go to Piccadilly Gardens, and that the 85 and the 86 buses are the ones she should get should she want to go there.

In other words, in all these three cases, the cognitive effect which according to the arguments of 4.2 is activated by *but* is activated in a context in which the speaker has achieved relevance in a way which does not involve the same cognitive effect, or in other words, in which the total relevance achieved by the speaker is not exhausted by the elimination of a single accessible assumption. While this happens to be the case in (33), (39) and (43), it is not the case either in the objection use of *but* in (76a) and (82) or the correction use in (58).

(76)   [speaker, who is in shock, has been given a whisky]
       (a) But I don't drink.
(82)   A: We had a very nice lunch. I had an excellent lobster.
       B: But what about the money?
(58)   He's not clever, but hardworking.

The fact that the intended relevance of the utterance in (76a) is exhausted by the elimination of the assumption in (90) is self-evident: the speaker has not communicated any other information which could achieve relevance in another way.

(90)   The speaker of (76a) can be expected to drink the whisky that is being offered.

The same is true of (82). However, it is also true of (83), where *however* is acceptable.

(83)   A: She's had a very difficult time this semester.
       B: However, I think she should hand in at least some of the work.

This would suggest that the fact that the speaker has not communicated information which he judges to be relevant in a way which does not involve the elimination of the assumption in (91) is beside the point.

(91)   She does not need to hand in any work.

Rather, the point is that whereas in (82) B will be taken to be suggesting that the information communicated by A is of no relevance at all, in (83) he will be taken to be suggesting that the information that has been communicated by A has some relevance, or in other words, that he has accepted the guarantee of relevance communicated by A. In other words, the hearer is intended to recognize that the context includes assumptions whose relevance comes with a guarantee that is accepted by the speaker, and whose cognitive effects do not include the elimination of (91).

   The speaker of (58) has, of course, communicated information which, in principle, could achieve relevance in a way that does not involve the elimination of (92).

(92)   He is clever. (= 62)

For example, from the information that he is not clever, the hearer might derive the assumption that he will not pass the examination he is about to sit. However, as I argued in 4.2.3, when this information is communicated in an utterance such as (58) – that is, an utterance with a reduced second clause – the hearer is encouraged to assume that the cognitive effect activated by *but* in the interpretation of the segment it introduces and the cognitive effect that the speaker intends her to derive from the first segment are one and the same. In this respect, the correction example in (58) must be distinguished from the counterfactual example in (68).

(68)   I would have liked to go on holiday this year, but I couldn't afford it.

For although the falsity of (93) is made manifest by the first segment, it is evident this segment does not itself achieve relevance as a correction and that the speaker can be interpreted as having communicated information which he believes is relevant in a way that does not include the elimination of (93).

(93)   I went on holiday this year.

In other words, this utterance, in contrast with (58), satisfies the conditions for the acceptable use of *however*. Hence the acceptability of (94):

(94)   I would have liked to go on holiday this year; however, I couldn't afford it.

   The fact that *but* can be used both in utterances such as (33), (39), (43) and in utterances such as (76a) and (58) suggests that it cannot be said to encode any information about the contexts in which the effect of contradiction and elimination is achieved. This is in line with the analysis in 4.2. Moreover, it is in line with the assumption underlying my original account of semantic constraints on relevance, namely, that they are restricted to information about cognitive effects. However, the fact that *however* is acceptable in utterances such as (33), (39), (43) and (83), but not in utterances such as (76a) or (58), would suggest that it does not simply encode the information that the hearer is expected to follow an inferential route which results in the contradiction and elimination of an accessible assumption A, but also that there is a restriction on the context in which this cognitive effect is derived. Specifically, it restricts the recovery of this effect to contexts which include assumptions which carry a guarantee of relevance accepted by the speaker and whose cognitive effects do not include the elimination of A. If this is right, then the notion of a semantic constraint on relevance must be broadened to incorporate constraints on contexts as well as constraints on cognitive effects.

4.3.3   nevertheless

The analysis of *nevertheless* must not only account for its unacceptability in objections such as (76c) and (95) or corrections such as (95), but also a range of utterances in which both *but* and *however* are acceptable, for example (96–9).

(76)   [speaker, who is in shock, has been given a whisky]
        (c) But/?Nevertheless I don't drink.
(95)   A: I had a very nice lunch. I had an excellent lobster.
        B: But/?Nevertheless what about the money?
(96)   He's not clever, but/?nevertheless hardworking.
(97)   A: Do all the buses from this stop go to Piccadilly Gardens?
        B: The 85 and the 86 do, but/however/?nevertheless the 84 and 87 go
        to Cross Street.
(98)   [mother's response to hungry child's request for food]
        There's a pizza in the fridge, but/ however/?nevertheless leave some
        for tomorrow.
(99)   I've just received a copy of Anne's latest paper. But/ However/?Nev-
        ertheless it's in French.

The key to the meaning of *nevertheless* will be found in whatever it is that distinguishes these utterances from the ones in which *nevertheless* is acceptable, for example, the ones below:

(74a)   I am sure she is honest. Nevertheless, the papers are missing.
(100)   A: She's had a very difficult time this semester.
         B: Nevertheless, she should hand in at least some of the work.
(101)   It is natural that learners in the early stages of learning should feel a
         need to stay firmly in familiar territory. Nevertheless, the unpredictable
         nature of much communication is a feature of naturally occurring lan-
         guage, and teachers have a responsibility to gradually expose learners
         to such language and enable them to develop strategies which will help
         them cope.
                [from a typescript on communicative methods in language teaching
                originally cited in Blakemore 2000]

Yorick Wilks (personal communication) has suggested that *nevertheless* is distinguished from *but* by the fact that it is a rhetorical device or that it is appropriate in rhetorical contexts. This does not amount to an analysis of *nevertheless*,
for there are many expressions and constructions which have been described
as 'rhetorical' – for example, epizeuxis (or repetition) or so-called rhetorical
questions – but whose contribution has very little to do with the one made by

nevertheless. Nevertheless, it seems that this suggestion may point us in the right sort of direction.

Let us return to the paragraph you have just read, where the last sentence is prefaced by *nevertheless*, and ask what was going on here. It is, I presume, mutually manifest that I am attempting to ask the question, 'What is the meaning of *nevertheless* and how is it different from the meaning of *but*?' Given this context, I am further assuming that I am justified in thinking that you will recognize that my aim in describing an answer suggested by someone else was to raise the question, 'Is this suggestion tenable?', or, in other words, that this question is not simply mutually manifest but highly accessible. Moreover, I am assuming that the utterance following my representation of this suggestion (that is, the second sentence of the paragraph) will be interpreted as suggesting that the answer to this question is, 'No, it is not tenable.' In other words, my use of *nevertheless* in the final sentence of the paragraph was based on the assumption that the preceding utterance communicated an answer to a mutually manifest (and highly accessible) question. It is this answer, of course, which is contradicted and eliminated by the utterance introduced by *nevertheless*. In other words, having given you one answer to a question which I assumed was mutually manifest, I then gave you another which contradicted it.

You are, of course, justified in thinking that I have set you up. On the other hand, I believe that what I have just described will be recognized as a typical example of a *nevertheless* context. (Moreover, I believe that it will enable us to explain the sense in which *nevertheless* operates as a rhetorical device.) Let us return to the acceptable uses of *nevertheless* in (74a), (100) and (101).

The fact that the speaker of (74a) (repeated below) is reassuring the hearer that he does not doubt the honesty of the woman referred to suggests that it must be understood as part of a dialogue in which the question of the woman's honesty has arisen, if not explicitly, implicitly. This reassurance could be taken to suggest that the missing papers had nothing to do with this woman. However, this suggestion is contradicted by the *nevertheless* segment, and the speaker will be understood to be suggesting that while he is not accusing the woman of dishonesty, he is accusing her of having something to do with the loss of the papers.

(74a)   I am sure she is honest. Nevertheless, the papers are missing.

Similarly, (100) (repeated below) can be understood as part of a dialogue in which the participants are discussing the question of whether a student should be absolved from the course requirements regarding assessed work. A's contribution could be interpreted as a reason for waiving the rules entirely, a suggestion which is contradicted by B.

(100)   A: She's had a very difficult time this semester.
          B: Nevertheless, she should hand in at least some of the work.

Notice that the discussion of these examples has not assumed that the question whose answer is being contradicted by the *nevertheless* segment is one that is posed explicitly in the preceding discourse. This may be the case, of course. But it is equally acceptable for it to be a question which is inferred by the hearer on the basis of contextual assumptions and the principle of relevance. Thus the writer of the passage in (101) (repeated below) will be understood to be addressing the question raised by the utterance which preceded it, namely (102).

(102)   Inexperienced language learners often express fears about jumping into conversations in a foreign language because they fear the unexpected.

(101)   It is natural that learners in the early stages of learning should feel a need to stay firmly in familiar territory. Nevertheless, the unpredictable nature of much communication is a feature of naturally occurring language, and teachers have a responsibility to gradually expose learners to such language and enable them to develop strategies which will help them cope.

For example, this question could be taken to be 'How should teachers deal with language learners' fear of the unexpected', and the answer suggested by the first segment of (101) could be 'they should protect them from unexpected problems'. As in the previous examples, this answer is contradicted by the segment introduced by *nevertheless*.

Within the framework of speech act theory (see Searle 1969, Bach and Harnish 1979), it is not clear how the utterance introduced by *nevertheless* in these examples could be regarded as an answer to a question. For according to this account, questions are requests for information, and hence must be posed explicitly. As we shall see in the following chapter, the phenomenon of implicit questions is not restricted to utterances involving *nevertheless*. For example, the second segment of (103) can be understood as an answer to a WH question (for example, 'Why?') which has been raised by the first.

(103)   She's going back to France next week. Her contract has expired.

For these phenomena, it seems that we need not an account of what it means for a speaker to produce an utterance which has a particular kind of illocutionary force, but rather an account of what it means for someone to have a particular kind of thought.

In fact, as Sperber and Wilson (Wilson and Sperber 1988, Sperber and Wilson 1995) point out, not all interrogative utterances are requests for information: consider, rhetorical questions, expository questions, examination questions, speculative questions, for example. They argue that within relevance theory it is possible to give a unitary account of interrogative utterances in terms of the notion of *interpretive use* (Sperber and Wilson 1995:224–31). For Sperber and Wilson, there is a basic sense in which every utterance is an interpretation: it is a public representation of a private representation, that is, a thought. The relationship between the propositional form of an utterance and the thought it represents is not one of identity, but rather of resemblance, so that literal resemblance is a limiting case rather than the norm. Hence the possibility of metaphor, for example.[8] Whereas in cases of descriptive language use, the thought interpreted is entertained as a description of a state of affairs (the one which would make it true), other utterances must be analysed as interpretations of thoughts which are themselves interpretive representations of other thoughts. Ironic utterances, varieties of reported speech, fall within this category. And so do interrogative utterances. However, while ironic utterances and reported speech are interpretations of thoughts which are interpretive representations of attributed thoughts, an interrogative utterance is an interpretation of a thought which is a representation of a thought which the speaker believes to be *desirable* – that is, relevant – to someone (not necessarily herself). In other words, the thought interpreted by an interrogative utterance is a representation of an answer which the speaker believes would be relevant to someone if true. Since this thought is not necessarily a representation of an answer which is relevant to the speaker, this analysis is able to account for interrogative utterances which are not requests for information. And since this thought is not necessarily a thought which is publicly represented by an utterance, this analysis, in contrast with the speech act theoretic one, is also able to account for implicit questions.

Returning to *nevertheless*, we can now say what it means to say that the utterance introduced by *nevertheless* is understood as an answer to a question which has been raised (explicitly or implicitly) by the preceding discourse or which has been made relevant through the interpretation of the preceding discourse. An utterance U is relevant as an answer to a question if there is a mutually manifest assumption in the context which is an interpretation of some desirable proposition p and p is communicated (explicated or implicated) by U.

---

[8] For a fuller discussion of this, see Sperber and Wilson (1985/6), Sperber and Wilson (1995:231–7).

My suggestion is that not only is the utterance introduced by *nevertheless* relevant in this way but it is relevant as an answer in a context which includes a contradictory assumption which is relevant as an answer to the same question.

While this is invariably the case for utterances prefaced by *nevertheless*, utterances containing *but* and *however* may be acceptable in contexts which do not satisfy this condition. Recall the example in (97), where the use of *nevertheless* is unacceptable.

(97)   A: Do all the buses from this stop go to Piccadilly Gardens?
        B: The 85 and the 86 do, but/however/?nevertheless the 84 and 87 go
        to Cross Street.

For *nevertheless* to be acceptable the second segment would have to be construed as an answer to a question in a context which includes a contradictory answer to the same question. The problem is that while it can be construed as communicating information which is relevant as an answer to a question which is answered by the first segment, namely, the one asked by A, it cannot be interpreted as contradicting the answer communicated by the first segment. As I argued in 4.2.2, this segment suggests that the 85 and the 86 are the only buses from the stop that go to Piccadilly Gardens.

In (98) (repeated below), the first segment is relevant as an answer to the child's question, 'Is there anything to eat?' While the second segment eliminates the assumption that might have been derived from the first, namely, that the child can eat all of the pizza, the effect of this is not to contradict the answer to this question. There is still something for the child to eat. Nor is it possible to construe the first segment as an answer to the question 'Can I eat the whole pizza?'.

(98)   [mother's response to hungry child's request for food]
        There's a pizza in the fridge, but/however/?nevertheless leave some
        for tomorrow.

Examples (75) and (99) (repeated below) can be explained in the same way.

(75)   [in response to: Have you got my article?]
        (a) Yes, but the last page is missing.
        (b) Yes. However, the last page is missing.
        (c) Yes. ?Nevertheless, the last page is missing.
(99)   I've just received a copy of Anne's latest paper. But/ However/?Never-
        theless it's in French.

These differences seem to suggest that while the use of *nevertheless* is linked to the cognitive effect of contradiction and elimination, it also encodes a restriction on the contexts in which this effect is recovered. At the same time, the fact that *nevertheless* cannot always be substituted for *however* suggests that this restriction cannot be the same as the one encoded by *however*. As we have seen, *nevertheless* is acceptable only in contexts in which there is an assumption whose truth is an issue, or in other words, in contexts in which the elimination of the assumption amounts to accepting one answer (the speaker's) rather than another. It is in this sense that *nevertheless* operates in a rhetorical context.

This account of the differences between *but*, *however* and *nevertheless* is in line with the suggestion made by Blass (1990) that a discourse connective may have a cluster of functions some of which may be shared by other connectives. Thus while the function of contradiction and elimination is shared by all these expressions, *however* and *nevertheless* have additional functions which are not encoded by *but*. The point is that these additional functions must be defined in terms of restrictions on the contexts in which the cognitive effect of contradiction and elimination is achieved, and hence that the notion of a semantic constraint on relevance is more complex than the one proposed in my earlier work (Blakemore 1987). However, it is more complex in a way which is consistent with the cognitive theory from which it derives. As I argued in the previous chapter, the possibility of procedural encoding is a consequence of the fact that the inferential phase of utterance understanding involves the construction and manipulation of conceptual representations. Since the results of this phase of understanding depend not only on the activation of particular inferential routes (for example, contradiction and elimination or independent strengthening), but also on the activation of contextual assumptions, it seems reasonable to assume that the information encoded by a linguistic expression or construction may activate either an inferential route or a particular kind of context or, indeed, both.

4.4   *Well*

4.4.1   *The elusiveness of* well

Over the course of this chapter I have given the impression that *but* has received more attention than any other English expression classified as a discourse marker. However, this impression requires qualification. While *but* may be the favourite among those philosophers and linguists who are interested in the question of how non-truth conditional meaning can be accommodated in a theory of meaning, linguists with an interest in the role that these expressions play in discourse are more interested in *well*. Thus *well* not only features in more general accounts of discourse connectives or markers (for example, Halliday and Hasan 1876, Schiffrin 1987, Bolinger 1989, Fraser 1990), but it has also been the focus of a range of papers (for example, Murray 1979, Owen 1981, Watts 1989, Jucker 1993 and Schourup 2001) and, indeed, a book (Carlson 1984). One could speculate on the reasons for semanticists' relative lack of interest in *well*, which is, after all, non-truth conditional in the same way as any of the expressions analysed as conventional implicatures. The popularity of *but* may derive from the fact that it contrasts with truth functional *and*. However, it is not entirely clear why *well* does not feature alongside expressions such as *so*, *therefore* or *however* in discussions of conventional implicature. One possibility is that in contrast with these expressions, it is impossible to say what *well* conventionally implicates. As we shall see below, the meaning of *well* is frustratingly elusive and appears to change with each of its uses. Another possibility is that *well* is regarded as a species of interjection that has more in common with expressions such as *ouch* or *hm* or *oh*. And indeed, as we shall see, it has been claimed that *well* is allied with interjections (see Schourup 2001).

In this section I do not aim to give a comprehensive review of the (expanding) literature on *well*. However, in order to locate my own proposal for the analysis of *well* in this research, I shall discuss examples of what I take to be two broad trends. Whereas for some writers, *well* signals that something has gone wrong with the discourse, or, in other words, that things are *not* well, for others, it signals that all *is* well. As we shall see, what is well or not well is spelt out in a variety of ways. For example, while both Schiffrin (1987) and Jucker (1993) analyse the use of *well* in terms of a signal that something is not well, Schiffrin sees it as a signal that the speaker has diverged from *coherence*, while Jucker sees it as a signal that the speaker has diverged from *relevance*. Similarly, while Bolinger (1989) and Carlson (1984) take the use of *well* to indicate the speaker's acceptance of something, Bolinger takes this to be the acceptance of a norm (which may vary from situation to situation), while Carlson takes it to be the acceptance of a move in a dialogue game.

My analysis of *well*, developed in 4.4.4, could be said to follow in the steps of Carlson and Bolinger rather than Schiffrin and Jucker in that it claims that *well* encodes the information that the utterance it introduces is consistent with the principle of relevance, and hence that things are well. However, in contrast with both Bolinger and Carlson, I shall argue against the semantic identity of the discourse marker *well* and the adverb *well*. In particular, I shall argue that while the adverb encodes a constituent of a conceptual representation, the discourse marker encodes a procedure. At the same time, however, I shall show that the kind of procedural information encoded by *well* must be distinguished from the sort of information which is encoded by *but*, *nevertheless* and *however*, and hence that the analysis of *well* shows that the notion of procedural meaning must be considerably broader than the one introduced in 4.1, where it is tied to the activation of a particular cognitive effect or a particular inferential route.

As we have seen, the existence of expressions (such as *but* or *so*) which activate a particular inferential route is justified by the communicative principle of relevance: they ensure the recovery of the intended cognitive effects for a minimum cost in processing. However, it is difficult to see why there should be an expression which indicates relevance when, according to relevance theory, every utterance (or more generally, every act of ostensive communication) communicates a presumption of its own optimal relevance in any case. I shall argue that the answer to this question lies in the communicative principle of relevance itself, and that this also provides the explanation for Schourup's (2001) observation that the use of *well* must be tied to the speaker rather than the hearer.

As Jucker (1993) has observed, the elusiveness of *well* derives from the range of purposes it seems to serve in different contexts. Thus for example, it can preface both questions (e.g. (104)) and answers to questions (e.g. (105)).

(104)   PASSENGER: A £1.20 return please.
         BUS-DRIVER [after failing to get the ticket machine to work several times]: Sorry, it's a brand-new machine and it's playing up.
         PASSENGER: Well, what do I do?

(105)   A: How long have you two been married?
         B: Well, actually we're not.

In an argument it may introduce a counter-argument (e.g. (106)), a direct denial (e.g. (107)), or an utterance which communicates concessive dissent (e.g. (108)).

(106)   – A dog is capable of great loyalty. In order to develop his own character to the best advantage he needs an outlet for that affection, for that feeling of loyalty. Linda looked at him thoughtfully. – Isn't the same true of a woman? she asked. – I wouldn't know. I've never been a woman. – You've never been a dog, she retorted. – Well, he told her, I've studied dogs. – All right, she said, with an amused smile. You win.
         (Gardner, *The Case of the Musical Cow*, cited in Carlson 1984:43)

(107)   – It seems to me an excellent plan. – Well, I disagree. Holder-Watts sounded sulky.
         (Moyes, *Black Widower*, cited in Carlson 1984:42)

(108)   A: Anna's much taller than Verity.
         B: Well, she *is* two years older.

Speakers can use *well* in both defensive responses (e.g. (109)) and diffident responses (e.g. (110)).

(109) A: Why did you accept the money?
       B: Well, I couldn't see any reason why I shouldn't.
(110) A: Would you like to stay to dinner?
       B: Well, that would be lovely. Are you sure?

It can appear in (antagonistic) refusals (e.g. (111)) and in a consent to a request (e.g.(112)).

(111) Jack flushed. – We want meat. – Well, we haven't got any meat . . .
                       (Golding, *Lord of the Flies*, cited in Carlson 1984:45)
(112) A: Mum, can I go down to the park with my roller-blades?
       B: Well, I don't see why not.

Speakers may use it to correct wording (e.g. (113)) or a strategy (e.g. (114)):

(113) This programme is not for the fainthearted. Well, it's not about the
       fainthearted anyway.
                                                       (Radio 4, 26 July 2000)
(114) A: Can I phone you later?
       B: I won't be in.
       A: Well, can I e-mail you then?

Within a single contribution, *well* can be used by a speaker whose form of words is a less than faithful representation of what he thinks (e.g. (115)), or by a speaker who is emphasizing a point (e.g. (116)), or by a speaker who has felt the need to establish that his reference to an individual has succeeded (e.g. (117)).

(115) A: What do you think of my dress?
       B: It's very, well, colourful.
(116) A: It must be rather disturbing when your cat goes around spraying all
          the time, though, mustn't it?
       B: It's not so bad if it's a female that's spraying, but if you have a good
          tomcat that's spraying, well, it can empty the room, it can empty the
          house.
                                                         (from Watts 1989:51)
(117) Do you remember Tom? Well, he's just bought a motorbike.

On its own, it can be used (with the appropriate intonation) as a question (e.g. (118)), or to indicate astonishment or surprise (e.g. (119)), or to indicate the speaker's reluctance to say anything at all (e.g. 120)).

(118)   [hearer returns after finding out examination results]
         Well?
(119)   [someone has just left the room after losing their temper]
         Well. [intonation fall]
(120)   A: Have you done the essay?
         B: Well. [intonation rise]

And then, of course, there is the double *well well* indicating mild curiosity, and the cliché associated with (British) policemen, *well, well, well*.

4.4.2   well = 'all is not well'

Some treatments of *well* have not aimed to find a unitary explanation for all these uses. For example, Lakoff (1973) restricted her analysis to the use of *well* in question–answer exchanges. She argued that *well* is used by a speaker in an answer to a question if he 'senses some sort of insufficiency in his answer, whether because he is leaving it to the questioner to fill in information on his own or because he is about to give additional information himself' (1973:463). Thus the speaker of (121B) (adapted from Lakoff 1973:459) would be taken to be suggesting that his answer is not a complete answer on its own (presumably because he believes that there were extenuating circumstances).

(121)   A: Did you kill your wife?
         B: Well, yes.

Similarly, *well* can be used in response to a question to which the hearer does not have the complete or precise answer.

(122)   A: How long is she going to be away?
         B: Well, I'm not exactly sure. About three weeks.
(123)   A: Are you from Wellington?
         B: Well, I was born there.

As Lakoff observed, the insufficiency in some cases is not always attributed to the utterance prefaced by *well*, but is felt by the user of *well* to have occurred in the utterance or action to which his utterance is a response (1973:463). This seems to be the case in the question–answer exchange in (105) above, where B's inability to give a straightforward answer derives from the fact that A has incorrectly assumed that B and his partner are married. However, it is also the case in other types of exchanges. Recall, for example (108), where B's response indicates that A's assumption that there is something remarkable about the fact that Anna is taller than Verity is incorrect. And in (104), where *well* introduces a question, the passenger seems to be suggesting that the bus-driver's explanation is insufficient in that it does not help her understand what she is expected to do in the situation.

However, Lakoff's notion of insufficiency is too narrow to accommodate other uses of *well*, for it is invariably insufficiency of *information*. Although the speaker of (110B) (repeated below) could be said to be communicating his recognition that there is something inadequate about his answer to A's invitation, this could not be described in terms of a failure to give 'the information sought' (see Lakoff 1973:458).

(110)   A: Would you like to stay to dinner?
        B: Well, that would be lovely. Are you sure?

Within a coherence-based approach to discourse (see chapter 5) the notion of insufficiency may be unpacked in terms of a failure to achieve coherence, or at least a failure to achieve coherence in a way that is anticipated by the hearer. Thus Schiffrin (1987) argues that '*well* anchors the speaker precisely at those points where upcoming coherence is not guaranteed' (1987:126) or that *well* is appropriate precisely at those points when 'the coherence options offered by one component of talk differ from those of another' (1987:127). In this way, the use of *well* constitutes evidence for the claim that speakers are alive to the need to achieve coherence and that hearers' understanding of utterances depends on their recognition of the 'coherence option' that the speaker has chosen. For according to this approach, the assumption underlying the use of *well* is that any divergence from coherence must be marked by the speaker.[9]

We will be examining this approach to discourse and discourse understanding in more detail in the following chapter. Here it is sufficient to say that Schiffrin seems to assume that each conversational move or utterance is governed by the requirement to produce an utterance which is coherent in the sense that it stands in an identifiable coherence relation with the preceding discourse, and that there is at each stage a menu of possible coherence relations to choose from, or in other words, a number of different means of achieving coherence. Moreover, it is assumed that the coherence relation chosen in a particular case (the coherence option) is determined in some (unspecified way) by the previous discourse. Thus *well* is used when the speaker chooses a continuation which diverges from the expectations set up by the preceding discourse.

---

[9] As we will see in chapter 5, it has been argued more generally that all interruptions can be accounted for within a coherence-based framework in this way (see for example Tsui 1991).

The problem is that *well* can be used to introduce an utterance which is *not* a continuation of preceding discourse. For example, it is possible to open a conversation with the utterance in (124).

(124)   Well, what would you like to do today?

Or consider (125), produced in a situation in which speaker and hearer are leaving a building after having failed to get the information they require:

(125)   Well, that wasn't much help.

Moreover, as we have seen, *well* can be used as a fragment either within a discourse or discourse-initially. Recall (118–19):

(118)   [hearer returns after finding out examination results]
         Well?
(119)   [someone has just left the room after losing their temper]
         Well. [intonation fall]

Since there is no preceding discourse in any of these examples, it seems impossible to analyse *well* as encoding the information that the utterance it prefaces is not coherent in a way which is consonant with the expectations set up by the preceding discourse.

It has been argued that these utterance-initial uses of discourse connectives can be explained by saying that they connect the utterance with an imagined utterance (see, for example, Knott and Dale 1994). However, as Schourup (2001) points out, it seems that in many instances the speaker would be regarded as responding to a non-verbal situation rather than an imagined utterance. This certainly seems to be the case in (125), as it is in Schourup's example in (126), produced by a speaker who has just opened the bedroom curtains.

(126)   Well, isn't it beautiful outside.
                    (Schourup 2001:1027)

In any case, it is extremely difficult to see how this defence could work in the case of fragmentary utterances such as (118–19).

Oddly, Jucker's (1993) relevance theoretic analysis is subject to the same sort of criticisms. I say 'oddly' because Sperber and Wilson's (1995) notion of relevance is not exclusively a property of verbal stimuli. Nor can it be construed as a relation between utterances or segments of a text. An utterance is relevant in a context of assumptions which may include assumptions derived through perception or assumptions derived from memory. However, Jucker claims that '*well* signifies that the most immediately accessible context is not the most relevant one for the interpretation of the impending utterance' (1993:435) and hence that the hearer is expected to 'reconstruct the background against which he can process the upcoming utterance' (1993:438).

As Schourup (2001) points out, it may be possible to reformulate Jucker's proposal in terms which do not refer to successive utterances. And indeed, Jucker seems to do this himself when he claims that '*well* indicates that the addressee has to reconstruct the background against which he can process the upcoming utterance' and that 'what seems to be the most relevant context is not appropriate' (1993:428). However, as we have just seen, sometimes there is no upcoming utterance. Perhaps more fundamentally, it seems that not all uses of *well* indicate that there is something inadequate or insufficient about the utterance it prefaces, and hence that neither Schiffrin's coherence-based approach nor Jucker's relevance theoretic one provides a fully comprehensive account. For example, in (117) (repeated below) the relevance of the first segment lies in the way it makes a particular context accessible for the interpretation of the second. More particularly, it ensures that the referent of *Tom* is accessible.

(117)   Do you remember Tom? Well, he's just bought a motorbike.

It is difficult to see how *well* could be interpreted as signalling that the hearer is to renegotiate this context: the context made accessible by the first segment simply *is* the context for the interpretation for the next. By the same token, it is difficult to see how the second segment diverges from expectations of coherence set up by the first.

Similarly, it is not clear that the hearer is being asked to renegotiate the context in an utterance such as (127), produced in a situation in which the audience are all sitting expectantly waiting for a well-known person to begin her lecture:

(127)   Well, as you all know, our speaker today is . . .

Nor is it clear how Jucker (or, indeed, Schiffrin) would analyse the use of *well* in Schourup's example in (128):

(128)   A: What's 221 divided by 13?
         B: Um, let me think . . . OK, that's 17.
         A: How did you work it out?
         B: Well, first I divided 13 into 22. Then I subtracted the remainder, and that left 9.
         A: Then I . . .

                                              (Schourup 2001:1053)

As Schourup says, the pupil's answer is an earnest one, designed to do the question justice, and hence there seems to be no sense in which he would regard it as insufficient.

4.4.3   well = 'all is well'

Bolinger (1989) and Carlson (1984) give a range of examples which they claim are evidence against the view that *well* encodes insufficiency of some kind. Although their analyses are couched in very different kinds of theoretical frameworks, they both argue for an analysis in which the meaning of the discourse marker *well* is related to its meaning in adverbial uses such as the one in (129).

(129)   She did very well at school this year.

Thus Bolinger (1989) argues that the only difference between the meaning of *well* as it is used in (129) and the meaning of *well* as its discourse marker uses is that in these latter uses its meaning has been 'transferred from the locutionary sphere ("relatively good, relatively strong") to the illocutionary sphere ("matched to a standard or a norm")' (1989:332). The norms which Bolinger has in mind are not norms governing discourse or communication, but range from norms of behaviour to norms in the physical world. Thus, for example, while he glosses the use of *well* in examples such as (130) as 'In view of the normal state of affairs, this bowls me over', he analyses its use as a prompt in examples such as (131) in terms of its role in invoking a norm of proper behaviour.

(130)   Well, I never, look who is here.
(131)   Well?

In contrast, Carlson analyses *well* as signalling the speaker's acceptance of a move in a *dialogue game*, or in other words that things are well or acceptable in the sense that the utterance provides an acceptable strategy for continuing the dialogue. Hence his rule 'Begin a dialogue move with *well* only if you accept a game situation in which the move is entered' (1984:29). Carlson's use of the word 'game' is not intended to be metaphorical: his analysis derives from an approach to discourse analysis in which conversation is reconstructed as a game in the sense of the mathematical theory of games (Carlson 1983). He conceives of this game as having an epistemic aim: it involves 'a number of players, engaged in a co-operative dialogue on antecedently agreed problems or topics of interest (represented as direct questions in their minds) and who are trying to come to a common understanding about epistemically optimal answers to the questions by means of observation, inference and exchange of opinion' (1984:6). While strategies in an idealized game situation are determined only by a number of internal aims which Carlson captures in a number of conversational maxims (e.g. 'Accept only what is true', 'Prefer agreement among players', 'Do not admit contradiction' and 'Prefer a short dialogue'), in a real-life dialogue strategies are also affected by external motivations such as ulterior preferences and plans, hopes and fears, likes and dislikes. It is the conflict between the idealized and the real, the internal aims and the external aims which, according to Carlson, gives rise to the use of *well*. For such conflict causes a break in the conversational routine, an aberration from the expected path of optimal play (see Carlson 1984:30), and it is this which motivates the use of *well*.

To say that the use of *well* is motivated by an interruption to the conversational routine is not to say that it *encodes* the information that all is not well. According to Carlson, *well* simply encodes the information that the speaker finds the game situation acceptable, and the fact that the game situation is less than optimal falls out as a conversational implicature. His argument is that since there is nothing to be gained by commenting on the acceptance of a game, the use of *well* would violate the maxim of least effort ('Prefer a short dialogue'). This implies that when *well* is used, the audience is justified in asking what calls for the extra effort. The answer, according to Carlson, is a situation in which acceptance of a game situation is problematic or in which 'someone or something causes an aberration from the expected path of optimal play' (1984:30). Thus while *well* encodes acceptance, it is motivated by either acceptance of a sub-optimal game situation or acceptance of an exceptional game situation.

In this way, argues Carlson, the use of *well* enables the speaker to draw attention to the features of the game situation which are problematic or defective while allowing him to continue the play. For example, in (108) (repeated below) B's use of *well* enables him to draw attention to the fact that A's utterance is based on contextual assumptions which should have included the information that the two girls are not the same age.

(108)   A: Anna's much taller than Verity.
          B: Well, she *is* two years older.

Alternatively, a player may wish to shift the topic, transfer his turn to another player, or close the dialogues, situations which, according to Carlson, 'deserve exceptionally careful evaluation, which makes them natural contexts for *well*' (1984:31).

While I believe that Carlson is right to distinguish between what *well* encodes and what motivates its use, I do not believe that his general approach to discourse can be maintained. In particular, it is not clear that discourse is always directed towards antecedently agreed problems or questions of interest. Indeed, it is not clear that we can always identify the direction of a discourse at all. If the overall aim of a discourse or dialogue were to find an answer to an antecedently agreed question or set of questions represented in the minds of the participants in the discourse, then these questions would be part of the context for the interpretation of the discourse. However, as Sperber and Wilson (1995:15–21, 39–46) have shown, the context for the interpretation of utterances is not set up in advance but constructed as part of the interpretation process so that it becomes a result of interpretation rather than a prerequisite for it (see also Blakemore 1992:16–22).

Carlson might argue that this is simply an example of the way in which real-life discourse diverges from idealized discourse. However, the assumption that actual discourse can be regarded as something that happens by default raises some difficult questions. If actual discourse is the result of diverging from the internal aims or rules which define the ideal, then we would need to know what constitutes an acceptable divergence from the ideal, or in other words, what constrains the speaker's strategy when external factors intervene. For the point is that not every break in the conversational routine *is* acceptable. Applying this to the use of *well*, we need to know what makes an utterance containing *well* an acceptable means of failing to meet the ideals set by the rules governing the game.

4.4.4   well *and optimal relevance*

In this section, I shall argue that the key to the analysis of *well* lies in the communicative principle of relevance itself. In contrast with Jucker's (1993) relevance theoretic account which argues that *well* encodes *deviation* from optimal relevance and hence is an instruction to renegotiate the context, this account will propose that the information it encodes amounts to a green light for going ahead with the inferential processes involved in the recovery of cognitive effects, and the renegotiation of the context may be, but is not always, a consequence of interpreting the utterance in accordance with the constraint which *well* encodes. In this way, this account, in contrast with Jucker's, is consistent with the fundamental relevance theoretic assumption that the communicative principle of relevance is an exceptionless generalization about ostensive inferential communication rather than a norm which people either follow or violate. As Sperber and Wilson (1995) say,

> communicators do not 'follow' the principle of relevance; and they could not violate it even if they wanted to. The principle of relevance applies without exception: every act of ostensive communication communicates a presumption of

> relevance. It is not the general principle, but the fact that a particular presump-
> tion of relevance has been communicated by and about a particular act of com-
> munication, that the audience uses in inferential communication. (1995:162)

In contrast, Grice's (1989) and Carlson's (1984) maxims are norms which although they are generally followed, are sometimes violated to achieve a particular effect. In analysing *well* as a means of indicating that optimal relevance
has not been achieved, Jucker (1993) is treating Sperber and Wilson's principle
more like a Gricean maxim.

As I explained in chapter 3, in saying that the principle of relevance is an exceptionless generalization about ostensive inferential communication, Sperber
and Wilson are not saying that the presumption of relevance communicated
is never false. Speakers may be mistaken about the contextual and processing
resources of hearers, and as a result the utterances they produce may fail to
be optimally relevant. The point is that hearers are able to form beliefs about
speakers' beliefs about what their audiences would find relevant, or in other
words, that hearers are able to use the presumption of relevance communicated
by a particular utterance in its interpretation even when it is false. Of course,
if a speaker has a particularly poor record as a communicator, the hearer may
not bother attending to the utterance at all. However, even poor communicators
communicate on the assumption that they are being optimally relevant.

If the principle of relevance is an exceptionless generalization and every act
of communication communicates a presumption of its own optimal relevance,
then why should a speaker use an expression to indicate that the utterance that
contains it is optimally relevant? The answer to this question can be found in
the communicative principle of relevance itself, and, more particularly, in the
definition of optimal relevance. So let us return to this principle and recall what
it entitles a hearer to expect. As Sperber and Wilson (1995:271) point out, since
a hearer will not pay attention to an utterance at all unless it achieves a level of
relevance which makes it worth paying attention to, a rational communicator
must intend the hearer to expect a level of relevance at least as high as this. This
is encapsulated in the first clause of the (1995) definition of the presumption of
optimal relevance:

(132)   *Presumption of optimal relevance*
   (a)   The ostensive stimulus is relevant enough for it to be worth the hearer's
         effort to process it.

At the same time, however, a rational communicator will know that the hearer
will not invest the effort needed for comprehension unless he achieves a degree

of relevance much higher than this. This means that it is to the communicator's advantage that the hearer should expect that the level of relevance should be as high as possible both on the effect side and the effort side. If this were the only consideration, then a hearer would be entitled to expect an utterance which yielded the maximum number of cognitive effects for the minimum amount of processing effort. However, it is not, of course, the only consideration. Hearers know that speakers are not always in a position to produce the utterance which is maximally relevant to the hearer. They are not able to give information that they have not got or that they feel they should not give (for ethical or legal reasons, for instance). Nor are they always capable of producing an utterance in the most hearer-friendly manner possible. In other words, speakers are constrained by what Sperber and Wilson (1995) describe as their own abilities and preferences. In other words, according to Sperber and Wilson, 'it is necessary for the first clause of the presumption of optimal relevance [given in (132a)] to be manifest to the addressee, and it is advantageous for the second clause [given in (132b)] to be manifest too' (Sperber and Wilson 1995:271–2).

(132)   *Presumption of optimal relevance*
  (b)   The ostensive stimulus is the most relevant one compatible with the speaker's abilities and preferences.

Since (132) encapsulates a fact which is known to every communicator and every hearer, it follows that 'whenever a communicator makes it mutually manifest that she is trying to communicate by means of a given stimulus, she thereby makes it mutually manifest that she intends a presumption of relevance is communicated' (Sperber and Wilson 1995:272).

The question, then, is why should a hearer who is not expecting maximal relevance but optimal relevance find it relevant to know that the speaker is not aiming at maximal relevance? At first, it seems that, broadly speaking, the presumption of relevance allows for two kinds of answer, and, consequently a distinction between two uses of *well*, the first deriving from the speaker's estimation of the hearer's processing abilities and the second deriving from the speaker's recognition of the constraints on his own capacities. However, this distinction becomes difficult to maintain when we come to look at actual cases in detail, which is not surprising once one recognizes that in a relevance theoretic framework the responsibility for ensuring successful interpretation lies with the speaker and hence that any constraints on the processing abilities of the hearer become the speaker's problem.

However, let us for the moment treat the two types of case separately. According to the second clause of the presumption of relevance, the hearer can expect the speaker to have produced the most relevant utterance compatible with his preferences and abilities. For the purposes of this discussion, let us forget the fact that the level of relevance attempted may be affected by the speaker's preferences and capacities and consider what it means for a speaker to produce an utterance which is the most relevant one for the hearer. In particular, let us consider what would count as the most relevant utterance from the point of view of the effort that the hearer is expected to expend in the derivation of cognitive effects. Since the cost of processing an utterance increases with the cost of accessing the context required for the derivation of the intended cognitive effects, it is in the interests of a speaker aiming to maximize relevance to produce an utterance whose cognitive effects can be derived in a context which he has grounds for thinking is immediately accessible to the hearer. It might be the case that he has grounds for thinking that this context is already accessible to the hearer or that his utterance will trigger highly accessible assumptions. Indeed, it might be the case that the speaker has ensured that these assumptions are accessible to the hearer by making them accessible, for example, by jogging her memory about an individual or event which the speaker believes may have been forgotten:

(133)   Remember Tom?

On the other hand, it might be the case that although the speaker has grounds for thinking that assumptions about Tom are now amongst the hearer's immediately accessible assumptions, there may be reasons for thinking that the hearer recognizes that they are intended to play a role in the derivation of the cognitive effects that she is intended to derive from a following utterance. It may be that a question such as (133) is taken as a genuine request for information. Or it may be that the hearer has no idea of why the preparatory utterance was produced in the first place. Or it may be that the speaker is not sure that even with the preparation, the hearer is able to derive the intended effects. In such a case, it would be in the speaker's interests (and of course, in the hearer's interests) to signal that the following utterance is relevant in the context which has been made accessible. Hence the use of *well* in (117) (repeated below).

(117)   Remember Tom? Well, he's just bought a motorbike.

In other words, *well* is being used to encourage the hearer to process the utterance for relevance in a context which the speaker believes would not have otherwise yielded a maximally relevant interpretation.

It seems that this kind of account can accommodate those cases which Carlson (1984:51) classified as 'transition' uses, in which *well* plays a role in 'easing recognition of the resulting topic shift'. Hence its use in Watts' example in (116) and the planned reformulation in (113) (repeated below).

(116)   A: It must be rather disturbing when your cat goes around spraying all the time, though, mustn't it?
B: It's not so bad if it's a female that's spraying, but if you have a good tomcat that's spraying, well, it can empty the room, it can empty the house.

(from Watts 1989:51)

(113)   This programme is not for the fainthearted. Well, it's not about the fainthearted anyway.

(Radio 4, 26 July 2000)

However, it is also able to accommodate cases where the speaker has grounds for believing that the context required for the interpretation of the information he wants to communicate is not accessible to the hearer at all. Recall for example (104):

(104)   PASSENGER: A £1.20 return please.
BUS-DRIVER [after failing to get the ticket machine to work several times]: Sorry, it's a brand-new machine and it's playing up.
PASSENGER: Well, what do I do?

It seems that in this case, the use of *well* derives from the passenger's belief that while she was aware of the driver's predicament (and hence the reason for his apology), the driver had not addressed her own problem, namely, how was she to travel to (and home from) work without a ticket. In other words, *well* signals that her question is relevant, but only on condition that the driver turns his attention from his problem to hers.

The analysis of examples such as (104) provides a clue to the role of *well* in interrogative fragmentary utterances such as the one in (118) (repeated below).

(118)   [hearer returns after finding out examination results]
Well?

It is possible, of course, that the hearer was bursting to tell the speaker the results. However, the use of *well* signals that the speaker believes that the hearer was not aware of the speaker's desire to know the result, or, in other words, that the hearer did not recognize that the answer to the implicit question was relevant. As Bolinger (1989:312) points out, this use of *well* can be insulting in certain situations. Thus in Bolinger's example, a waiter who addresses a patron with an 'unadorned' *well?* seems to suggest that the patron was not aware of the waiter's desire to know what he wanted to order and hence that the waiter should not have had to ask. Alternatively, the speaker might be taken to be asking whether there is anything at all that the hearer could say that the speaker would find relevant.

Although the passenger may have taken the driver's utterance in (104) as evidence that he did not have the contextual assumptions necessary for understanding her problem, it is not necessarily the case that she was intending to suggest that he should have had them. This does, however, seem to be the speaker's intention when *well* is used in arguments and disagreements. For example, in (108) (repeated below) B evidently believes that A's utterance is relevant only if she believes that there is little or no difference in age between the two girls.

(108)   A: Anna's much taller than Verity.
         B: Well, she *is* two years older.

In this way, the use of *well* could be said to encourage the hearer to recognize a contextual assumption which the speaker believes that she should have recognized was relevant but did not. Similarly, in the examples given by Carlson (1984), the use of *well* in arguments and counter-arguments is intended to signal that the utterance is relevant as a premise in an argument which the hearer had failed to recognize on her own. Recall (106):

(106)   – You've never been a dog, she retorted. – Well, he told her, I've studied dogs. – All right, she said, with an amused smile. You win.
                        (Gardner, *The Case of the Musical Cow*, cited in Carlson 1984:43)

So far all of the cases seem to conform to Jucker's (1993) observation that *well* is used when the hearer is expected to renegotiate the context. However, in each case this 'renegotiation' is a consequence of the hearer's recognition that the speaker is aiming at optimal relevance. As we have seen, the speaker's assumption that his utterance is relevant to the hearer is based on his estimation of the hearer's contextual resources. However, this does not mean that optimal relevance is achieved only when the required contextual assumptions are among the assumptions already entertained by the hearer. It means that the speaker's estimation of what is relevant to the hearer depends on what assumptions are manifest to her, or, in other words, on what assumptions the hearer is capable of entertaining at a given moment. In some cases, the required assumptions may be among the assumptions in the hearer's memory; in other cases, they may be triggered by the utterance itself; in some cases the speaker may have to make them manifest to the hearer. Strictly speaking, there is no negotiation of the context – and hence no renegotiation either. The speaker simply takes the responsibility for the success of the communication either by producing an utterance which yields the intended cognitive effects in a context of assumptions which the hearer is capable of entertaining or by reorienting the hearer to a context of assumptions which will yield the intended interpretation. Those cases which Jucker has described in terms of the renegotiation of contextual assumptions are better described in terms of reorienting hearers for the purpose of achieving optimal relevance. However, as Carlson (1984) recognized, one must draw a distinction between what justifies the use of *well* and what it encodes. What it encodes is the information that the utterance is relevant. What justifies its use – in the utterances just discussed – is the speaker's belief that certain assumptions are not manifest to the hearer.

In fact, as we have seen, there is a whole range of cases in which the use of *well* is *not* motivated by the speaker's desire that the hearer 'renegotiate' the context. These are cases in which the speaker recognizes that the level of relevance that he can achieve is affected by constraints that he himself is under. Recall that according to the second clause of the presumption of optimal relevance, the hearer is only entitled to expect a level of relevance that is consistent with the speaker's preferences and abilities. If the presumption of optimal relevance is mutually manifest to speaker and hearer as Sperber and Wilson (1995) argue, it can be assumed that it is mutually manifest to speaker and hearer that the hearer's expectations of relevance must take the speaker's capabilities and preferences into account. At the same time, however, it cannot necessarily be assumed that it is mutually manifest that the level of relevance attempted on a particular occasion has been affected by the speaker's own preferences and capabilities and hence that the utterance is not the one which the speaker believes would have been maximally relevant to the hearer. Since an utterance which is not maximally relevant for the hearer will entail processing effort not required otherwise and since it is always in the speaker's interests to minimize the hearer's processing costs inasmuch as this is compatible with his interests and preferences, it will be in the speaker's interests that the hearer should know that the level of relevance attempted has been constrained by the speaker's preferences and capabilities.

Perhaps the most straightforward illustration of how *well* plays a role here are cases such as (122), where B takes A's question as evidence that he would find it relevant to have a more precise specification of the time she is going to be away than he is able to provide.

(122)   A: How long is she going to be away?
         B: Well, I'm not exactly sure. About three weeks.

As Lakoff's example in (121) shows, it is possible to use *well* even when the utterance appears to be the one which the hearer would find the most relevant.

(121) A: Did you kill your wife?
       B: Well, yes.

However, the use of *well* leads the hearer to derive further assumptions which, while they are not relevant from the hearer's point of view, are relevant if one takes the speaker's preferences into account (in this case, the desire to demonstrate he is not a cold-blooded killer). In this way, the hearer is led to entertain assumptions (about the circumstances of B's behaviour) which he would not have derived had the speaker simply answered 'Yes'.

Clearly, there is a wealth of difference between morality and tact. However, it seems that the use of *well* in examples such as (110) is also motivated by the speaker's wish to communicate that his answer is to be interpreted as being constrained by a preference for not wishing to impose himself on his hosts.

(110) A: Would you like to stay to dinner?
       B: Well, that would be lovely. Are you sure?

In the same way, the use of *well* in (115) allows the speaker to communicate doubts about the dress which would not have been communicated by the response in (B′).

(115) A: What do you think of my dress?
       B: It's very, well, colourful.
       B′: It's very colourful.

Here it is evident that B's answer is a rather less than frank representation of his thoughts. A frank answer (for example, 'It's gaudy and tasteless') would, of course have achieved far more cognitive effects and hence would have been the most relevant one from the hearer's point of view (by virtue of being the least welcome). The choice of the word *colourful*, which generally has positive connotations, was presumably determined by a desire to appear polite or perhaps to avoid an argument. At the same time, however, the use of *well* indicates that his choice of answer has been constrained by his own preferences and capabilities – in this case, his preference to seem polite – and, as a result, A will know that in spite of the use of a word with positive connotations, B has doubts about the dress.

Schourup (2001) has argued that an utterance containing *well* can only be interpreted as a representation of the speaker's own thoughts, and that in this sense *well* 'ties an utterance they preface to the current speaker' (2001:1041).

Thus for example, he claims that whereas in (134) B's utterance must be understood as representing his own thought and not as an attempt to 'ventriloquize' A's, in (135) B can be understood as 'filling in' A's thought.

(134)   A: I never miss a day's illness.
           B: Well, you deserve a longer vacation.
(135)   A: I never miss a day's illness.
           B: So you deserve a longer vacation.
                          (Schourup 2001:1041)

As (136) and (137) show, Schourup's point here cannot be that *well* cannot be used in an utterance which achieves relevance as an attributive representation of another speaker's thought. In (136) the hearer is expected to recognize the proposition expressed as an attributive representation on the basis of contextual assumptions and the principle of relevance, while in (137) the speaker makes his intentions explicit.

(136)   A: What did the report have to say about her?
           B: Her performance is rather, well, amateurish.
(137)   The report said that her performance was quite, well, amateurish.

However, notice that while both B's response in (136) and the utterance in (137) are relevant as a representation of another person's thoughts or utterance, the use of *well* cannot itself be interpreted as being attributed to anyone other than the speaker. The fact that it is used before the word *amateurish* seems to suggest that its role is to comment on the particular contribution of this word to the relevance of the utterance.[10] Thus its use might have been motivated by the fact that the speaker's decision to use *amateurish* as a representation of the report's judgement was governed less by his aim of producing a faithful representation than by his aim of finding a diplomatic representation. Alternatively, it might have been motivated by his desire to ensure that the hearer recognizes that this is the report's word and not his. In contrast, as we have seen in 4.1 and 4.2, the meanings of *so* and *but* may be included in what is being attributed to another speaker. Recall (3) and (4).

(3)   Tom thinks that Sheila is rich but unhappy. But I have always thought that all rich people are unhappy.
(4)   Peter thought that Mary had a holiday, so he should have one too.

---

[10] Schourup (2001:1038) points out that *well* is unique among adverbial discourse connectives in being able to 'focus down' on the choice of a particular word or phrase.

As I have argued, in these utterances the speaker's use of *but* and *so* indicate that he is attributing a certain inference to someone in the sense that the cognitive effects that they activate are to be attributed to someone other than the speaker. The question is, why can't *well* be used in this way?

The answer lies in the fact that in contrast with *so* and *but*, *well* does not activate a particular cognitive effect but simply encodes the speaker's guarantee that his utterance yields cognitive effects.[11] An utterance may be relevant as an interpretation of someone else's thought or utterance. Moreover, it may yield cognitive effects which are relevant as an interpretation of the assumptions derived by another speaker. However, a speaker cannot be expected to guarantee the optimal relevance of another person's utterance or thoughts. The guarantee of relevance communicated by a speaker can only be a guarantee of relevance for his own utterance. As we have seen, this guarantee is communicated by any speaker who is manifestly engaged in ostensive inferential communication. However, a speaker may recognize that there are circumstances in which his utterance will be recognized as being consistent with the principle of relevance only if certain assumptions which are manifestly not manifest to the hearer are made manifest. These may be assumptions which the hearer uses in the derivation of cognitive effects, or they may be assumptions about the speaker's interests and preferences. Since it is in the speaker's interests that the hearer take up the guarantee of relevance he is communicating and invest effort in the derivation of cognitive effects, it will be in his interests in such circumstances for him to provide a linguistically encoded signal that there are cognitive effects to be derived, or, in other words, that all is well.

Well could be regarded as a signal simply in the sense that it provides a green light for the hearer, a sign to go ahead with the inferential processes involved in the derivation of cognitive effects. Considered in this way, it would contribute to implicit content along with *but*, *however* and *so*, but in a far more general

---

[11] Schourup (2001) notes that although *so* and *well* share a prompting use in (i) and (ii), there is an important difference in the way they are interpreted.

  (i) A: I learned three new words today.
      B: So?
  (ii) A: I learned three new words today.
      B: Well?

Whereas in (i) B will be understood to be asking A what follows from her remark (see Blakemore 1992:139), in (ii) B will be understood to be asking for the three words. This difference is explained if *so* is understood to be activating a particular cognitive effect (contextual implication), and *well* is understood to signal that B would find the answer to the question raised by A's utterance (what are the three words?) relevant.

sort of way. On the other hand, it could be regarded as a signal in the sense that it activates a higher-level explicature of the form in (138).

(138)   The speaker believes U is relevant (where U is the utterance containing *well*).

Schourup (2001) has proposed that in contrast with *so* and *but*, *well* contributes to explicatures. However, he analyses it as contributing to an explicature of the form in (139), and is in this way suggesting that it behaves as a kind of illocutionary particle.

(139)   The speaker is saying with consideration p (where p is the proposition expressed).

Schourup admits that this is only a vague characterization of what is conveyed. And, indeed, the problem is that as it stands, it is difficult to see how such an explicature would contribute to the relevance of the utterance, or, more generally, how the hearer is expected to gain from its recovery. As I hope I have shown in this section, there are circumstances in which there is much to be gained by a signal from the speaker that his utterance yields a level of relevance consistent with the guarantee communicated by every act of ostensive inferential communication. Given such a signal, the hearer will make whatever assumptions are required in order to recover an interpretation consistent with this guarantee. However, whether this is a signal in the sense that it leads a hearer to entertain a higher level explicature of the form in (138), or whether it simply amounts to a kind of go-ahead sign, requires further research. Whichever it is, it is clear that *well* does not encode a procedure in the same way in which expressions such as *but*, *however*, *after all* and *so* do, and hence that the notion of procedural meaning must be broader than the one that we started with at the beginning of this chapter.

5 *Relevance and discourse*

5.1   The location of discourse on the theoretical map

As I have said in my introduction, this book is about the two properties which have brought discourse markers into the forefront of pragmatics research. On the one hand, expressions classified as discourse markers are said to be non-truth conditional, which means that they play a role in discussions of the non-unitary nature of linguistic meaning and the relationship between semantics and pragmatics. On the other, they are generally claimed to signal connections in discourse, which means that they play a role in the discussion of how we account for the unity of discourse. So far the emphasis has been on the first property. However, the section on *well* (4.4) should have reminded us that I have yet to discuss the second.

In fact, it seems that discussions of the non-truth conditionality of discourse markers rarely make reference to their role in discourse, while discussions of role in discourse rarely include an investigation of their non-truth conditionality. Indeed, it seems that some writers whose concern is with their analysis within a discourse perspective classify expressions as discourse markers in a way which cuts across the distinctions that we have been discussing in the previous chapter. For example Knott and Dale (1994) include within their list of expressions they call *cue markers* both truth conditional expressions (for example, *because, and, then*) and expressions which are regarded as non-truth conditional (for example, *but, furthermore, hence*). The same point can be made about Schiffrin's (1987) list of discourse markers, which includes both truth conditional and non-truth conditional expressions. For Fraser (1990, 1996), discourse markers are always non-truth conditional. However, like Knott and Dale and Schiffrin, he includes in his list expressions which, according to the criteria outlined in chapter 3, encode concepts (for example, *as a result*) and expressions which encode inferential procedures (for example, *however, so*).

It would seem that the framework I have proposed for the analysis of expressions such as *after all, so, but, however, nevertheless* and *well* is guilty of similar single-mindedness. There is virtually no mention in the preceding chapter of discourse at all. Moreover, in restricting my attention to expressions which encode procedures I have ignored a large range of expressions which according to many writers do play a role in signalling connections in discourse, for example, *as a result* or *then*. This chapter is *not* an attempt to remedy this apparent oversight: my thesis is that while I have not said all that needs to be said about the expressions discussed in the preceding chapter, a complete analysis does not need to say anything at all about the discourse connections they encode. By the same token, the analysis of expressions such as *then* or *as a result* need not make reference to discourse connections either. More fundamentally, a theory of verbal communication should not be construed as the study of discourse at all.

For many readers, this last claim will be regarded as a very large step backwards. The whole point of the various enterprises that go under the name of 'discourse analysis' was to take the study of language beyond the narrow boundaries set by grammar, whose domain was perceived to be the study of the sentence. To ignore discourse is to ignore the undeniable fact that we have intuitions about the way in which sentences are combined. Thus while both (1) and (2) consist of grammatical sentences, only (2) would count as an acceptable discourse.

(1)   As your payment is made by direct debit, you do not need to take any action. British Gas will use existing wires, cables and meters for your electricity supply. In addition, from 1 October 2001 the variable base rate has also changed from 6.75% to 6.50% a year. If you want to cancel later, please call us on the same number. This will be collected on or just after October 2001, and each subsequent month from your bank/building society.

(2)   We will arrange for you to be sent a new prepayment card which you should start using from your supply start date. We will be writing to you soon to tell you when your supply start date is. When you receive your new prepayment card, you must either destroy the old one or return it to your previous supplier. If you continue using your old prepayment card, you will not be benefiting from our low priced electricity.

Furthermore, to ignore discourse is to ignore the way in which judgements about the acceptability of discourse depend on the 'relevant features of the speaker's and hearer's (or writer's and reader's) material, social and ideological environment' (Halliday and Hasan 1976:20). As Schiffrin (1994) points out, the study of grammar is inherently decontextualized.

To say that relevance theory does not regard discourse as an object of study is not to say that relevance theory has nothing to say to those people who describe themselves as students of discourse and discourse phenomena. The aim of the previous two chapters was to show what relevance theory does regard as a legitimate object of study. In this chapter, I shall attempt to show how some so-called discourse phenomena – coherence and the function of discourse markers – can be re-analysed in relevance theoretic terms.

In this section, I shall distinguish between a number of theoretical paradigms in linguistics and attempt to show how they yield different approaches to the study of discourse. My ultimate aim is to locate relevance theory on the theoretical map, and to see if we can identify the points where it converges with and diverges from what I shall call 'coherence-based' approaches to verbal communication. Because I am drawing this map from the perspective of relevance theory, I may draw distinctions that cross-cut more traditional distinctions. However, any theoretical map is drawn from some theoretical perspective, and will draw distinctions that are not recognized in other theoretical paradigms. For example, Schiffrin's (1994) map, which I shall discuss in some detail, is clearly drawn from a functional perspective, and consequently she conflates what I – and indeed most linguists in the Chomskyan tradition – consider to be two quite distinct approaches to linguistic theory. What is important is to understand where and why these maps do not overlap.

Although it is generally agreed that the study of discourse takes us beyond the study of the sentence, it seems that in some cases we are not taken all that very far at all. According to some approaches, discourse is contrasted with the sentence, but the difference lies solely in its size or length. Thus Harris (1951), who, according to Schiffrin (1994), was the first linguist to refer explicitly to 'discourse analysis', claimed that discourse is the next level in a hierarchy of morphemes, clauses and sentences. This view has persevered. For example, in his introductory textbook, Salkie (1995) suggests that the best way to understand text and discourse analysis is 'to compare it with another area of linguistics: grammar' (1995:ix): while grammar is 'basically about how words combine to form sentences', 'text and discourse analysis is about how sentences combine to form texts' (1995:ix).

Given this conception of discourse, it is not surprising to find that the identification of structural relations between the segments or units of a discourse play a central role in the analysis of texts and discourses. Nor is it surprising that these structural relations are analysed by analogy with the structural relations exhibited in a sentence. Thus Hovy (1990) claims that 'one of the first observations one makes when analysing discourse is that it exhibits internal structure'

(1990). This notion of discourse structure is to be understood by analogy to syntactic structure so that discourse is analysed into clause-length segments linked by structural relations into larger segments, and so on. In other words, discourse, like a sentence, exhibits hierarchical structure. 'At the top level, the discourse is governed by a single root node if it is coherent ... In every coherent discourse, juxtaposed segments are related depending on the underlying inter-relationships among their contents' (Hovy: 1990). On this approach, discourse markers or connectives are defined in terms of the role they play in 'marking' these structural relations between segments, and the key to their analysis lies in the classification of the kinds of relations that exist between text segments. And, indeed, as we shall see, recent research in the study of discourse has been dominated by proposals for the classification of the structural relationships that can exist between the segments of texts.

There is considerable disagreement about what a segment of discourse is. Some writers, for example, Redeker (1991) and Fraser (1996), see discourse connections as existing between utterances, and distinguish discourse markers from co-ordinators and subordinators which encode connections within utterances. In contrast, Halliday and Hasan (1976), Hovy (1990), Knott and Dale (1994) do not make this distinction and list expressions such as *and* and *because* alongside expressions such as *as a result* and *however*. Other writers avoid syntactic units altogether and argue that language is produced in intonational units which reflect the organization of information (and do not necessarily correspond to syntactic units) (Chafe 1987).[1] However, in all these approaches it is assumed that there is such a thing as discourse and that it can be divided up into units.

The idea that discourse markers encode structural relationships between segments of text or discourse is inspired by Halliday and Hasan's (1976) *Cohesion in English*. This seems at odds with their insistence that a text is 'a unit of language *in use*' (my emphasis) rather than 'a grammatical unit like a clause or a sentence' (1976:1–2). Given their view that a text is not some kind of super-sentence, it is difficult to reconcile the Hallidayan commitment of writers such as Hovy with their search for structural relations between units of text that are analogous to the hierarchical structure of sentences.

It seems that the explanation may lie in the fact that although Halliday and Hasan do not think of a text as a grammatical unit, they do assume that there is a system of rules which relate linguistically patterns of connection – that is *cohesion* – with texts in exactly the same way as a grammar is said to pair

---

[1] For further discussion of this issue, see Unger (1996).

sounds and meanings. Thus they argue that 'although a text does not consist of sentences, it is realized by or encoded in sentences' (1976:2).

As Halliday and Hasan point out, a hearer or reader may base her judgement about textual unity on non-linguistic situational factors – or, on the 'relevant features of the speaker's and hearer's (or writer's and reader's) material, social and ideological environment' (1976:20). However, at the same time they argue that these context-dependent (or external) aspects of textuality fall within the domain of linguistics since they are encoded by language in exactly the same way as the linguistically determined (or internal) aspects of a text are. Thus while cohesion is part of that coding system by which 'meanings are realized (coded) as forms, and forms are realized in turn (recoded) as expressions' (1976:5), there is also a code (or 'register') by which a 'set of configurations' is associated with 'a particular CLASS of contexts' (1976:26). This means that although Halliday and Hasan may have taken us beyond the notion of a grammatical unit, they have not really taken us beyond the notion of a coding system.

It seems that for Schiffrin (1994), it is the attention to context which distinguishes functionalist approaches (such as Halliday and Hasan's and her own) from structuralist approaches (such as Harris 1951) which are 'decontextualized'. For her, utterances are 'units of language production (whether spoken or written) that are inherently contextualized' (1994:41). This definition, she claims, avoids the question of 'whether (or how) they [utterances] are related to sentences or to other units such as propositions, turns or tone units' (1994:41). While this may be so, it seems that Schiffrin regards utterances as units of some kind. The difference between her functionalistist approach and the one she calls 'structuralist' or 'formalist' is that whereas the structuralist view sees discourse markers as encoding connections between structural units, the functionalist approach regards them as marking connections between units of behaviour. More generally, whereas according to the structuralist view, discourse is an abstract object analogous to the sentence, according to the functionalist view, it is a product of behaviour.

As Schiffrin herself warns, distinctions such as the one she draws between structural and functional approaches to language are drawn at the risk of oversimplification. However, it seems important to point out that as she has presented it, the distinction cross-cuts another distinction that is fundamental to the theoretical framework underlying this book, namely, the distinction between those approaches for whom the object of study – language or discourse – is something external to the human mind and those approaches for whom the object of study is internal to the human mind. The fact that Schiffrin's distinction cross-cuts this distinction is evident from her decision to classify Chomsky, who of course is the source of the *E-language* versus *I-language* distinction just drawn, along with Harris in the structuralist camp.

According to Schiffrin, 'formalist' definitions of discourse view discourse as sentences, while functional definitions view it as language use. If Chomsky is a 'formalist' (or structuralist), then he would, by Schiffrin's criterion, advocate the study of sentences. I have never found a reference in Chomsky to a definition of discourse – although he has very occasionally mentioned pragmatics (Chomsky 1980). However, it is clear from what he says about his approach to language that he would never advocate the study of sentences. For Chomsky, linguistics is the study not of sentences, which he regards as abstract artifacts of our linguistic knowledge, but of grammar. While Chomsky's theory of grammar has changed radically over the years – from grammar as a set of rules, through grammar as a set of principles and parameters right through to the current minimalist notion of Universal Grammar as a set of computations relating the two interface levels of PF (Phonological Form) and LF (Logical Form), at every stage, a grammar is not a description of the properties of sentences that have been produced, but rather a theory of the speaker's knowledge of her language, and is constrained by the aim of explaining linguistic knowledge in terms of properties of the human mind.

Schiffrin does acknowledge that the 'formalist' approach views language as a mental phenomenon and hence must be contrasted with the functionalist approach which sees it as a societal phenomenon. Nevertheless it is not clear that she has understood the significance of Chomsky's (1986) own description of his contribution to linguistics in terms of a move from the study of language as an externalized object (*E-language*) to the study of language as an internalized system (*I-language*), or in other words, a move from the study of behaviour of sentences to the study of the language-user's knowledge of her language, or linguistic competence.

As we have seen, for Harris (1951) discourse is rather like a big sentence – the next unit up after the clause – and it is these units which are themselves the object of study. By Chomsky's criterion, this is an externalized view of language. However, the fact that Schiffrin sees utterances as the products of behaviour, and that she sees discourse analysis in terms of the investigation of these objects rather than the investigation of those properties of the human cognitive system which enable people to understand utterances in discourse, suggests that her view is also an externalized view – although perhaps for a different reason.

The fact is that in spite of what Schiffrin says about the effect that Chomsky has had on the study of discourse, there has not been an analogous move in the study of discourse – at least not by the authors she cites. The move in the case of discourse would be a move from the study of discourse itself (whether this be defined in the structural terms advocated by Harris (1951) or Hovy (1990)) to the study of discourse competence, or in other words, to the study of the knowledge that underlies our ability to integrate linguistic and non-linguistic knowledge for successful communication. As we have seen (in chapter 1), this sort of move has been attempted in pragmatics by Kasher (1991a, 1991b, 1991c). And indeed, Chomsky himself has talked about pragmatics competence (Chomsky 1980).

As I have explained in chapter 1 and chapter 3, the theoretical framework underlying the analyses given in the preceding chapter is not a theory of pragmatic competence in the sense defined by Chomsky or Kasher, but rather a theory of pragmatic processing, or in other words, performance. However, it should by now be clear that this is not a theory of linguistic performance, contrasted with linguistic competence. It is not concerned with those factors which result in false starts, mishearings, variations in pronunciation. Nor is it performance in the sense of Leech (1983) or Mey (1993). For them, a theory of performance is concerned with social features of language use (for example, social class, gender, age) insofar as assumptions about these enter into the processes involved in determining the speaker's communicative intentions. Relevance theory is a cognitive performance theory, and as such is concerned with the actual cognitive processes involved in the interpretation of utterances. It is a theory of the system that actually does the interpretive work.

It is not clear how this approach would be accommodated in the paradigm described by Schiffrin. Clearly, it is not functional, since it does not regard language as a societal phenomenon. Nor does it see the task of pragmatics as the analysis of actual language use. The fact that it accepts many of the fundamental assumptions attributed by Schiffrin to the structuralist tradition, specifically, that grammar is an autonomous system which is acquired on the basis of a genetically determined human (that is, species specific) capacity, would, I assume, lead Schiffrin to classify it as structuralist. However, its structuralist assumptions are not, as Schiffrin suggests, reflected in an acceptance of the particular definition of discourse which she attributes to structuralist approaches. For the object of study is not an externalized object characterized by its organizational or structural properties, but the cognitive processes involved in understanding.

The discussion so far has given the impression that the study of discourse is inconsistent with an internalist approach to language and communication, or that one cannot talk of discourse and cognition in the same breath. However, there is an approach to discourse which does precisely that. Not only does it embed the study of discourse within the study of human cognition, but it supports its claims with experimental evidence. Thus for example, Sanders, Spooren and Noordman (1992) stress that an account of what makes a discourse coherent 'has to be psychologically plausible' (1992:1) and argue for a taxonomy of coherence relations which is a 'psychological model' for the interpretation of coherence relations (1992:30). Coherence relations, they argue, must be 'cognitive entities' (1992:3) and not simply an analytic tool, and they describe a variety of experiments which they claim show that this is in fact the case. Thus for example, they mention Haberlandt's (1982) experiments which show that on-line processing is affected by whether relations are marked explicitly, and they see their own experiments as providing psycholinguistic evidence for the existence of a taxonomy of coherence relations that classifies them in terms of four 'cognitively salient' primitives (1992:1). At the same time, however, Sanders, Spooren and Noordman base their research on the assumption that comprehension consists in 'the construction of a mental *representation of the discourse* by the reader' (or hearer) (1992:1, my emphasis). In another article Sanders and Noordman (2000) speak of constructing 'a representation of *the information*' (2000:37, my emphasis); however, it is unclear what they mean by this, and in any case they go straight on to speak of a 'text representation' (2000:37). In other words, there is a fundamental assumption that there is something – a text or a discourse – that is processed, and that the aim of processing is to recover a coherent representation of that text or discourse.

It is not entirely clear what kind of object these authors believe a text or discourse is – except, of course, that it exhibits discourse or coherence relations and hence has structural properties. In some cases, it seems, the text representation is a representation of what they call 'semantic' relations whose source is in relationships that exist in the external world (for example, temporal and causal relations), while in other cases it is a representation of what they call 'pragmatic' or illocutionary' relations whose source is in the relationship between people's beliefs, desires and intentions.[2] However, the point seems to be not just that people have assumptions about temporal or causal relationships between states of affairs in the world, but rather that they identify relationships in the text or discourse which have their source in such relationships. Thus an interpretation is not so much a representation of a speaker's beliefs and assumptions about, for example, temporal relationships between states of affairs, but a representation of structural relationships in the discourse or text itself. My difficulty with

---

[2] This distinction seems to be similar to Halliday and Hasan's (1976) distinction between ideational (or semantic) and internal relations. See Blakemore (1997b) for discussion.

this approach as a cognitively grounded approach to communication is that the coherence relations which hearers identify as part of a cognitive representation are identified as part of a representation of something (that is, discourse) which is not itself explained in cognitive terms.

It is true, of course, that relevance theorists speak of understanding utterances (and, sometimes, indeed, of understanding discourse), and of deriving interpretations of utterances (and sometimes discourse). However, there is a fundamental difference between the two approaches. For relevance theorists, utterances (and discourse) are simply public phenomena which are produced as representations of private phenomena (thoughts). An interpretation of an utterance is an interpretive assumption about the thoughts that the speaker intends to communicate, or, in other words, an interpretive representation of the speaker's thoughts. Thus a hearer constructs a representation of the utterance only in the sense that she constructs a representation of the speaker's thoughts. This representation is not mediated by the representation of any kind of structural object such as a text or discourse. In particular, it is not mediated by a representation of structural relations between utterances. The point of processing is not (*contra* Sanders, Spooren and Noordman) to derive an acceptable representation of the discourse, but to enlarge the mutual cognitive environment of speaker and hearer. As we shall see, the inferential processes involved in utterance interpretation may involve assumptions about temporal or causal relationships between events in the world or about relationships between the speaker and hearer. However, within a relevance theoretic framework, these assumptions are not construed as assumptions about relationships in the discourse or text itself.

5.2 Discourse connections

5.2.1 *Approaches to discourse coherence*
In this section, I shall return to the assumption that utterance interpretation *is* about deriving assumptions about relationships in the discourse and that discourse markers encode these connections. As I have said, my aim is not to dispute the claim that people have intuitions about coherence, but to ask whether these intuitions play a role in the way utterances are understood. Obviously, if it could be shown that our understanding of utterances is a consequence of the organization of discourse, then it is clear that it is worth looking at the organization of discourse in order to discover what this organization consists in. If on the other hand, our intuitions about the organization of discourse are a consequence of the way we understand utterances, then we should instead

be trying to discover the constraint(s) on comprehension processes from which our intuitions about the organization of a sequence of utterances can be derived.

In fact, it seems that some writers are less concerned with how comprehension or understanding is achieved than they are with the question of what distinguishes a text from a non-text, or, in other words, that for some writers, a theory of text/discourse *is* a theory of what makes a text a text. Thus, for example, the primary aim of writers such as Grimes (1975), Longacre (1983) and Pike and Pike (1983) seems to be restricted to providing the means for distinguishing a text from a non-text. However, there are also writers who see textual or discourse organization as an essential part of a theory of discourse comprehension. Thus for example, Mann and Thompson (1987, 1988) have claimed that the hearer's search for textual organization plays an essential role in the recovery of implicatures, Hobbs (1979) has claimed that reference assignment is the consequence of the search for discourse organization and Asher and Lascarides (1995) have argued that disambiguation is a product of the search for discourse relations. More generally, it is argued that the relations between segments or spans of text are what people actually use in interpreting it.

According to Knott (1996), the distinction I have just made is analogous to Chomsky's (1964) distinction between syntactic theories which are descriptively adequate and those which have explanatory adequacy. Thus a theory which can decide whether a text is coherent or not is, according to Knott, 'descriptively adequate', while a theory which is descriptively adequate and can in addition explain why it is that readers and writers have judgements of coherence has 'explanatory adequacy' (Knott 1996:6). In fact, it is not clear whether these two distinctions are analogous. However, the question to be discussed in 5.2.2 is whether understanding utterances does depend on the ability to make judgements analogous to judgements about syntactic well-formedness or, in other words, whether we make judgements about the coherence of texts in order to achieve understanding.

Not all writers who see verbal comprehension as being governed by the search for coherence define coherence in terms of structural relationships between segments of discourse. Indeed, as Samet and Schank (1984) have shown, it is possible to construct texts in which there are discourse relations between adjacent pairs but which are nevertheless nonsense:

(3)   In a little Danish town, two fishmongers exchanged blows. Anders, by far the stronger, had a cousin in prison. Anders was twice the age of the cousin. When he was first convicted Anders was living in Italy. Anders has a wife who lost her bathing cap. Her car is at this moment double parked.

                                                                    (Samet and Schank 1984)

While such examples show that *local* discourse relations are not sufficient by themselves to account for the acceptability of texts, the question remains whether this means that we should develop a notion of *global* coherence in order to account for textual unity, and whether this notion can itself be defined in terms of local relations. While some writers (for example, Hovy 1990) argue that this is possible, other writers (for example, Giora 1997) take a different approach altogether, arguing that coherence must be defined in terms of a hierarchical structure of discourse topics. Giora's approach has been discussed in detail by Wilson (1998), who shows not only that the notion of topic-relevance is a derivative one, but that the phenomena discussed by Giora can be given a more satisfactory analysis within a relevance theoretic framework (see note 3 below). Here, however, I shall focus on local coherence relations between adjacent segments of text, for these are the relations which are said to be encoded by discourse connectives or markers.

5.2.2   Cohesion, coherence and discourse acceptability

As we have seen in 5.1, Halliday and Hasan's (1976) notion of cohesion was restricted to linguistically encoded relationships in the text. Halliday and Hasan's account of cohesion in English was not, of course, limited to discourse connectives: it includes anaphoric devices such as pronouns, ellipsis, repetition and substitution. However, it is now generally recognized that connectivity of form is neither necessary nor sufficient for textual well-formedness or acceptability. Thus both the connection said to be encoded by *so* in (4) and the temporal connection encoded by *then* in (5) could have been communicated non-linguistically.

(4)   There was £5 in his wallet. (So) he hadn't spent the money.

(5)   I cooked myself an egg and (then) started on my essay.

And as Hobbs (1978) points out, even though *he* in the second segment of (6) will be understood to refer to Jimmy Carter, the sequence will not be understood as an acceptable text.

(6)   Jimmy Carter proposed a massive energy programme. He used to cultivate peanuts.

(Hobbs 1978:5)

Moreover, as Hobbs' (1978) example in (7) shows, even when two sentences are related by a cohesive tie, the hearer has to go beyond her linguistic resources in order to recover an interpretation, since in principle *he* could refer either to John or Bill.

(7)   John can open Bill's safe. He knows the combination.

(Hobbs 1979:78)

Hobbs takes these examples to show that for an account of textual acceptability, we need to turn to connectivity of content (which may or may not be realized by cohesive ties) – or in other words coherence. As I have indicated, my interest in this approach lies mainly in Hobbs' further claim, which is made by a number of other theorists, that it is the search for coherence that leads to successful comprehension, and thus that it provides the key to a theory of discourse comprehension. However, let us first examine the assumption which underlies this approach, namely, that acceptability and coherence are one and the same.

In simple terms, Hobbs' claim is that in producing acceptable discourse, speakers make use of a menu of discourse or coherence relations. Having produced a segment of discourse U_1 he selects a relation R from the menu and then produces a segment U_2 which stands in relation R to U_1. By repeating this process the speaker will create an acceptable discourse in which each segment U is related to the next by an identifiable relation.

Clearly, the success of this sort of approach depends on a definitive list of coherence relations. However, the search for *the* set of discourse relations has resulted in a confusing picture in which each theorist uses a differently defined set of relations. For example, Hovy (1990) identifies seventy relations, Mann and Thompson's (1987) rhetorical structure theory is based on sixteen, and Hobbs himself, while he does not specify an exact number, claims that it is 'small' (Hobbs 1979:3). Not surprisingly, this confusion is matched by a corresponding disagreement over the definition of individual relations. For example, while a number of theorists agree that there is a relation of *elaboration*, not all of them agree on what it is. Thus while Hobbs' (1978, 1979) definition includes reformulations such as (8), Mann and Thompson (1987) classify elaborations, restatements and summaries as distinct relations.

(8)   From the style of a communication it is possible to infer such things as what a speaker takes to be the hearer's cognitive capacities and level of attention, how much help or guidance she is prepared to give him in processing her utterance, the degree of complicity between them, their emotional closeness or distance. In other words, a speaker not only aims to enlarge the mutual cognitive environment; she also assumes a certain degree of mutuality, which is indicated and sometimes communicated by her style.

(Sperber and Wilson 1995:217–8, cited in Blakemore 1997b)

Similarly, while Hobbs includes under elaboration 'such trivial moves as pure repetitions, repairs, tag questions, and the like' (Hobbs 1979:73), it is not clear that these fall within the scope of the definitions given by other writers.

Sanders, Spooren and Nordman (1993), who, as we have seen, adduce psycholinguistic experiments in support of their approach, argue that it is cognitively implausible for a speaker to have knowledge of all the relations that have been proposed and that from a cognitive point of view it is more attractive to generate the full set of coherence relations by combining the members of a set of four cognitively salient primitives: (i) basic operation (*causal* or *additive*); (ii) source of coherence (*semantic* or *pragmatic*); (iii) polarity (*negative* or *positive*); (iv) order of segments (*basic* or *non-basic*). As they point out, within this approach it is not possible to argue that every discourse connective is linked to a different discourse connection. In fact, it is rarely claimed that there is a one-to-one relationship between coherence relations and discourse markers or connectives. Within coherence-based approaches, the classification of discourse connectives is often based on broad categories so that clusters of connectives are associated with a single type of relation. Thus for example, the connectives *so*, *hence* and *therefore* are linked to a causal relation, while the connectives *however*, *but*, *yet* and *still* are associated with an adversative or contrastive relation.

As we have seen in the last chapter, it is not clear that this sort of approach can reflect the (often extremely subtle) distinctions between the meanings of certain discourse connectives. Recall for example, the differences between *but*, *however*, *nevertheless* and *yet* illustrated in the following:

(9)   She's not a linguist but/?however a logician.
(10)   Hi Frank. I've just received your message; but/however/?nevertheless it's in Dutch.
(11)   (a) Her husband is in hospital, but she's seeing other men. ≠
       (b) Her husband is in hospital, yet she's seeing other men.

(based on example from Kitis 1995)

It is difficult to see how these differences are captured in an analysis in which these expressions are associated with a relationship of contrast or adversity. Similarly, it is not clear how the differences in (12) and (13) are captured in an analysis in which *so* and *therefore* are associated with relation of consequence.

(12)   A: I'm just going to have a cup of coffee.
       B: So/?Therefore you're not going to the meeting?

(13)   You can't do anything about it now. So/?Therefore just go home and
        relax.

More recently Sanders and Noordman (2000) have argued that there is experimental evidence which supports the view that whereas coherence relations are
part of the discourse representation itself, discourse connectives merely 'guide
the hearer in selecting the right relation' (2000:56). While it seems right to
think of many of these expressions as guides to interpretation in the sense that
they encode a processing direction rather than an element of the interpretation
derived, it would seem that in treating, say, *but* and *however* as guides for selecting the relation of contrast we would be failing to identify those aspects
of their encoded meanings that distinguish the contributions they make to the
interpretation of the utterances that contain them. This suggests that either we
accept that not every aspect of the contribution made by these expressions can
be explained in terms of the role that they play in coherence or we conclude
that each of the expressions just listed is linked to a different coherence relation. The first suggestion leaves us with the problem of saying what role these
expressions play in addition to guiding the hearer in her search for coherence,
while the second leads to the proliferation of undefined coherence relations.

Let us leave the problem of the classification of coherence relations and return
to Hobbs' (1978, 1979) assumption that the acceptability of a text or discourse
depends on whether its segments are related by an identifiable coherence relation. As Blass (1990) has shown, the acceptability of a particular coherence
relation varies from context to context. Compare, for example, the sequences in
(14), which seem to satisfy both Mann and Thompson's and Hobbs' definitions
of elaboration.

(14)   (a) I read a book about coherence last night. It had a chapter about
            elaboration and there were a few pages about relevance.
        (b) I read a book about coherence last night. It had a cover and the
            pages were numbered consecutively.

Whereas it is possible to imagine how most readers of this book would find
(14a) acceptable, it is more difficult to imagine a context in which (14b) would
be considered acceptable.

Similarly, whether or not we classify restatements and repetitions as sub-
types of elaboration, it is clear that not all restatements and repetitions are
acceptable. For example, it would be inappropriate for a speaker to communicate
his excitement at seeing a mouse by producing the sequence in (15).

(15)   There's a mouse, a small grey furry rodent.

According to Mann and Thompson (1988), the intended effect of a restatement is simply that the hearer recognizes that a restatement is being made. However, it is difficult to see how this could provide a means either for distinguishing acceptable restatements from unacceptable ones, or for distinguishing the effects of a restatement such as (16) from a restatement such as (17).

(16)   (a) At the beginning of this piece there is an example of an anacrusis. (b) That is, it begins with an unaccented note that is not part of the first full bar.

(Blakemore 1997b)

(17)   (a) A well-groomed car reflects its owner. (b) The car you drive says a lot about you.

(Mann and Thompson 1988)

As we shall see in 5.3.4, it is possible to account for these differences in a relevance theoretic framework where an interpretation does not include the identification of coherence relations. The same kind of point can be made about repetitions (which Hobbs 1978 classifies as a type of elaboration). Thus while it is not difficult to think of a situation in which (18) is an acceptable sequence, the sequence in (19) would only be produced by an automated voice.

(18)   Look! Look! There's a mouse. A mouse.
(19)   The number you have dialled is unobtainable. The number you have dialled is unobtainable. The number . . .

Wilson (1998) has identified a slightly different point about the analysis of repetitions in terms of a structural relation between adjacent segments. As she points out, repetitions are not always adjacent, as they are in (18). Moreover, it is possible to have a repetition within a one clause utterance, as in (20).

(20)   That was a really really stupid thing to do.

She argues that since there is no obvious intonation break in an example such as (20), it is difficult to see how the repetition could be analysed in terms of a structural relation between two discourse segments. It might be argued that this is a different kind of repetition. However, it would seem more satisfactory to have an analysis which covers *all* cases of repetition – whether or not it occurs in adjacent segments.

These examples show that it is not enough for a speaker aiming at acceptability to produce an utterance that stands in an identifiable coherence relation to the preceding one. Coherence is not sufficient for acceptability. But nor is it necessary. As Blass (1990) has pointed out, an utterance may be part of what is, intuitively, an incoherent discourse but still be understood by the hearer. For example, B's response in (21) has both a coherent interpretation, in which it reports what she said, and an incoherent interpretation, in which it describes what B has just seen.

(21)   A: What did Sue say, then?
         B: Our train is leaving in thirty seconds.

The incoherent interpretation might be classified as an interruption, which could be analysed as some kind of exception to the principles which govern discourse. Thus Tsui (1991) analyses an interruption such as this as a violation of a 'coherence rule' which, unless it is justified, results in anti-social and impolite behaviour. This, of course, raises the question of what would justify such a violation. Giora (1997), who, as we have seen, does not believe that coherence is analysable in terms of a set of local coherence relations, regards the incoherent interpretation of an example such as (21) as unacceptable because it violates a 'relevance requirement' (which is *not* to be confused with Sperber and Wilson's principle of relevance which, as we have seen, is not subject to violation). This requirement requires that all the propositions of a well-formed discourse be related to a *discourse-topic proposition*.[3] At the same time, however, she suggests that violations of this requirement *are* acceptable provided that they are explicitly marked by an expression such as *by the way* or *incidentally*. The problem is that this would rule out the incoherent interpretation of B's response in (21), since it is not explicitly marked. Moreover, as Deirdre Wilson has pointed out, it would also allow exchanges such as the following:

(22)   A: What's the time, please?
         B: By the way, Beethoven was deaf.

Hobbs and Agar (1985) have attempted to accommodate interruptions and other such 'vagaries of naturally occurring discourse' (1985:230) within the formal framework of Artificial Intelligence. Their conclusion is that while the standard planning mechanism of AI needs to be modified in order to accommodate naturalistic material, 'with suitable tinkering, a planner can be made to include a modifiable knowledge base that represents shared as well as idiosyncratic knowledge' (1985:230). Indeed, they argue that the formal analysis of

---

[3] In her reply to Giora, Wilson (1998) points out that the notion of topic-relevance is derivative in a relevance theoretic account. Giora sees the function of a discourse topic as a means of providing access to the contextual information required for comprehension. However, Sperber and Wilson (1995) show that it is this contextual information rather than the discourse topic that is essential for comprehension. On the one hand, a text may be comprehensible when there is no explicitly stated topic. On the other hand, it may remain incomprehensible when there is an explicitly stated topic. See Sperber and Wilson (1995:742) for further discussion.

seemingly incoherent discourse is not only possible but also revealing in that it enables us to uncover hidden coherencies. These coherencies are not the local coherencies that we have just been discussing, but global coherencies governed by global plans which change as the conversation progresses.

Hobbs and Agar see a global plan as a formal structured representation 'of what the system is trying to accomplish in the world by carrying on the conversation and the means which it is using' (1985:216). The initial plan is, they argue, rarely complete: it will simply be one which enables the system to take the initial action. Thereafter the plan will develop in response to the actions of participants or changes in the environment. Their subsequent discussion shows that a central feature of this plan is the selection and negotiation of topic. As we have just seen, this notion is derivative within a relevance theoretic framework (see note 3). More generally, Hobbs and Agar's proposal becomes explanatory only if it can be explained what makes a global plan acceptable at any stage of the discourse, and in particular, what governs a speaker's decision about the means he uses given his own informative intentions and his assumptions about the hearer's knowledge. As we have seen in chapter 3, within relevance theory it is argued that every contribution made by a speaker is constrained by the aim of optimizing relevance. And as we shall see in 5.3.2, the principle of relevance constrains (and hence explains) so-called incoherent discourse in exactly the same way as it constrains (and explains) coherent discourse.

The emphasis in any coherence-based account, whether it is couched in terms of local coherence relations or in terms of topic-relevance, is on the acceptability of utterances which are part of a discourse sequence. However, as Blass (1990) observes, everyday discourse is full of perfectly acceptable utterances which, although they cannot be understood in isolation from the context, cannot be said to be part of any kind of sequence. For example, a hearer who interprets an utterance such as the one that used to be found at the foot of escalators in the London Underground must access and use certain contextual assumptions in order to understand that she is not prohibited from using the Underground because she does not have a dog.

(23)   Dogs must be carried.

It is unlikely that anyone would dispute this. However, it seems that within a coherence-based approach to discourse it must be assumed that acceptability of isolated utterances such as (23) must be constrained by different principles from the ones governing the acceptability of utterances that are part of a discourse sequence. For clearly, the acceptability of (23) cannot be governed by the speaker's aim of constructing a coherent text.

In the previous chapter we saw that expressions classified as discourse connectives (or markers) can in some cases be used discourse initially. Recall examples such as the following:

(24)   [speaker looks in his wallet and finds a £5 note]
        So I didn't spend all the money.
(25)   [speaker, who is suffering from shock, has been given a glass of whisky]
        But I don't like whisky.

Such examples would seem to pose a difficulty for an approach which analyses expressions such as *so* and *but* as encoding coherence relations. Like (23), they are acceptable, but do not stand in any identifiable coherence relation with the preceding text. Knott and Dale (1994) have argued that this difficulty is only apparent since utterances such as (24) and (25) must be 'interpreted as a reaction to a previously existing propositional attitude . . . and this is arguably a kind of discourse context' (1994:48). This seems to suggest that we can continue to think of *so* and *but* as encoding coherence relations if we think of the context for their interpretation as if it were a span of discourse, or, in other words, as if the utterance and its context constituted some kind of discourse sequence. For example, the utterance in (24) could be treated as if it were part of the discourse sequence in (26).

(26)   I have found a £5 note in my wallet. So I didn't spend all the money.

As I have argued elsewhere (Blakemore 1998), this approach leaves us with the question of why not all expressions classified as discourse connectives can be used in non-linguistic discourse connectives. In particular, it leaves us with the question of why apparently closely related discourse connectives are not equally acceptable in non-linguistic contexts. For example, as I have observed (Blakemore 1987), while *so* is appropriate in an utterance such as (24), *therefore* is not.

(27)   [speaker finds a £5 note in his wallet]
        ?Therefore I didn't spend all the money.

Similarly, as we have seen in the preceding chapter, *however* cannot be substituted for *but* in discourse initial contexts.

(28)   [speaker, who is in shock, is given a glass of whisky]
        ?However, I don't like whisky.

As we have seen, these differences can be accommodated in a framework which analyses these expressions as encoding a constraint on the relevance of the utterance that contains it.

More generally, it is not clear whether treating contextual assumptions as discourse is consistent with an account of utterance interpretation in which hearers use their assumptions about the world in inferential processes constrained by a general cognitive principle. As I have said earlier, it is not clear what status discourse would have in such a theory; however, it is clear that it is not discourse itself which enters the inferential processes involved in utterance interpretation. By the same token, it is not clear that Knott and Dale's extension of the concept 'discourse' to include context reflects what is normally meant by 'discourse' in theories of discourse. Cook (1989), for example, defines discourse as 'stretches of language perceived to be meaningful, unified and purposive' (1989:156). While it may be possible to extend this definition to non-linguistic communicative behaviour, it is difficult to see how it can be extended to phenomena which do not involve communicative intentions (for example, the discovery of a £5 note).

The fact that discourse is full of utterances which cannot be understood in isolation from the context, but which cannot be said to be part of a coherent text, suggests that instead of stretching the notions of discourse and context in order to accommodate utterances such as (24–5), we should develop an account of the role of the context in utterance interpretation that is general enough to explain the interpretation of all utterances – whether they are part of a discourse or not. Clearly, this account cannot be based on the assumption that utterance interpretation is constrained by the search for coherence, as for example Hobbs (1978, 1979) has claimed. The question, then, is whether we can capture our intuitions about the unity of discourse in an account that does not appeal to coherence relations.

5.3   Understanding without discourse relations

5.3.1   *Coherence and understanding*

In this section we shall turn our attention from discourse acceptability to discourse understanding, and in particular, to the claim that it is the search for coherence that leads to the successful comprehension of utterances. This claim has been articulated particularly clearly by Mann and Thompson (1987, 1988), who argue that the fact that two discourse segments stand in a particular coherence relation is part of what is intentionally communicated by the speaker, and the recognition of this relation is essential to the successful comprehension of the sequence by the hearer. More specifically, amongst the propositions implicitly communicated by a discourse sequence such as (29a) is the *relational proposition* in (30):

(29)   (a) I love to collect classic automobiles. (b) My favourite car is my 1899 Duryea.

(Mann and Thompson 1987)

(30)   Segment b is an elaboration of segment a.

In fact, according to their account, this relational proposition is the most central of all the propositions implicitly communicated by (29a), for its recovery is the key to the recovery of all the other propositions that it implicitly communicates. For example, this sequence implicitly communicates that an 1899 Duryea is a classic automobile. However, the hearer would not recover this proposition, it is argued, unless she had first recovered the implicit relational proposition in (30).

As I have observed (Blakemore 1997b), there is a striking resemblance between this approach to discourse understanding, on the one hand, and speech act theoretic approaches to pragmatics, on the other. For just as Mann and Thompson claim that coherence relations are part of what is intentionally communicated by a speaker, speech act theorists claim that the classification of speech acts plays an essential role in communication so that, for example, a speaker who wishes to issue a warning must communicate that she is making a warning, or a speaker who is making a guess must communicate that she is making a guess. Moreover, just as Mann and Thompson claim that a hearer will not understand an utterance unless she can first identify the coherence relation that is being communicated, in speech act theory it is claimed that a hearer will understand the utterance only if she can first identify the type of speech act being performed. Given this analogy, it seems appropriate to recall Sperber and Wilson's (1995) analogy between the classification of utterances and the classification of tennis strokes:

> it is one thing to invent, for one's own theoretical purposes, a set of categories to use in classifying the utterances of native speakers. It is quite another to claim that such a classification plays a necessary role in communication and comprehension. To see the one type of investigation as necessarily shedding light on the other is rather like moving from the observation that tennis players can generally classify strokes as volleys, lobs, approach shots, cross-court back hands and so on, to the conclusion that they are unable to perform or return a stroke without correctly classifying it. (1995:244)

As Sperber and Wilson say, this kind of move requires justification. We have already seen how this approach to discourse has been dominated by the same kind of questions about classification that have dominated speech act theoretic approaches to pragmatics. In the next three sections, I wish to ask whether the assumption that coherence is a prerequisite for understanding can be maintained. I shall argue that the sort of arguments Sperber and Wilson give against the claim that the success of utterance comprehension depends on the successful identification of the speech act performed apply equally to the claim that it depends on the successful identification of coherence relations: if a hearer identifies a coherence relation, then it is as a result of successful comprehension rather than a prerequisite for it.

5.3.2   Coherence and relevance
Let us recall the example in (21):

(21)   A: What did Sue say, then?
        B: Our train is leaving in thirty seconds.

As I have said, B's utterance in (21) has two possible interpretations – a coherent interpretation in which B is understood to be reporting what Sue said (and thus answering A's question), and an incoherent interpretation in which B is telling A that their train is about to leave (and thus not answering A's question). The question for the hearer in each case is: what context does B intend the hearer to interpret in?

As we have seen, the answer according to a coherence approach must be 'whatever context yields a coherent interpretation'. However, this will yield only the first interpretation and rule out the second. As Hobbs and Agar (1985) recognize, in natural discourse the second interpretation would be quite acceptable. What we need is an answer which explains, first, why both interpretations are possible, and, second, why in a certain sort of context the incoherent interpretation is preferred over the coherent.

The answer according to relevance theory is that the hearer will interpret the utterance in the context which yields an interpretation that is consistent with the principle of relevance in a way that the speaker could have manifestly foreseen. In other words, she will interpret it in the context that yields an optimally relevant interpretation. It will be recalled (from chapter 3) that an utterance is optimally relevant if and only if:

(a)   the utterance is relevant enough for it to be worth the hearer's effort to process it; and

(b)   the utterance is the most relevant compatible with the speaker's abilities and preferences.

It is not difficult to imagine a context in which the incoherent interpretation of B's utterance in (21) is optimally relevant. While the answer to A's question will manifestly be relevant to her, there are situations in which B's utterance might itself trigger an immediately accessible context which yields cognitive effects which will not be derivable for very much longer: the train will not wait; however A and B can always discuss what Sue said later (for example, on the train).

In this case, B's utterance is processed for relevance in a context which is distinct from the one in which A's utterance is interpreted. There are no contextual assumptions used in the interpretation of B's utterance that are used in the interpretation of A's. Moreover, the contextual assumptions used in establishing the relevance of B's utterance do not include the content of A's utterance or any contextual effects derived from it. It is this which according to Blass (1990) is the source of the incoherence. Putting this the other way round, if a discourse *is* coherent, then it is because there is continuity of context in the sense that assumptions made accessible by the interpretation of one segment are used in establishing the relevance of the next. Since the interpretation of information which has just been processed will provide a highly accessible context for the interpretation of an utterance, coherence can be regarded as a consequence of the hearer's search for optimal relevance.

If this is right, then it ought to be possible to show how particular coherence relations can be re-analysed in terms of a consequence of the way relevance is established. In the following two sections I shall give two examples of the way in which coherence relations may be re-analysed in relevance theoretic terms. The discussion of temporal relations in 5.3.3 draws upon work by Carston (1993, 2002), while the re-assessment of so-called restatement relations in 5.3.4 is based on my earlier work on restatement, exemplification and the analysis of apposition markers (Blakemore 1993, 1996, 1997b). However, I am focussing on these relations here not just because it is possible to show that in each case their identification is not a prerequisite for comprehension, but also because the expressions which are said to mark them (for example *then* and *in other words*) can be shown to encode quite different kinds of information from the information encoded by the expressions discussed in chapter 4. In this way, I hope to underline the point made in chapter 3 that the classification of all of these expressions as discourse connectives (or markers) obscures the fact that they make different kinds of contributions to the interpretation of the utterances containing them.

5.3.3   *Temporal relations*

As is well known, the fact that suggestions of temporal sequence can be communicated by conjoined sequences such as (31) and (32) led some theorists to claim that *and* should be construed as meaning *and then* in addition to the meaning that is captured by the truth table definition for its logical counterpart &.

(31)   She jumped on her horse and rode into the sunset.

(32)   She gave up semantics and felt much happier.

The sequence in (32) is also understood to communicate a suggestion of causal sequence which, on the semantic analysis just described, would mean that *and* encodes something like *and as a result of that*. However, in this section I shall focus on the suggestion of temporal sequence.[4] It was of course, this sort of phenomenon, and more particularly, this sort of approach to it, which provided the main motivation for Grice's (1989) account of conversational implicature. His account provides a strategy for maintaining a minimal truth functional semantics for natural language *and* in the face of examples such as (31) and (32). According to this strategy, the non-truth functional suggestions of temporal and causal sequence are due to general properties of discourse or communication which Grice encapsulated in the maxims of conversation. The particular maxim which, according to Grice, accounts for these suggestions requires that speakers present their material in an orderly manner, which in the case of a narrative means that their utterances should match the chronology of the events being described.

The advantage of this explanation of the interpretation of utterances such as (31) and (32) is that it is not construction specific. It applies equally to non-conjoined sequences such as (33) and (34).

(33)   She jumped on her horse. She rode into the sunset.

(34)   She gave up semantics. She felt much happier.

However, as Blakemore and Carston (1999) have pointed out, Grice's maxim is specifically about utterances which are intended to locate events in time, and not all utterances are intended to narrate events. For example, while the sequence in (35) has an interpretation in which the event of Ben tripping over the wire follows the event of Ben breaking his leg, it has another (more likely) interpretation in which the leg-breaking event follows the tripping event, or, in

---

[4] In fact, my general approach can be applied straightforwardly to the causal suggestions communicated by so-called narrative sequences. For a more extensive discussion, see Blakemore and Carston (1999), Carston (2002).

other words, in which the order of events does *not* match the order in which the events are presented.

(35)   Ben broke his leg. He tripped over a wire.

As Herb Clark (cited in Gazdar 1979) points out, this interpretation is not available for the corresponding conjoined utterance in (36).

(36)   Ben broke his leg and he tripped over a wire.

This raises the question of why the parallel between juxtaposed sequences and conjoined sequences breaks down, and, indeed, the main aim of Blakemore and Carston's paper is to provide an explanation for a range of interpretive discrepancies between *and*-utterances and their juxtaposed counterparts. However, they also point out that there is a range of conjoined sequences in which the order of the conjuncts appears to be the opposite of the chronological order assumed to hold between the events described. Consider, for example (37–9):

(37)   A: Did Mary do all of her education in the States?
        B: No, she did her BA in London and her A levels at home in Leeds.
(38)   A: Did John break the vase?
        B: Well, the vase broke and he dropped it.
                              (example due to Larry Horn, Carston 1998:145)
(39)   A: Bob wants me to get rid of these mats. He says he trips over them
           all the time. Still, I don't suppose he'll break his neck.
        B: Well, I don't know. JOHN | broke his LEG | and HE | tripped on a
           PERSian RUG |
           [upper-case indicates accented syllables; | marks intonation
           phrases; note that a fall–rise intonation is likely on *John* and *he*]
                              (from Carston 1998:146)

As Blakemore and Carston (1999) point out, such examples would seem to suggest that the interpretive discrepancies between conjoined utterances and their non-conjoined counterparts cannot be explained by saying that *and* encodes temporal sequence (*contra* Bar-Lev and Palacas 1980).

The problem with Grice's (1989) maxim of manner is that it does not say anything about sequences which cannot be interpreted as narrative sequences. Dowty's (1986) temporal discourse interpretation principle (given in (40)) and Cooper's (1986) discourse strategy (given in (41)) face the same problem.

(40)   Temporal discourse interpretation principle (Dowty 1986)
         Given a sequence of sentences $S_1, S_2 \ldots S_n$ to be interpreted as a nar-
         rative discourse, the reference time of each sentence S_i is interpreted
         to be:
         (a) a time consistent with the definite time adverbial in S_i if there are
         any;
         (b) otherwise, a time which immediately follows the reference time of
         the previous utterance S_{i-1}.
(41)   Discourse strategy (Cooper 1986)
         Move forward the connection for tensed verbs in main clauses as the
         discourse progresses.

It is assumed that these proposals would be accompanied by a pragmatic explanation for those discourses which do not conform to them. In other words, they
treat the narrative interpretation as a default and non-narrative interpretations
are recovered as contextually determined cancellations of the default. However,
as Smith (1990) points out, it would seem that we would obtain a more general
explanation of these sorts of phenomena if we retained a single minimal semantics for the past tense and derived both chronological and non-chronological
interpretations of past-tense utterances as a consequence of the same general
cognitive principle which governs the interpretation of all ostensive communicative acts.

According to Carston (1993, 1998, 2002) the chronological interpretation of a
conjoined utterance such as (31) is a consequence of the way in which the hearer
uses contextual information to develop the linguistically determined semantic
representation into a proposition which can achieve optimal relevance. Her
argument is that the linguistically determined semantic representation of these
utterances under-determines their propositional content in just the same way
as the linguistic meaning under-determines the explicit content of uttterances
such as those in (42) or (43):

(42)   On the table.
(43)   Paracetemol is better.

As we have seen, in order to recover an interpretation that is consistent with the
principle of relevance, the hearer must use contextual information to recover
the intended explicit content of these utterances. That is, she must use contextual information to enrich the linguistically determined semantic representation
delivered by the grammar. Carston argues that the same kind of pragmatically

determined inferential enrichment processes enable the hearer of a conjoined utterance such as (31) to recover a propositional form such as (44):

(44)   (a) She$_i$ got on [her horse]$_j$ at time t_n. (b) At time t_{n+1} she$_i$ rode on [her horse]$_j$ into the sunset.

Similarly, she argues that the hearer of an utterance such as (45) will recover the enriched propositional form in (46).

(45)   The taxi got stuck in a traffic jam and I missed most of the syntax lecture.

(46)   (a) [The taxi got stuck in a traffic jam]$_i$. (b) As a result of that$_i$ I missed most of the syntax lecture.

As Carston explains, these interpretations can be explained in terms of the fact that ready-made scripted knowledge makes the contextual assumptions that give rise to it highly accessible. In other words, the utterances achieve relevance because their conjuncts represent components of a scenario which itself is an instance of a more general stereotypical scenario. Thus (31) will be understood to map on to a cognitive unit in which one event (jumping on a horse) is a necessary precursor for another (riding into the sunset), and its relevance will lie, partly at least, in 'the reinforcing effect [it has] on the schema as a whole and the modifications it might introduce to sub-parts of the schema' (Carston 1998:212).

    If an utterance is to achieve relevance in this way, that is, by interacting with a highly accessible narrative script, then it would follow from the principle of relevance that a speaker will present the propositions representing those events in a chronological order, thereby saving the hearer unnecessary processing effort. Notice that this is not to say that utterances are interpreted according to specific sequencing principles that require them to present their description of events in the order in which they occurred (*contra* Grice 1989). It is simply to say that they are interpreted in accordance with the assumption that they are consistent with the principle of relevance.

    Given this account, it might be asked how a hearer approaches the interpretation of an utterance for which she has no highly accessible script, for example, the utterance in (47).

(47)   Mary put on her tutu and pruned the apple trees.
                            (from Blakemore and Carston 1999)

As Carston (1998) argues, it seems that while the hearer may find the interpretation of such utterances difficult, she will take the natural processing track – that is, the one in which the order of events matches the one in which they are presented. She takes this to be a result of the way human cognition is set up. In particular, it is the result of the fact that it is natural, and hence, less costly, to process all informational units – whether they are ostensively communicated or not – as chronological. After all, she argues, in interpreting visual and auditory stimuli occasioned by the natural world we cannot help but interpret them to a significant extent in the order in which they occurred if only because this is the order in which they impinge on our receptors.

This could be taken as a cognitive justification for treating the chrono-logical interpretation of sequences as the default interpretation, and the non-chronological interpretations of sequences such as (35) and (37–9) as violations of the default. In other words, it could be seen as cognitive justification for the claim that the interpretation of these sequences is governed by a principle of temporal sequencing which can be violated in particular circumstances. How-ever, this would be to misconstrue what Carston is saying here. The point is that the speaker's aim *in every case* is to achieve optimal relevance. In some cases optimal relevance may be achieved by recounting how events happened over time. It follows from the principle of relevance that if this is the way in which the speaker intends to achieve optimal relevance, then he will present the events in the order in which they happened, thus saving the hearer from gratuitous processing effort. However, there are cases in which it is manifest that the speaker is achieving optimal relevance in another way. For example, in (35) (repeated below) the speaker may achieve optimal relevance by commu-nicating that the first segment is an explanation for the event represented in the second, or, in other words, by communicating that the second segment is relevant as an answer to a question which is raised by the first, namely, 'How?'

(35)   Ben broke his leg. He tripped over a wire.

Notice that a speaker who aims to achieve optimal relevance in this way cannot be said to be communicating that the second segment of his utterance stands in some sort of explanation or elaboration relation to the first (see Hobbs 1979, Mann and Thompson 1987, 1988). The hearer will have understood the second segment provided that she interprets it as an answer to the question raised by the first – that is, provided that the first segment makes it manifest that the answer to the question 'how?' is relevant. Clearly, the hearer may describe the speaker as having provided an explanation for the event described in the first segment, or even as having elaborated on the information in the first segment. However, this description, if given, will be a consequence of having understood the utterance and not a prerequisite for understanding. In other words, the information that the second segment is an explanation or elaboration will contribute nothing to relevance.

As I noted earlier, this sort of interpretation is not available for the corresponding conjoined utterance. This is not surprising if the speaker of a conjoined utterance is understood to be guaranteeing the optimal relevance of the conjoined proposition expressed rather than each individual conjunct (see Blakemore 1987). Since questions and answers are by their very nature planned as separate utterances, each carrying the presumption of relevance individually, it would be impossible for the speaker to guarantee the relevance of a conjoined proposition in a sequence such as (35).

However, as we have seen, there are conjoined sequences which do not achieve optimal relevance as descriptions of events over time. Recall for example (37–9).

(37)   A: Did Mary do all of her education in the States?
        B: No, she did her BA in London and her A levels at home in Leeds.
(38)   A: Did John break the vase?
        B: Well, the vase broke and he dropped it.
                                        (example due to Larry Horn, Carston 1998:145)
(39)   A: Bob wants me to get rid of these mats. He says he trips over them all the time. Still, I don't suppose he'll break his neck.
        B: Well, I don't know. JOHN | broke his LEG | and HE | tripped on a PERSian RUG |
        [upper-case indicates accented syllables; | marks intonation phrases; note that a fall–rise intonation is likely on *John* and *he*]
                                        (from Carston 1998:146)

As Blakemore and Carston (1999) point out, these cases should not be regarded as examples of reverse or backwards temporal ordering, because they are not intended or understood as narrative cases: the order of the conjuncts is either not relevant at all or it is determined by considerations which have nothing to do with chronology. Thus in (37) the order of the conjuncts does not matter: the speaker is simply communicating a conjoined proposition which is relevant by virtue of being a single answer to a single question, namely, the question suggested by the negative response, 'So where else did she do parts of her education?' In (38) the order is determined by the speaker's desire to communicate that she is not willing to take responsibility for the assumption that John broke the vase, or that this is a conclusion for which the hearer alone must take responsibility. And in (39) the order is determined by the speaker's desire to contradict A's assumption that none (or virtually none) of the people who have broken bones are people who have tripped over rugs. In each case, the speaker will be understood to be guaranteeing the relevance of a conjoined proposition rather than the relevance of each individual conjunct.

Let us now return to cases of conjoined and non-conjoined sequences which are understood as temporal sequences, for example (31).

(31)   She jumped on her horse and rode into the sunset.

It will be recalled that according to Carston's analysis, a hearer will have understood (31) provided she recovers the propositional form in (44).

(44)   (a) She$_i$ got on [her horse]$_j$ at time t_n. (b) At time t_{n+1} she$_i$ rode on [her horse]$_j$ into the sunset.

As we have seen, the hearer's recovery of (44) is a consequence not of her recognition that the two segments are related by a temporal relation, but of her search for an interpretation that is consistent with her assumption that the speaker has aimed at optimal relevance. In other words, the recovery of a relational proposition (see Mann and Thompson 1987, 1988) expressing the coherence relation intended by the speaker plays no role in the inferential processes involved in its interpretation. Indeed, for a hearer who has recovered (44) the recovery of such a relational proposition would require gratuitous processing effort, and would, therefore, be ruled out by the principle of relevance.

If there is no coherence relation of temporal sequence between the two segments of utterances such as (21), then how are we to explain the function of *then* in (48)?

(48)   She jumped on her horse and then rode off into the sunset.

It would, I believe, be generally agreed that *then* contributes to the truth conditional content of (48), since it will be true if and only if the conditions in (49) obtain.

(49)   (a) She jumped on her horse.
        (b) She rode off into the sunset.
        (c) The event in (a) preceded the event in (b).

This is, of course, captured in the propositional form in (44). On the other hand, there seems to be no constituent corresponding to a concept encoded by *then* in the propositional form in (48). All we have is two time references t_n and t_{n+1}. In other words, it seems that although the meaning of *then* contributes to the proposition expressed by (48), it does not actually encode a constituent of that proposition.

The account of procedural meaning developed in chapter 4 focussed on those expressions which activate assumptions which are part of the implicit content of the utterances that contain them. This account built on my original account of semantic constraints on relevance (Blakemore 1987) which was intended as a relevance theoretic re-assessment of Grice's notion of conventional implicature. However, as I explained in chapter 3, Wilson and Sperber (1993) have argued that the notion of procedural encoding can be generalized so that it constrains any phase of inferential encoding, whether explicit or implicit. In particular, they have argued that Kaplan's (1989) arguments for treating indexicals such as *they* or *I* as being directly referential can be construed as arguments for treating them as linguistic constraints on explicit (truth conditional) content. According to these arguments, the pronoun *I* does not encode the concept 'the speaker', but encodes a rule for determining its content in any given context: 'Indexicals are directly referential. The rules tell us what is referred to. Thus they *determine* the content for a particular occurrence of an indexical. But they are not *part* of that content' (Kaplan 1989:523). Thus the explicit content of the utterance in (50) is not (51), but (52), where the value of x is constrained by the meaning of *he*.

(50)   He is happy.
(51)   Some male person is happy.
(52) x is happy

In other words, the meaning of *he* narrows down the hearer's search space for the value of x.

It seems to me that *then* could be analysed along similar lines. That is, the meaning of *then* is not a concept which appears in the propositional form recovered by the hearer, but is a means of narrowing down the hearer's search space for the value of the time reference for the event described. Obviously, further research is required before this can become anything more than speculation. This research would have to incorporate the investigation of other indexical temporal adverbs (for example, *now*) as well as those temporal adverbs which seem to be composed of an expression encoding a concept together with an indexical (for example, *after that*, *before that*). It would also have to include the investigation of a range of uses of *then* which are not identical with the one illustrated in (48), but which may well be related to it, for example:

(53)   Now then, what's the problem?
(54)   I haven't been happy with your attendance at classes or the standard of your essays. And then there is the matter of your exam mark.
(55)   Put your jersey on. Then you won't have to carry it.
(56)   If you attended class more regularly, then your marks would be better.
(57)   So we're not going to the pub, then?

My point here, however, is that this research follows from the framework developed in chapter 3 in which linguistic meaning is classified not according to its role in marking connections in discourse, but according to the kind of input it provides for the inferential phase of comprehension.

5.3.4   Restatement

At first sight, it would appear that reformulations such as the one in (16) would be ruled out by the principle of relevance.

(16)   (a) At the beginning of this piece there is an example of an anacrusis.
(b) That is, it begins with an unaccented note that is not part of the first full bar.

(Blakemore 1997b)

(17)   (a) A well-groomed car reflects its owner. (b) The car you drive says a lot about you.

(Mann and Thompson 1988)

In an unplanned discourse, a reformulation may achieve relevance following the speaker's recognition that the original formulation failed to achieve optimal relevance, that is, as a kind of repair. However, it may not be clear why a speaker who is aiming at optimal relevance should intentionally present both the original and the reformulation, as I have just done in the sentence you have just read. It could be said that given the hearer's assumed unfamiliarity with the term *repair* or *anacrusis* (in (16)), the reformulation achieves relevance by virtue of helping the hearer process the original. However, the principle of relevance entitles the hearer of an utterance to assume that it yields adequate contextual effects for no gratuitous processing effort. If the reformulation alone achieves the same cognitive effects as the original but for less processing effort, what is the point of producing both? Why produce an utterance which one knows will require reformulation?

As I have argued elsewhere (Blakemore 1993, 1997b), there are a number of ways in which planned reformulations may achieve relevance. Thus the reformulation in (16) achieves relevance by virtue of communicating information about the meaning of the term *anacrusis* in addition to the information it communicates about the piece of music. The interpretation of (17) (which I assume is an advertisement for car polish) is more complicated. The first segment is a pun, and thus presents the hearer with a puzzle. The second segment is an interpretation of only one of the readings for the first, and thus provides a solution to the puzzle posed by the first. However, the second segment on its own would not have captured the hearer's attention in the way that the first segment does. Nor would it have yielded the cognitive effects about the shiny qualities of well-groomed, highly polished cars. In other words, the extra processing costs entailed by the reformulation in (17) are offset by the way it captures the attention of the hearer and by the cognitive effects yielded by the first segment that are not yielded by the second segment alone.[5]

However, it seems that in neither case would the extra processing costs be offset by these extra cognitive effects unless the hearer recognized that the utterance *was* a restatement. In other words, it seems that in these cases the identification of the coherence relation *is* a prerequisite for understanding the utterance, as coherence approaches predict. But let us consider what it means exactly for a hearer to recognize that one utterance is a restatement or reformulation of another. Writers such as Mann and Thompson (1987, 1988) appeal to this notion, but simply assume that we know what it means. Thus their criterion for distinguishing a summary from a restatement is 'bulk': the restatement relation holds between segments of equal 'bulk', while a summary relation is a restatement which is shorter in 'bulk'. However, these definitions are not accompanied by a criterion for measuring 'bulk'.

In my work on reformulations and reformulation markers (Blakemore 1993,1997b), I have argued that reformulations are one example of the way that utterances may be relevant as representations of utterances which they resemble. As Sperber and Wilson (1995) point out, all sorts of phenomena can be used as representations in this way, for example, pictorial representations and mimes. Since no two phenomena are exactly alike, a communicator must expect the hearer to identify the respects in which the resemblance holds. In the case of an utterance which is used to represent another, the resemblance may hold by virtue of resemblances in phonetic and phonological form, or resemblances in lexical and syntactic form, or resemblances in logical properties. For example, all the utterances in (60) could be produced as answers to (59) in a situation in which the director had produced the utterance in (58):

(58)   We will have to let her go.
(59)   What did the director say?
(60)   (a) We will have to let her go.
        (b) They'll have to let her go.
        (c) She's fired.
                    (Blakemore 1997b)

---

[5] For a more detailed relevance theoretic account of the effects of puns in advertising, see Tanaka (1992, 1994).

(60a) is a direct quotation and represents the director's utterance by virtue of resemblances in linguistic and semantic structure. (60b) has a different semantic structure (since it uses the third-person pronoun instead of the original first-person pronoun), but the two utterances share a common propositional form. (60c) has neither the same linguistic structure nor the same propositional form of the original. However, its propositional form may still be said to resemble the propositional form of the original in the sense that it is not difficult to imagine a context in which it gives rise to the same contextual implications. In such cases where the resemblance involves the sharing of logical and contextual implications, Sperber and Wilson (1995) say that the utterance can be said to be relevant as an *interpretation* of a propositional form or thought.

As Sperber and Wilson (1995) explain, a speaker who produces an utterance which is relevant as a representation of another utterance cannot be taken to be creating expectations of truthfulness since he is not using that utterance descriptively. He can only be taken to be creating expectations of *faithfulness*. Faithfulness is a matter of degree, the degree of faithfulness being determined by the extent to which the two propositional forms share logical and contextual implications, and the degree of faithfulness attempted will vary from situation to situation, for what is the optimally relevant representation of a thought or utterance in one situation is not necessarily the optimally relevant representation in another. In particular, the optimally relevant representation of a thought or body of thought is not necessarily a fully identical representation. Consider, for example, this summary of Sperber and Wilson's (1995) notion of interpretive resemblance. It would not be relevant for me to reproduce pages 231 to 237 of their book word for word, for I am only concerned with those aspects of their account which have implications for the analysis of reformulations. The summary I have produced is based on my (possibly incorrect) assessment of what the reader will need to know in order to understand the main point that I want to make about the interpretation of utterances that we have been calling reformulations. In other words, I have made a decision about the level of faithfulness that is necessary in order to achieve my intended cognitive effects for the minimum processing effort. This is not a decision about 'bulk' (see Mann and Thompson 1987), but rather a decision about the effort that is required in order to obtain cognitive effects. As I have explained (Blakemore 1997b), such decisions may take into account the hearer's vocabulary, her processing resources at the time, or her contextual assumptions. In each case, the utterance made is constrained by the same principle that constrains any utterance – whether it is a reformulation or not.

So what is the point that I want to make about the utterances that we have been calling reformulations? I have argued that an utterance that achieves relevance as a reformulation achieves relevance by virtue of being an interpretation of another representation. The question of whether an utterance is relevant as an interpretation (rather than as a description) is not a question about how it is connected to the preceding text, but a question about the relationship between the proposition it expresses and the thought it represents. In other words, a speaker who recognizes an utterance as a reformulation has not recognized that it is a segment of discourse which stands in some relationship with another, but has recognized a relationship between propositional representations. Obviously, this relationship is not like a temporal relationship in that it cannot be perceived out there in the world. However, this is not to say that the relationship is *internal* (in the sense defined by Halliday and Hasan 1976). The notion of interpretive representation occupies a central place in Sperber and Wilson's (1995) account of the communication of propositional attitudes. However, this is a cognitive account in which language is seen as a vehicle for the communication of thoughts, desires and beliefs, rather than a speech act account in which language is seen as a vehicle for action. Thus the interpretation of utterances such as (16) and (17) is not explained in terms of a language user who is using language to achieve perlocutionary effects, but rather in terms of the ways in which humans use representations not only of the world, but also of thoughts.

Given this re-analysis of utterances such as (16) and (17), what can we say about expressions that are said to mark restatement relations, for example, *in other words* or *that is*? Within the framework of relevance theory, Blass (1990) has argued that the analysis of the Sissala hearsay particle re as a marker of interpretive use is able to explain a wider range of uses than traditional modal analyses (for example, Palmer 1986). Thus, for example, in contrast with modal analyses, Blass' analysis can account for the use of re to mark irony, which in relevance theory is analysed as a particular example of the interpretive use of utterances. Blass' work, together with other work on so-called hearsay markers (for example, Slobin and Aksu's 1982 work on the Turkish marker -*mis*), suggests that languages have developed linguistically encoded means for encouraging hearers to interpret utterances as interpretive representations of thoughts attributed either to other speakers or to themselves at other times. Indeed, Wilson and Sperber (1993) have suggested this sort of analysis for the English discourse particle *huh* as it is used in (61).

(61)   Peter's a genius, huh.

Given that restatement can be analysed in terms of the interpretive use of rep-resentations, could we not analyse expressions such as *in other words* along similar lines?

Blass' analysis of re is a procedural analysis. That is, it encodes a constraint on the construction of a higher level explicature. Similarly, Wilson and Sperber's suggestion in the case of *huh* is that it encodes a procedure for the construction of a higher-level explicature of the form in (62).

(62)   The speaker does not believe that p (where p is the proposition ex-pressed by the utterance).

In contrast, the expression *in other words*, as it is used in (63), does not have the properties which I have argued characterize procedural encoding.

(63)   A: I'm afraid I will have to let you go.
        B: In other words, I'm fired.

For example, a procedural account of *in other words* would be difficult to reconcile with the fact that it can appear in semantically complex expressions such as *to put it in other words*. Moreover, in contrast with the examples of procedural encoding discussed in chapter 4 of this book, expressions such as *that is* and *in other words* have synonymous counterparts which clearly must be analysed as contributing to the conceptual content of the utterances that contain them. Consider, for example:

(64)   He asked me to put it in other words.
(65)   That is the same as saying I'm fired.

Following Wilson and Sperber's (1993) arguments for illocutionary adverbials, the simplest hypothesis would be that the discourse markers and their truth conditional counterparts encode the same concepts. The difference is that in their discourse marker use, they encode constituents of higher-level explicatures which communicate the speaker's belief that the propositional form of the utterance they preface is relevant as a faithful representation of the propositional form of another utterance.

Conclusion

Research on discourse markers has been dominated by taxonomy and classification. As I have shown in the final chapter of this book, this is matched by a corresponding focus on the classification of coherence or discourse relations. In neither case has this concern with classification yielded an account of discourse markers that is universally accepted by those who are working with them. Indeed, as I remarked in the introduction to this book, it is not even agreed what *the* set of discourse markers for any given language is. It seems that in general, classifications are made at a descriptive level: the aim is to describe the role that these expressions play either in constructed examples of acceptable uses (see Halliday and Hasan 1976) or in naturally occurring discourse (see Schiffrin 1987, 1994). In these approaches, the evidence for any generalization made is always positive. Thus there is not a single example of an unacceptable use of a conjunctive cohesive device in Halliday and Hasan's book, and, since Schiffrin's examples are all examples of actual uses, there are no unacceptable uses of the expressions she classifies as discourse markers either. However, as is so often the case in linguistics, we often learn more about the meanings of these expressions from the fact that they *cannot* occur in a particular context than the fact that they can occur in another. Thus, for example, it is difficult to see how one could learn anything about the subtle differences in meaning between *but*, *however* and *nevertheless* discussed in chapter 4 without appealing to contexts in which their use is not acceptable.

It could be claimed that my suggestion that there are clusters of discourse connectives with similar (but not identical) meanings (for example, the ones just mentioned) is in the same taxonomic spirit. However, as I hope my discussion in chapter 4 has shown, my investigation of these expressions was based on theoretical assumptions about the role of inference in utterance understanding. The fact that there are expressions which are linked to the cognitive effects of contextual implication, strengthening and denial and elimination, follows, first, from the fact that linguistically encoded meaning provides an input to inferential processes, and, second, from the fact that it is possible to encode information either about the conceptual representations that undergo these processes or about the processes themselves. At the same time, it is clear that procedural information cannot be limited to information about cognitive effects. Constraints on implicatures may also include information about the contexts in which cognitive effects are derived (see, for example, my analyses of *however* and *nevertheless*). Indeed, it seems that there may be expressions classified as discourse markers which, although they encode procedures, are not linked to any particular cognitive effect (see my analysis of *well*). And if my suggestion about the analysis of *then* turns out to be correct, there are discourse markers which encode procedural constraints on explicit content. Finally, as the last section has shown, not all expressions classified as discourse connectives/markers can be analysed in terms of procedural encoding. There are so-called discourse markers which encode constituents of conceptual representations.

The picture that emerges from this approach is one in which there is no single category of discourse markers. Should this be construed as a recommendation that research on discourse markers should cease forthwith? If this means research on discourse markers as a class or category, then yes. However, if this means research on the expressions that have been called discourse markers, then, most emphatically, no. This book has been concerned with a number of fundamental questions about the relationship between linguistic form and pragmatic interpretation. Inevitably there are many loose ends. In particular, while I believe that I have got a bit closer to understanding the ways in which linguistic form may contribute to the inferential process involved in utterance understanding, there is still much work to be done before we have a full understanding of the notion of procedural encoding. All the expressions I have mentioned in this book and a great many expressions that I have not mentioned will play a central role in this research.

Bibliography

Anscombre, J.C. 1983. *L'argumentation dans la langue*. Brussels: Pierre Mardaga.

Anscombre, J.C. and Ducrot, O. 1977. Deux 'mais' en français? *Lingua* 43, 23–40.

1989. Argumentativity and informativity. In M. Meyer (ed.) *From metaphysics to rhetoric*. Dordrecht: Kluwer, 71–87.

Asher, N. and Lascarides, A. 1995. Lexical disambiguation in a discourse context. *Journal of Semantics* 12, 69–108.

Austin, J.L. 1962. *How to do things with words*. Oxford: Clarendon Press.

Bach, K. 1994. Conversational implicature. *Mind and Language* 9, 124–62.

1999. The myth of conventional implicature. *Linguistics and Philosophy* 22.4, 327–66.

Bach, K. and Harnish, R. 1979. *Linguistic communication and speech acts*. Cambridge, MA: MIT Press.

Banfield, A. 1982. *Unspeakable sentences: narration and representation in the language of fiction*. Boston: Routledge.

Bar-Lev, Z. and Palacas, A. 1980. Semantic command over pragmatic priority. *Lingua* 51, 137–46.

Bell, D.M. 1998. Cancellative discourse markers: a core/periphery approach. *Pragmatics* 8.4, 515–41.

Blakemore, D.L. 1987. *Semantic constraints on relevance*. Oxford: Blackwell.

1989. Denial and contrast: a relevance theoretic analysis of 'but'. *Linguistics and Philosophy* 12, 15–37.

1990. Performatives and parentheticals. *Proceedings of the Aristotelian Society* 91.3, 197–213.

1991. Review of Recanati, 1987, *Meaning and force*. *Mind and Language* 4.3, 235–45.

1992. *Understanding utterances*. Oxford: Blackwell.

1993. The relevance of reformulations. *Language and Literature* 2.2, 101–20.

1995. Relevance theory. In J. Verscheuren *et al. Handbook of pragmatics*. Amsterdam: John Benjamin, 443–52.

1996. Are apposition markers discourse markers? *Journal of Linguistics* 32, 325–47.

1997a. On non-truth conditional meaning. *Linguistische Berichte. Sonderheft* 8, 92–102.

1997b. Restatement and exemplification: a relevance theoretic re-assessment of elaboration. *Pragmatics and Cognition* 5.1, 1–19.

186

1998. On the context for so-called discourse markers. In J. Williams and K. Malmkjaer (eds.) *Context in language understanding and language learning.* Cambridge: Cambridge University Press, 44–60.

2000. Procedures and indicators: 'nevertheless' and 'but'. *Journal of Linguistics* 36.3, 463–86.

Blakemore, D. and Carston, R. 1999. The pragmatics of *and* conjunctions: the non-narrative cases. *University College London Working Papers in Linguistics* 11, London: University College, 1–20.

Blass, R. 1990. *Relevance relations in discourse: a study with special reference to Sissala.* Cambridge: Cambridge University Press.

Bolinger, D. 1989. *Meaning and form.* London: Longman.

Burge, T. 1974. Demonstrative constructions, reference, and truth. *The Journal of Philosophy* 71, 205–23.

Carlson, L. 1983. *Dialogue games: an approach to discourse analysis.* Dordrecht: Reidel.

1994. 'Well' in dialogue games: a discourse analysis of the interjection 'well' in idealized conversation. Amsterdam: John Benjamins.

Carston, R. 1988. Implicature, explicature and truth theoretic semantics. In R. Kempson (ed.) *Mental representations: the interface between language and reality.* Cambridge: Cambridge University Press, 155–81.

1993. Conjunction, explanation and relevance. *Lingua* 90, 27–48.

1995. Quantity maxims and generalised implicature. *Lingua* 96, 213–14.

1997a. Enrichment and loosening:complementary processes in deriving the proposition expressed? *Linguistische Berichte. Sonderheft* 8, 103 27.

1997b. Informativeness, relevance and scalar implicature. In R. Carston and S.Uchida (eds.) *Relevance theory: applications and implications,* 179–236.

1998. Pragmatics and the explicit–implicit distinction. University of London PhD thesis.

1999. The semantics/pragmatics distinction: a view from relevance theory. In K. Turner (ed.) *The semantics–pragmatics interface from different points of view.* Amsterdam: Elsevier, 85–125.

2000a. The relationship between generative grammar and (relevance theoretic) pragmatics. *Language and Communication* 20, 87–103.

2000b. Explicature and semantics. *University College London Working Papers in Linguistics* 12, London: University College, 1–44.

2002 *Thoughts and utterances: the pragmatics of explicit communication.* Oxford: Blackwell.

Chafe, W. 1987. Cognitive constraints on information flow. In R. Tomlim (ed.) *Coherence and grounding in discourse.* Amsterdam: John Benjamins, 21–51.

Chomsky, N. 1964. *Current issues in linguistic theory.* The Hague: Mouton.

1980. *Rules and representations.* Oxford: Blackwell.

1986. *Knowledge of language.* New York: Prager.

1992. Explaining language use. *Philosophical Topics* 20, 205–31.

Clark, B. 1991. Relevance theory and the analysis of non-declarative sentences. University of London PhD thesis.

1993. Relevance and pseudo-imperatives. *Linguistics and Philosophy* 16, 79–121.

Cook, V. 1989. *Discourse*. Oxford: Oxford University Press.

Cooper, R. 1986. Tense and discourse location in situation semantics. *Linguistics and Philosophy* 9, 17–36.

Dascal, M. and Katriel, T. 1977. Between semantics and pragmatics: the two types of 'but' – Hebrew 'aval' and 'ela'. *Theoretical Linguistics* 4, 143–72.

Davidson, D. 1967. Truth and meaning. Reprinted in Davidson 1984.

　　1984. *Inquiries into truth and interpretation*. Oxford: Clarendon Press.

Donnellan, K. 1966. Reference and definite descriptions. *Philosophical Review* 77, 281–301.

Dowty, D. 1986. The effects of aspectual class on the temporal structure of discourse: semantics or pragmatics? *Linguistics and Philosophy* 9, 37–61.

Fodor, Jerry. 1983. *The modularity of mind*. Cambridge, MA: MIT Press.

　　1998. *Concepts: where cognitive science went wrong*. Oxford: Clarendon Press.

Foolen, A. 1991. Polyfunctionality and the semantics of adversative conjunctions. *Multilingua* 10.1/2, 79–92.

Fraser, B. 1990. An approach to discourse markers. *Journal of Pragmatics* 14, 383–95.

　　1996. Pragmatic markers. *Pragmatics* 6, 167–90.

　　1998. Contrastive discourse markers in English. In A. Jucker and Y. Ziv (eds.) *Discourse markers: descriptions and theories*. Amsterdam: John Benjamins, 301–26.

Frazier, L. 1987. Sentence processing: a tutorial overview. In M. Coltheart (ed.) *Attention and performance* XII. Hillsdale, NJ: Lawrence Erlbaum.

Frege, G. 1918. Thought. In B. McGuiness 1984 (ed.) *Gottlob Frege: collected papers on mathematics, logic and philosophy*. Oxford: Blackwell, 351–72.

Gazdar, G. 1979. *Pragmatics, implicature and logical form*. London: Academic Press.

Giora, R. 1997. Discourse coherence and theory of relevance: stumbling blocks in search of a unified theory. *Journal of Pragmatics* 27, 17–34.

　　1998. Discourse coherence is an independent notion: a reply to Deirdre Wilson. *Journal of Pragmatics* 29, 75–86.

Grice, H.P. 1989. *Studies in the way of words*. Cambridge, MA: Harvard University Press.

Grimes, J.E. 1975. *The thread of discourse*. Janua Linguarum Series Minor 207, The Hague: Mouton.

Haberlandt, K. 1982. Reader expectations in text comprehension. In J.F. Le Ny and W. Kintsch (eds.) *Language and language comprehension*. Amsterdam: North Holland, 239–49.

Halliday, M.A.K. and Hasan, R. 1976. *Cohesion in English*. London: Longman.

Harris, Z. 1951. *Methods in structural linguistics*. Chicago: University of Chicago Press.

Heim, I. 1982. The semantics of definite and indefinite descriptions. PhD dissertation, University of Massachusetts, Amherst.

Higashimori, I. 1994. A relevance theoretic analysis of *even, sae/sura/mo/remo/ddemo/datte/made*. *English Literature Review* (Kyoto Women's University) 38, 51–80.

Higginbotham, J. 1988. Contexts, models and meanings: a note on the data of semantics. In R. Kempson (ed.) *Mental representations: the interface between language and reality*. Cambridge: Cambridge University Press, 29–48.

　　1989. Elucidations of meaning. *Linguistics and Philosophy* 12.4, 465–517.

1994. Priorities in the philosophy of thought. *Aristotelian Society Supplementary Volume* 68, 85–106.

Hobbs, J. 1978. Why is discourse coherent? In F. Neubauer (ed.) *Coherence in natural language texts*. Hamburg: Buske, 29–70.

1979. Coherence and co-reference. *Cognitive Science* 3, 27–90.

Hobbs, J. and Agar, M. 1985. The coherence of incoherent discourse. *Journal of Language and Social Psychology* 4.3/4, 213–32.

Horn, L. 1984. Towards a new taxonomy for pragmatic inference: Q-based and R-based implicature. In D. Schiffrin (ed.) *Meaning, form and use in context: linguistic applications (GURT '84)*. Washington: Georgetown University Press.

1988. Pragmatic theory. In F. Newmeyer (ed.) *Linguistics: the Cambridge survey I*. Cambridge: Cambridge University Press, 113–45.

1989. *A natural history of negation*. Chicago: University of Chicago Press.

Hovy, E. 1990. Parsimonious or profligate approaches to the question of discourse structure relations. *Proceedings of the 5th International Workshop on Natural Language Generation*, 128–34.

Ifantidou-Trouki, E. 1993. Sentential Adverbs and Relevance. *Lingua* 90, 69–90.

1994. 'Evidentials and relevance'. University of London PhD thesis.

Itani, R. 1993. The Japanese sentence-final particle 'ka': a relevance theoretic approach. *Lingua* 90.1/2, 129–47.

Iten, C. 2000a. The relevance of argumentation theory. *Lingua* 110.9, 665–701.

2000b. 'Non-truth conditional' meaning, relevance and concessives. University of London PhD thesis

Jackendoff, R. 1972. *Semantic interpretation in generative grammar*. Cambridge, MA: MIT Press.

Jucker, A.H. 1993. The discourse marker *well*: a relevance theoretic account. *Journal of Pragmatics* 19, 435–52.

Kamp, H. and Reyle, U. 1993. *From discourse to logic*. Dordrecht: Kluwer.

Kaplan, D. 1997. What is meaning? Explorations in the theory of meaning as use. Research paper.

1989. Demonstratives. In J.H. Almog *et al.* (eds.) *Themes from Kaplan*. New York: Oxford University Press, 565–614.

Kasher, A. 1991a. Pragmatics and Chomsky's research program. In A. Kasher (ed.) *The Chomskyan turn*. Oxford: Blackwell, 122–49.

1991b. On pragmatic modules: a lecture. *Journal of Pragmatics* 16, 381–97.

1991c. Pragmatics and the modularity of mind. In S. Davis (ed.) *Pragmatics: a reader*. Oxford: Oxford University Press, 567–82.

Katz, J. 1977. *Propositional structure and illocutionary force: a study of the contribution of sentence meaning to speech acts*. Hassocks: Harvester Press.

Kitis, E. 1995. Connectives and ideology. Paper delivered at the 4th International Symposium on Critical Discourse Analysis: Language, Social Life and Critical Thought, University of Athens.

Knott, A. 1996. A data-driven methodology for motivating a set of coherence relations. PhD dissertation, University of Edinburgh.

Knott, A. and Dale, R. 1994. Using linguistic phenomena to motivate a set of coherence relations. *Discourse Processes* 18.1, 35–62.

Kuno, S. 1980. Functional syntax. In E. Moravcsik and J. Wirth (eds.) *Current approaches to syntax. Syntax and semantics 13*. New York: Academic Press, 117–36.

1987. *Functional syntax: anaphora, discourse and empathy*. Chicago: Chicago University Press.

Lakoff, R. 1971. If's, and's and but's about conjunction. In C. Fillmore and D.T. Langendoen (eds.) *Studies in linguistic semantics*. New York: Holt, Rinehart & Winston, 114–49.

1973. Questionable answers and answerable questions. In B.B. Kachru *et al.* (eds.) *Papers in honor of Henry and Renee Kahane*. Urbana, IL: University of Illinois Press.

Leech, G. 1983. *Principles of pragmatics*. London: Longman.

Levinson, S. 1983. *Pragmatics*. Cambridge: Cambridge University Press.

2000. *Presumptive meanings*. Cambridge, MA: MIT Press.

Lewis, D. 1972. General semantics. In D. Davidson and E. Harman, G. (eds.) *Semantics of natural language*. Dordrecht: Reidel, 169–218.

1979. Scorekeeping in a language game. In R. Bauerle *et al.* (eds.) *Semantics from different points of view*. Berlin: Springer, 172–87.

Longacre, R.E. 1983. *The grammar of discourse*. Dallas, TX: Summer Institute of Linguistics.

Mann, W.C. and Thompson, S. 1987. Relational propositions in discourse. *Discourse Processes* 9, 57–90.

1988. Rhetorical structure theory: towards a functional theory of text organization. *Text* 8.3, 243–81.

Mey, J. 1993. *Pragmatics: an introduction*. Oxford: Blackwell.

Moeschler, J. and Reboul, A. 1994. *Dictionnaire encyclopédique de pragmatique*. Paris: Seuil.

Murray, D. 1979. Well. *Linguistic Inquiry* 10, 727–32.

Neale, S. 1992. Paul Grice and the philosophy of language. *Linguistics and Philosophy* 15, 509–59.

1999. Coloring and composition. In R. Murasugi and R. Stainton (eds.) *Philosophy and linguistics*. Boulder, CO: Westview, 35–82.

Nolke, H. 1990. Pertinence et modalisateurs d'énonciation. *Cahiers de linguistique français* 11.

Owen, M. 1981. Conversational units and the use of 'well...'. In P. Werth (ed.) *Conversation and discourse: structure and interpretation*. London: Croom Helm, 99–116.

Palmer, F. 1986. *Mood and modality*. Cambridge: Cambridge University Press.

Pike, K. and Pike, E. 1983. *Text and tagmeme*. London: Francis Pinter.

Prince, E. 1985. Fancy syntax and 'shared knowledge'. *Journal of Pragmatics* 9, 65–82.

1988. Discourse analysis: a part of the study of linguistic competence. In F. Newmeyer (ed.) *Linguistics: the Cambridge survey, Vol. II*. Cambridge: Cambridge University Press, 164–82.

1997. On the functions of left-dislocations in English discourse. In A. Kamio (ed.) *Directions in functional linguistics*. Amsterdam: John Benjamins, 117–43.

Quirk, R. *et al.* 1972. *A grammar of contemporary English.* London: Longman.

Radford, A. 1997. *Syntactic theory and the structure of English.* Cambridge: Cambridge University Press.

Recanati, F. 1987. *Meaning and force.* Cambridge: Cambridge University Press.

1989. The pragmatics of what is said. *Mind and Language* 4, 295–329.

Redeker, G. 1991. Linguistic markers of discourse structure. *Linguistics* 29, 1139–72.

Rieber, S. 1997. Conventional implicatures as conventional implicatures. *Linguistics and Philosophy* 20.1, 50–72.

Rouchota, V. 1998. Procedural meaning and parenthetical discourse markers. In A. Jucker and Y. Ziv (eds.) *Discourse markers: descriptions and theory.* Amsterdam: John Benjamins, 97–126.

Salkie, R. 1995. *Text and discourse analysis.* London: Routledge.

Samet, J. and Schank, R. 1984. Coherence and connectivity. *Linguistics and Philosophy* 7, 57–82.

Sanders, T., Spooren, W. and Noordman, L. 1992. Towards a taxonomy of discourse relations. *Discourse Processes* 15, 1–35.

Sanders, T. and Noordman, L. 2000. The role of coherence markers and their linguistic markers in text processing. *Discourse Processes* 29.1, 37–60.

Schiffrin, D. 1987. *Discourse markers.* Cambridge: Cambridge University Press.

1994. *Approaches to discourse.* Oxford: Blackwell.

Schourup, L. 1999. Discourse markers. *Lingua* 3.4, 227–65.

2001. Rethinking 'well'. *Journal of Pragmatics* 33, 1025–60.

Searle, J. 1968. Austin on illocutionary and locutionary acts. *Philosophical Review* 77, 405–24.

1969. *Speech acts.* Cambridge: Cambridge University Press.

Slobin, D. and Aksu, A. 1982. Tense, aspect and modality in the use of the Turkish evidential. In P. Hopper (ed.) *Tense–aspect: between semantics and pragmatics.* Amsterdam: John Benjamins, 185–200.

Smith, N.V. 1990. Observations on the pragmatics of tense. *University College London Working Papers in Linguistics* 2, 82–112.

Sperber, D. 1975. *Rethinking symbolism.* Cambridge: Cambridge University Press.

1994. The modularity of thought and the epidemiology of representations. In L. Hirschfield and S. Gelman (eds.) *Mapping the mind: domain specificity in cognition and culture.* New York: Cambridge University Press, 36–67.

Sperber, D. and Wilson, D. 1985/6. Loose talk. *Proceedings of the Aristotelian Society* 56, 153–71.

1986, second edn 1995. *Relevance: communication and cognition.* Oxford: Blackwell.

1987. Precis of *Relevance. The Behavioural and Brain Sciences* 10.4, 697–210.

1997. The mapping of the mental and the public lexicon. *University College London Working Papers in Linguistics* 9, 107–25.

Stainton, R. 1994. Using non-sentences: an application of relevance theory. *Pragmatics and Cognition* 2, 269–84.

1997. Utterance meaning and syntactic ellipsis. *Pragmatics and Cognition* 5, 51–78.

forthcoming. In defense of non-sentential assertion. Research paper, Carleton University.

Stanley, J. 2000. Context and logical form. *Linguistics and Philosophy* 23, 391–434.
　　2002. Making it articulated. *Mind and Language*, 17.1 and 2, *Special Issue on Pragmatics and Cognitive Science*, 149–68.
Strawson, P.F. 1973. Austin and 'locutionary meaning'. In I. Berlin *et al.* (eds.) *Essays on J.L. Austin*. Oxford: Clarendon Press, 46–68.
Stubbs, M. 1983. Discourse analysis: the sociolinguistic analysis of natural language. Chicago: University of Chicago Press.
Tanaka, K. 1992. The pun in advertising. *Lingua* 87.1/2, 91–102.
　　1994. *Advertising language: a pragmatic approach to advertisements in Britain and Japan*. London: Routledge.
Tsui, A. 1991. Sequencing rules and coherence in discourse. *Journal of Pragmatics* 15, 111–29.
Unger, C. 1996. The scope of discourse connectives: implications for discourse organization. *Journal of Linguistics* 32, 403–38.
Urmson, J. 1966. Parenthetical verbs. In A. Flew (ed.) *Essays in conceptual analysis.* London: Macmillan, 192–212.
Watts, R. 1989. Taking the pitcher to the 'well': native speakers' perception of their use of discourse markers in conversation. *Journal of Pragmatics* 18, 203–37.
Wharton, T. 2001. Natural codes. *University College London Working Papers in Linguistics* 12, 173–214.
Wilson, D. 1975. *Presuppositions and non-truth conditional semantics.* London: Academic Press.
　　1994. Relevance and understanding. In E. Brown *et al.* (eds.) *Language and understanding.* Oxford: Oxford University Press, 35–58.
　　1998. Discourse, coherence and relevance: a reply to Rachel Giora. *Journal of Pragmatics* 29, 57–74.
Wilson, D. and Sperber, D. 1979. Ordered entailments: an alternative to presuppositional theories. In C.K.Oh and D. Dineen (eds.) *Syntax and semantics 11: presuppositions.* New York: Academic Press.
　　1981. On Grice's theory of conversation. In P. Werth (ed.) *Conversation and discourse.* London: Croom Helm, 155–78.
　　1988. Mood and the analysis of non-declarative sentences. In J. Dancy, J. Moravcsik and C. Taylor (eds.) *Human agency: language, duty and value.* Stanford, CA: Stanford University Press, 77–101.
　　1992. Verbal irony. *Lingua* 87.1/2, 53–76.
　　1993. Linguistic form and relevance. *Lingua* 90.1/2, 1–25.

General index

ad hoc concept formation 66–7, 68
adverbials, sentence 34, 41–5, 75–6,
83–3, 183; in sub-sentential utterances
87–8; speech act theoretic analysis of
41–5; VP adverbs and 44–5, 83–4
after all 48, 78, 89–90, 95–6, 97, 149
and 49, 72, 99–103, 105–7, 117, 118,
171–2, 174–6
argumentation theory 27–8
attributed thought 58, 93–4, 114, 146;
see also interpretive use

but 12, 13, 26, 27, 32–3, 46, 48, 49, 50,
52, 58, 83, 84, 88, 90, 92–4, 129, 146,
147, 149; in attitude contexts 53, 91,
114; concessivity and 104–8;
contradiction and elimination and 95,
100–3, 104–15, 119–22; contrast and
54–5, 98–103, 115, 161; correction and
105, 109–13, 117–19, 121; discourse
initial 105, 109, 118, 121, 166; ironic
uses of 93–4, 114; manifestness and
107–15; in objections 118–19, 121;
vs. *and* 49, 99–103, 105–7, 117; vs.
however 96, 115–22, 128, 166; vs. *in
contrast* 102–3; vs. *nevertheless*
96, 115–16, 123–8; vs. *whereas*
102–3; vs. *yet* 107

causal discourse markers 161; *because*
149; *as a result* 150; *see also so*
causal relations 159, 171
cognitive effect 61, 94–5; contextual
implication 61, 95; strengthening
61, 89–90, 95–6; contradiction and

elimination 61, 95, 100–3, 104–15,
119–22, 124–5, 127–8
cognitive environment 69
cognitive principle of relevance: *see*
principle of relevance
coherence 156, 157–60; discourse
acceptability and 162–7; global
159; interruptions and 164–5;
local 159; relevance and 164,
169–70
coherence relations 54, 157–8;
acceptability of 162–3; causal 159,
171; classification of 156, 160–2;
contrastive 161; discourse
understanding and 167–9;
elaboration 160, 162–3, 175;
psychological reality of 156, 161;
temporal 159, 171–7
cohesion 152–3, 159
communication: approaches to 59–60;
explicit vs. implicit 71; ostensive
51–2, 62
communicative principle of relevance:
see principle of relevance
competence: linguistic 23, 26; vs.
performance 8; pragmatic 8, 14,
21–3, 26
conceptual meaning: vs. procedural 4,
78–9, 82–8, 89, 183; truth conditions
and 4; non-truth conditional 81;
semantic compositionality and 88,
183
concession 100, 104–5
conjoined utterances 99–103, 105–7,
117, 118, 171–7; *see also and*

193

Name index

198